S
EA
RCH
ENGINE
VISIBILITY

SHARI THUROW

New
Riders

201 West 103rd Street, Indianapolis, Indiana 46290

An Imprint of Pearson Education

Boston ■ Indianapolis ■ London ■ Munich ■ New York ■ San Francisco

Look for This Related Title from New Riders:

Speed Up Your Site: Web Site Optimization

Andrew B. King

0-7357-1324-3

See a chapter excerpt from *Speed Up Your Site*
in the back of this book.

Search Engine Visibility

Copyright © 2003 by New Riders Publishing

International Standard Book Number: 0-7357-1256-5

Library of Congress Catalog Card Number: 2001098262

Printed in the United States of America

First edition: January 2003

07 06 05 04 03   7 6 5 4 3 2 1

Interpretation of the printing code: The rightmost double-digit number is the year of the book's printing; the rightmost single-digit number is the number of the book's printing. For example, the printing code 03-1 shows that the first printing of the book occurred in 2003.

Trademarks

Warning and Disclaimer

Publisher
David Dwyer

Associate Publisher
Stephanie Wall

Editor in Chief
Chris Nelson

Production Manager
Gina Kanouse

Senior Product Marketing Manager
Tammy Detrich

Publicity Manager
Susan Nixon

Senior Development Editor
Lisa Thibault

Project Editor
Jake McFarland

Copy Editor
Jill Batistick

Indexer
Lisa Stumpf

Proofreader
Jessica McCarty

Composition
Wil Cruz

Manufacturing Coordinator
Dan Uhrig

Interior Designer
Aren Howell

Cover Designer
Alan Clements

Contents at a Glance

Table of Contents

About the Author

 **Shari Thurow** is a sought-after speaker and trainer on the topics of search engine–friendly web site design, web copywriting, and link development. A popular speaker at Search Engine Strategies, web site design, and online marketing conferences worldwide, Shari's sessions are very popular and four-star rated.

Shari Thurow is the webmaster and marketing director for GrantasticDesigns.com. She has been designing and promoting web sites since 1995, and she is outsourced to many firms throughout the United States. She has a 100 percent success rate for getting client sites ranked at the top of search engine and directory queries.

Shari has designed and successfully marketed web sites for businesses in fields such as medicine, finance, science, biotechnology, software, computers, online stores, e-commerce, real estate, manufacturing, art and design, marketing, insurance, employment, education, and law. Shari is also the founder of the I-Design Discussion List, which discusses all aspects of effective web design, including look and feel, navigation, ease of use, database management, and download speed.

Shari has been featured in many publications, including *PC World*, *Crain's Chicago Business, Inc.*, *MacWorld*, and *ComputerUser.com*. She has also received numerous design awards and content awards, including top web site honors from Lycos, Business 2.0, and *Computer User Magazine*.

❖

In loving memory of my grandfather, Harold Paul Thurow,
and my father-in-law, Richard Crowell.

❖

About the Technical Reviewers

These reviewers contributed their considerable hands-on expertise to the entire development process for *Search Engine Visibility*. As the book was being written, these dedicated professionals reviewed all the material for technical content, organization, and flow. Their feedback was critical to ensuring that *Search Engine Visibility* fits our readers' need for the highest-quality technical information.

 **Mikkel deMib Svendsen** has years of professional experience with search engines: in search engine optimization; as manager of the largest Scandinavian search engine; and as vice president of product development at Ankiro, which is Denmark's leading search product company. He also consults with many European portals and search engines on search-related projects.

Mikkel was a long-term moderator at Search Engine Forums, where he established and managed these two forums: *Dynamic Pages, Frames, and Stuff* and *Non-English Search Engines.* He is known as the resident authority on advanced problems with frames, dynamic pages, Flash, cloaking, and so on.

In addition, Mikkel served as co-chair of Search Engine Strategies Copenhagen 2001. Working with Detlev Johnson, he was responsible for organizing the speakers and sessions for the conference.

Web site: www.demib.com
Email: Mikkel@joyzone.dk

 **Craig Fifield** is the product manager for Microsoft bCentral's small business web site optimization and submission service, Submit It! (www.submit-it.com).

Craig's career in Internet marketing began in early 1996. As marketing manager for U.S. Architectural Products, Inc., he built and optimized his first web site. Within two months, the site began to bring in more leads than the company's entire national sales team.

Due to this early success, Craig left his position as marketing manager for U.S. Architectural Products, Inc. in 1997 to work for Submit It! as a search engine optimization consultant to small businesses. This constant one-to-one interaction with customers gave him an in-depth understanding of the issues customers face when optimizing. He used this knowledge to make numerous product improvements and ultimately became the product manager of Submit It!.

Craig currently spends most of his time writing about search engine optimization, optimizing sites, and endlessly developing ways to improve the Submit It! service.

Jim Stob is the CEO of Position Technologies, Inc., one of today's fastest growing dot-com companies. The company provides search engine marketing technologies to more than 8,500 domains on the World Wide Web. Position Technologies' leading-edge product, Position Pro™, is the industry standard for web site content analysis.

Since 1998, Position Technologies has amassed a Who's Who list of top-tiered clients who are very satisfied with their services. Position Technologies has direct partnerships with Inktomi, FAST Search, AltaVista, and Teoma/AskJeeves. Jim and Position Technologies have been featured at numerous search engine marketing conferences worldwide.

Acknowledgments

This book took years of testing and experience to get to a final product. It also took the knowledge and support of some very important people.

First, I would like to thank my two cybermentors, Danny Sullivan and John Audette. Back in 1995 when I created my first web site and was assigned the task to market it as well, I stumbled onto your sites. I was in awe of your knowledge, intelligence, and the way that you communicated your knowledge to your readers. I listened to everything you said and followed your advice. I learned by example. My success as a web designer and online marketer, my clients' successes, and this book can all be traced back to the day I discovered your sites. I thank you both for sharing your knowledge with me and others, for publishing my posts and my articles, and for allowing me to speak at your conferences. You are great cybermentors.

Thank you to all of the staff at New Riders—Stephanie Wall, Victoria Elzey, and Lisa Thibault. Your incredible patience, attention to detail, and enthusiasm were crucial in shaping this book. And thank you to my technical editors—Jim Stob, Craig Fifield, and Mikkel deMib Svendsen—for your attention to detail and for not letting me get away with anything that was not factually accurate. You are great technical editors, colleagues, and friends.

Thank you to all the folks at Internet.com—Karen DeWeese, Beth Ritter, Chris Elwell, Chris Sherman, Kendra Jaros, Alison Alessio, and Frank Fazio—for providing me with a venue to present this topic. You have been wonderful, supportive colleagues and friends.

A very special thanks goes out to the I-Search and Adventive community. Having a forum to share ideas and knowledge helped shape this book. I hope you have learned as much from me as I have learned from all of you.

I would also like to thank the representatives from the various search engines (Google, FAST Search, Inktomi, Overture, Teoma, and so on) and directories (Yahoo!, LookSmart, and Open Directory) for reviewing the book's content for accuracy.

Thank you to all my clients and non-clients who agreed to be showcased in this book. And thank you to my colleagues who had the kindness and generosity to listen to my ideas.

And last, but certainly not least, much love and gratitude goes out to my spouse and business partner, Grant Crowell. This book took a long time to write, especially with the ever-changing search engine environment. Grant took the time to take over many of my search engine marketing duties so that I would have time to write this book.

Tell Us What You Think

As the reader of this book, you are the most important critic and commentator. We value your opinion and want to know what we're doing right, what we could do better, what areas you'd like to see us publish in, and any other words of wisdom you're willing to pass our way.

As the Associate Publisher for New Riders Publishing, I welcome your comments. You can fax, email, or write me directly to let me know what you did or didn't like about this book—as well as what we can do to make our books stronger. When you write, please be sure to include this book's title, ISBN, and author, as well as your name and phone or fax number. I will carefully review your comments and share them with the author and editors who worked on the book.

Please note that I cannot help you with technical problems related to the topic of this book, and that due to the high volume of email I receive, I might not be able to reply to every message.

Fax: 317-581-4663

Email: stephanie.wall@newriders.com

Mail: Stephanie Wall
        Associate Publisher
        New Riders Publishing
        201 West 103rd Street
        Indianapolis, IN 46290 USA

Foreword

"If you build it, they will come," is the famous quote from the movie *Field of Dreams*. However, as all too many webmasters and designers have discovered, just building a web site is no guarantee of receiving visitors.

There are many ways that people may come to a web site, but one of the leading methods is through search engines. Survey after survey attests to the popularity of these tools with web surfers. How you build your web site can have a major impact on whether those users will find you through search engines.

Build it right, and you can easily tap into "natural" traffic and gain quality visitors for free, saving your money to spend on ads to target areas you don't naturally do well in. Build it wrong, and you'll find yourself in the morass of constantly trying to win the search engine game with strikes against you from the outset. You then should expect to spend significant time and money to raise your profile.

Building a site right doesn't need to be be hard. "Search engine friendly" design, which I've been preaching about through SearchEngineWatch.com since 1997, isn't about using a myriad of tricks to fool search engines into favoring your web site. Rather, making a site search engine friendly often means implementing small and easy changes that usually have a big impact in gaining search engine visibility.

Far too often, designers spend time ensuring that their web sites are compatible with the two major web browsers while ignoring what I call the "third browser" search engines. Building a site that's accessible and friendly to search engines that crawl the web is just as important as thinking about humans who use Internet Explorer and Netscape Navigator. Why? Because many of those humans will "tune in" to your web site by means of crawler-based search engines. If those crawlers have problems reaching you, they can't direct the human visitors you want to your web site.

Fortunately, building a site for the third browser of crawler-based search engines doesn't mean ostracizing your human visitors. In fact, thinking about crawlers can often make your site's usability for humans better than it was before.

Shari Thurow has been a leader in helping guide people toward better search engine design through her writing and speaking. She has consistently been one of the best-rated speakers at the Search Engine Strategies series of conferences produced by SearchEngineWatch.com. Now Shari has put her knowledge into book format, and it is a great companion for anyone involved in constructing web sites.

Search engine–friendly design isn't just about pleasing crawlers. How sites are listed in human-powered search engines can also be positively—or negatively—impacted by site design. Shari addresses these issues, as well as offering tips on improving the submission process to human-backed search engines.

Build it right with the help of this book, and you should indeed find that they come!

Danny Sullivan
Editor, SearchEngineWatch.com

Introduction

This book is a guide to help web designers, web developers, programmers, ad agencies, web design firms, online marketers, copywriters, and anyone who builds web sites, to build a better web site, one that can be found through search engines and directories.

The foundation of a successful search engine optimization campaign begins with a good, effective web site, one that delivers content for which site visitors are searching. That is what this book is about: building a strong foundation. Without a strong foundation, a search engine marketing campaign will ultimately fail, which costs web site owners time and money.

Therefore, this book does not teach you a "secret recipe" for each search engine and directory. It does not teach you a "magic formula" to get your site at the top of search engine results. Rather, it teaches you the foundation of a successful search engine marketing campaign, a foundation that works across all the search engines and that delivers long-term search engine visibility—not quick fixes.

This book is not based on my personal design preferences. Everyone has opinions on what constitutes good and bad design. I might look at a site and think it is ugly, but the site might actually be quite successful and get millions of dollars in sales. A beautifully designed site might get virtually no traffic and no sales. However, that's not what this book is based on. This book is based on my years of experience, expertise, and my 100 percent success rate at increasing search engine visibility, site traffic, and sales on my own site and client sites since 1995—without any spam penalties whatsoever.

It is based on the client data that I have gathered since 1995. One of the many jobs I've held over the years is as an online marketing manager at various web design firms. Even though I did not design every site at those firms, I did have to market many of them. I had access to site statistics for thousands of web sites. I was able to see the types of web site designs search engine spiders indexed easily and which designs gave them problems. I was able to see the types of sites directory editors accepted and rejected. With that knowledge, I was able to build web sites that search engines and directory editors liked.

However, that was never the ultimate goal. For a web site to be successful, its end users, or target audience, had to like the site. To my pleasant surprise, I found that sites that are naturally search engine friendly are also user friendly. Thus, this book is not based on my personal preferences; it is based on the years of data on actual user behavior. It will help you build a web site that is both search engine friendly and user friendly.

How This Book Is Organized

The best way to read this book is in order, from beginning to end, regardless of whether you are new to search engine marketing or are an expert. Why?

Too many search engine marketers, advertising agencies, and web design firms are focused on quick fixes and short-term results. This book focuses on the very core of a successful search engine marketing campaign.

In Part 1, "Before You Build," I define the different types of search services: search engines and directories. The two are quite different, but they are inextricably interrelated. The strategies for being listed well in search engines are different from being listed well in directories. Thus, it is important to know how search engines and directories work, and how they are interrelated.

Part 1 also addresses the basic components of a successful web site design and the foundation of an effective search engine optimization campaign. Site design and search engine visibility are also inextricably interrelated.

Part 2, "How to Build Better Web Pages," goes into great detail about the foundation of a successful search engine marketing campaign using a fictional web site. Each component of the foundation is addressed. This section contains information on how to write search engine–friendly copy for your whole web site and for individual HTML tags. Part 2 presents solutions to navigations schemes that are problematic, showing actual search engine–friendly web pages. In addition, it contains guidelines to building a solid link-development campaign.

Part 3, "Page Design Workarounds," is written for sites that have already been created. If your site uses frames, Flash, Dynamic Hypertext Markup Language (DHTML), Cascading Style Sheets (CSS), and other technologies, there are ways to make it more search engine friendly. This section helps you employ workarounds on your site without affecting the overall design.

Part 4, "After Your Site Is Built," outlines the submission process to both search engines and directories. It contains detailed checklists to use before submitting. In addition, the section provides tips, guidelines, and actual email letters to use in the event a submission is rejected.

Parts 1 through 4 teach you what to do. Part 5 tells you what *not* to do. Part 5, "Best Practices: The Dos and Don'ts of Search Engine Marketing," addresses best practices—what to do and what not do to. It also debunks common search engine marketing myths. The contents of this section can help you select a reputable search engine marketing firm and determine if the firm follows best practices.

Confused by any term in this book? I have also included a search engine glossary for quick reference.

Although many advanced designers and marketers might be tempted to skip straight to Part 3, I highly recommend starting at the beginning. A workaround helps a site that already has a good foundation, so you should make sure that the foundation is in place before employing a workaround.

Companion Web Site

To supplement this book, I have created a companion web site at www.searchenginesbook.com/. As you know, search engines change all the time, and some of the content in this book can become outdated as soon as search engines and directories change partnerships, new search engines emerge, and so on. The companion web site will contain the most recent tips and guidelines for optimization.

In addition, note that HTML code, style sheets, and JavaScript can be difficult to retype. Thus, I am creating the companion site for you to use in your site designs. For example, if I find that a rollover script is more search engine friendly than other scripts, I will post that information (and the code for the script) on the companion site for your use. Furthermore, search engines are becoming increasingly better at indexing different types of web pages and documents. As the search engines continually develop, so to will search engine–friendly web design tips. Any new or updated information will be presented on the companion site.

part 1

Before You Build

Introduction

Search engine optimization (SEO) is a powerful online marketing strategy. When done correctly, millions of online searchers can find your site among millions of top search results.

Many web site owners consider SEO as an after-thought—after a site has already been built. If you are about to create a new site or redesign an existing one, understanding how the search engines work, how your target audience searches, and how best to design your site from the onset can save your company thousands of dollars in time and expenses.

Why Search Engine Visibility Is Important

Search engines and directories are the main way Internet users discover web sites. Various resources confirm this statement, and the percentages generally range from 42 percent of Internet users to 86 percent.

A January 2001 study conducted by NPD Group, a research organization specializing in consumer purchasing and behavior, tested the impact of search engine listings and banner advertisements across a variety of web sites to determine which marketing medium was more effective. In each situation, search engine listings came out on top. They found consumers are five times more likely to purchase your products or services after finding a web site through a search engine rather than through a banner advertisement.

Jupiter Media Metrix, another Internet research firm, determined that 28 percent of consumers go to a search engine and type the product name as a search query when they are looking for a product to purchase online.

Search engines and directories average over 300 million searches per day. Therefore, regardless of whether the percentage value is as low as 28 percent or as high as 86 percent, millions of searches are performed every day. Properly preparing your web site for search engine visibility increases the probability that web searchers will visit your site.

Additionally, think about your own personal experience. Where do you go to search for information about a company or a product on the web? Where do you go to find a site whose web address you do not know or cannot remember? In these cases, you probably use a search engine or directory to find the information.

Web searchers are not random visitors. When searchers enter a series of words into a search engine query, they are actively searching out a specific product or service. Thus, the traffic your site receives from the search engines is already targeted. In other words, web searchers are self-qualified prospects for your business.

Of course, search engines are not the only way in which people discover web sites. People may find a web address in offline sources such as print, television, or radio. They might click a link to a web site in an email document or a banner advertisement. Word of mouth (referral marketing) also is a popular method of bringing visitors to sites. In addition, people locate sites by clicking links from one site to another, commonly known as surfing the web.

Because millions of people use the search engines and directories to discover web sites, maximizing your site's search engine visibility can be a powerful and cost-effective part of an online marketing plan. A properly performed search engine marketing campaign can provide a tremendous, long-term return on investment (ROI).

Understanding the Search Services

Search services can generally be categorized into two types of sources: directories and search engines. Many people confuse the two terms, often referring to Yahoo! as a search engine. (Yahoo! is a directory.)

The reason for the confusion is understandable. People see a Search button on a web site and assume that when they click the button, they are using a search engine. Both Yahoo! and Google have search boxes, as shown in Figure 1.1.

The search services use two main sources to obtain their listings. The first type of search service is called a directory, and a directory uses human editors to manually place web sites or web pages into specific categories. A directory is commonly called a "human-based" search engine.

The other type of search service is called a search engine, and a search engine uses special software robots, called *spiders* or *crawlers*, to retrieve information from web pages. This type of search service is called a "spider-based" or "crawler-based" search engine.

Figure 1.1
Although both Yahoo! and
Google enable people to
search, the information
they provide in their search
results is different.

Many search services are a hybrid of a search engine and a
directory. A hybrid search service usually gets most of its listings
from one source; thus, hybrid search services are classified according to the main source used. If a hybrid search service gets its
primary results from a directory and its secondary results from a
search engine, the search service is generally classified as a directory.

MSN Search is classified as a directory. Its primary results come
from the LookSmart database, and its secondary (fall-through)
results currently come from Inktomi, a search engine.

Most search engine marketers label both search engines and directories as "search engines," even though search engines and directories have unique characteristics. Web site owners need to understand the differences between the two terms because the strategies for getting listed well in search engines are quite different from the strategies for getting listed well in directories.

Search Engines

What differentiates a search engine from a directory is that the directory databases consist of sites that have been added by human editors. Search engine databases are compiled through the use of special software robots, called spiders, to retrieve information from web pages.

Search engines perform three basic tasks:

- Search engine *spiders* find and fetch web pages, a process called crawling or spidering, and build lists of words and phrases found on each web page.

- Search engines keep an index (or database) of the words and phrases they find on each web page they are able to crawl. The part of the search engine that places the web pages into the database is called an *indexer*.

- Search engines then enable end users to search for keywords and keyword phrases found in their indices. Search engines try to match the words typed in a search query with the web page that is most likely to have the information for which end users are searching. This part of the search engine is called the *query processor*.

How do search engines begin finding web pages? The usual starting points are lists of heavily used servers from major Internet service providers (ISPs), such as America Online, and the most frequently visited web sites, such as Yahoo!, the Open Directory, LookSmart, and other major directories. Search engine spiders will begin crawling these popular sites, indexing the words on every single page of a site and following every link found within a site. This is one of the major reasons it is important for a web site to be listed in the major directories.

What Is a URL?

A uniform resource locator (URL) is an address referring to the location of a file on the Internet. In terms of search engine marketing, it is the address of an individual web page element or web document on the Internet.

Many people believe a URL is the same as a domain name or home page, but this is not so. Every web document and web graphic image on a web site has a URL. The syntax of a URL consists of three elements:

- The protocol, or the communication language, that the URL uses.
- The domain name, or the exclusive name, that identifies a web site.
- The pathname of the file to be retrieved, usually related to the pathname of a file on the server. The file can contain any type of data, but only certain files, usually an HTML document or a graphic image, are interpreted directly by most browsers.

For example, the URL for a home page is commonly written as follows: http://www.companyname.com/index.html.

- The http:// is the protocol (Hypertext Transfer Protocol).
- The www.companyname.com is the domain name.
- The index.html is the pathname. In this example, it is a Hypertext Markup Language (HTML) document named index.

The URL for an About Us page for a company called TranquiliTeas is commonly written as this: http://www.tranquiliteasorganic.com/about.html.

- The http:// is the protocol.
- The www.tranquiliteasorganic.com is the domain name.
- The about.html is the path name.

As a general rule of thumb, whenever you see Add URL or Submit URL to the search engines, remember that every web page has a unique URL.

Figure 1.2 outlines the search engine crawling process for a single web page.

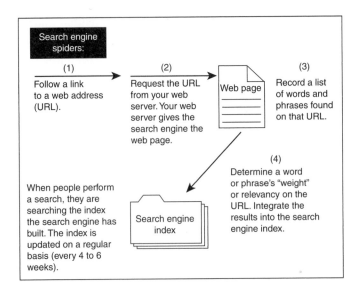

Figure 1.2

How search engines crawl web pages.

Because search engine spiders are continuously crawling the web, their indices are constantly receiving new and updated data. Search engines regularly update their indices about every four to six weeks.

The search engine index contains full-text indices of web pages. Thus, when you perform a search query on a search engine, you are actually searching this full-text index of retrieved web pages, not the web itself.

To determine the most relevant URL for a search query, most search engines take the text information on a web page and assign a "weight" to the individual words and phrases on that page. An engine might give more "weight" to the number of times that a word appears on a page. An engine might assign more "weight" to words that appear in the title tags, meta tags, and subheadings. An engine might assign more "weight" to words that appear at the top of a document. This assigning of "weight" to a set of words on a web page is part of a search engine's algorithm, which is a mathematical formula that determines how web pages are ranked. Every search engine has a different formula for assigning "weight" to the words and phrases in its index.

Search engine algorithms are kept highly confidential and change almost every day. Thus, no search engine optimization expert can ever claim to know an exact search engine algorithm at a specified point in time.

Submission Forms Versus Natural Spidering

Search engines also add web pages through submission forms, generally labeled as Add URL or Submit URL. The Submit URL form enables web site owners to notify the search engines of a web page's existence and its URL.

Unfortunately, unethical search engine marketers (called spammers) created automated submission tools that bombard submission forms with thousands of URLs. These URLs point to poorly written and constructed web pages that are of no use to a web site owner's target audience.

Most of the major search engines state that 95 percent of submissions made through the Add URL form are considered spam.

Because of the overwhelming spam problems, submitting a web page through an Add URL form does not guarantee that the search engines will accept your web page. Therefore, it is generally more beneficial for web pages to be discovered by a search engine spider during its normal crawling process.

However, a search engine optimization expert can do the following:

- Ensure that targeted words and phrases are placed in a strategic manner on the web pages, no matter what the current algorithms are.

- Ensure that spiders are able to access the web pages.

The key to understanding search engine optimization is comprehending Figure 1.2. Why? Because search engine spiders are always going to index text on web pages, and they are always going to find web pages by crawling links from web page to web page, from web site to web site. *Anything that interferes with the process outlined in Figure 1.2 will negatively impact a site's search engine positions.* If a search engine spider is not able to access your web pages, those pages will not rank well. If a search engine can access your web pages but cannot find your targeted keyword phrases on those web pages, those pages also will not rank well.

Pay-for-Inclusion Models

With a pay-for-inclusion model, a search engine includes pages from a web site in its index in exchange for payment. The pay-for-inclusion model is beneficial to search engine marketers and web site owners because (a) they know their web pages will not be dropped from a search engine index, and (b) any new information added to their web pages will be reflected in the search engines very quickly.

This type of program guarantees that your submitted web pages will not be dropped from the search engine index for a specified period of time, generally six months or a year. To keep your guaranteed inclusion in the search engine's index, you must renew your payment.

Submitting web pages in a pay-for-inclusion program does *not* guarantee that the pages will appear in top positions. Thus, it is best that pages submitted through pay-for-inclusion programs be optimized.

Search engine marketers find pay-for-inclusion programs save them considerable time and expense because a web page cannot rank if it is not included in the search engine index. Furthermore, pay-for-inclusion programs enable dynamic web pages to be included in the search engine index without marketers having to implement costly workarounds.

Pay-for-Placement Models

In contrast to pay-for-inclusion models, a pay-for-placement search engine guarantees top positions in exchange for payment. With pay-for-placement search engines, participants bid against each other to obtain top positions for specified keywords or keyword phrases. Typically, the higher the bid, the higher the web page ranks.

Participants are charged every time a person clicks through from the search results to their web sites. This is why pay-for-placement search engines are also referred to as "pay-per-click" search engines. Participants pay each time a person clicks a link to their web site from that search engine.

Many pay-for-placement search engines have excellent distribution networks, and the top two or three positions are often displayed in other search engines and directories. Paid placement advertisements are generally marked on partnered sites as "Featured Listings," "Sponsored Links," and so on.

If no one bids on a particular search term, the free, fall-through results are generally displayed from a search engine partner. For example, currently, the fall-through results for Overture.com come from Inktomi.

Participating in pay-for-placement programs can get expensive. Part 3, "Page Design Workarounds," discusses how to best utilize this type of service.

Search Engine Optimization Strategies

Search engine optimization is the process of designing, writing, coding (in HTML), programming, and scripting your entire web site so that there is a good chance that your web pages will appear at the top of search engine queries for your selected keywords. Optimization is a means of helping your potential customers find your web site.

To get the best overall, long-term search engine visibility, the following components must be present on a web page:

- Text component
- Link component
- Popularity component

All the major search engines (Google, FAST Search, MSN Search, and other Inktomi-based engines) use these components as part of their search engine algorithm. Figure 1.3 illustrates the "ideal" web page that is designed and written for the search engines.

Very few web pages can attain the "ideal" match for all search engine algorithms. In reality, most web pages have different combinations of these components, as illustrated in Figure 1.4.

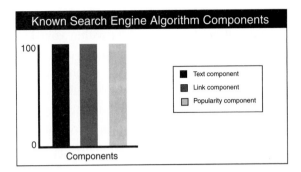

Figure 1.3
Known search engine
algorithm components:
text, link, and popularity.

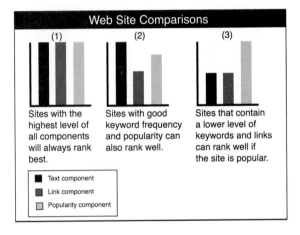

Figure 1.4
Web site comparisons.

Sites perform well in the search engines overall when they have (a) all the components on their web pages and (b) optimal levels of all the components.

Text Component—An Overview

Because the search engines build lists of words and phrases on URLs, it naturally follows that to do well on the search engines, you must place these words on your web pages in the strategic HTML tags.

The most important part of the text component of a search engine algorithm is keyword selection. For your target audience to find your site on the search engines, your pages must contain keyword phrases that match the phrases your target audience is typing into search queries.

After you have determined the best keyword phrases to use on your web pages, you will need to place them within your HTML tags. Different search engines do not place emphasis on the same HTML tags. For example, Inktomi places some emphasis on meta tags; Google ignores meta tags. Thus, to do well on all the search engines, it is best to place keywords in all the HTML tags possible, without keyword stuffing. Then, no matter what the search engine algorithm is, you know that your keywords are optimally placed.

Keywords need to be placed in the following places:

- Title tags

- Visible body text

- Meta tags

- Graphic images (the alternative text)

The title tag and the visible body text are the two most important places to insert keywords because all the search engines index and place significant "weight" on this text.

Keywords in Your Domain Name

Many search engine marketers believe that placing keywords in your domain name and your filenames affect search engine positioning. Some search engine marketers believe that this strategy gives a significant boost whereas others believe that the boost is miniscule.

One reason people believe the position boost is significant is that the words or phrases matching the words you typed in a query are highlighted when you view the search results. This occurrence is called *search-term highlighting* or *term highlighting*.

Search engines and directories might use term highlighting for usability purposes. The process is done dynamically using a highlighting application. This application simply takes your query words and highlights them in the search results for quick reference. Term highlighting merely indicates that query terms were passed through the application. In other words, in search results, just because a word is highlighted in your domain name does not necessarily mean that the domain name received significant boost in search results.

Many other factors determine whether a site will rank, and the three components (text, link, and popularity) have more impact on search engine visibility than using a keyword in a domain name.

Link Component—An Overview

The strategy of placing keyword-rich text in your web pages is useless if the search engine spiders have no way of finding that text. Therefore, the way your pages are linked to each other, and the way your web site is linked to other web sites, does impact your search engine visibility.

Even though search engine spiders are powerful data-gathering programs, HTML coding or scripting can prevent a spider from crawling your pages. Examples of site navigation schemes that can be problematic include the following:

- **Poor HTML coding on all navigation schemes:** Browsers (Netscape and Explorer) can display web pages with sloppy HTML coding; search engine spiders are not as forgiving as browsers.

- **Image maps:** Many search engines do not follow the links inside image maps.

- **Frames:** Google, Inktomi, and Lycos follow links on a framed site, but the manner in which pages display in search results are not ideal.

- **JavaScript:** The major search engines do not follow many of the links, including mouseovers/rollovers, arrays, and navigation menus, embedded inside JavaScript.

- **Dynamic or database-driven web pages:** Pages that are generated through scripts or databases, or that have a ?, &, $, =, +, or % in the URL, pose problems for search engine spiders. URLs with CGI-BIN in them can also be problematic.

- **Flash:** Currently, only Google and FAST Search can follow the links embedded in Flash documents. The others cannot.

Therefore, when designing web pages, be sure to include a navigation scheme so that the spiders have the means to record the words on your web pages. Usually that means having two forms of navigation on a web site: one that pleases your target audience visually and one that the search engines spiders can follow.

For example, let's say that a web site's main navigation scheme is a series of drop-down menus coded with JavaScript. Figure 1.5 illustrates why sites without JavaScript in the navigation scheme consistently rank higher than sites with JavaScript in the navigation scheme.

In Figure 1.5, note that both the text and the popularity component levels are equal in all three graphs. A web page that uses JavaScript in its navigation can rank well in the search engines as long as a spider-friendly navigation scheme (text links, for example) is also present on the web page. However, because some scripts can "trap" a spider (prevent it from indexing the text on a web page), the link component level is lower than a site that does not use JavaScript in its navigation.

Figure 1.5
How a site with JavaScript and a site without JavaScript might rank in the search engines.

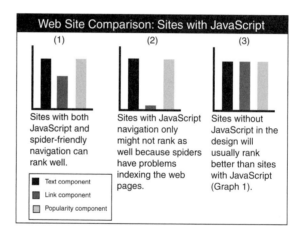

Popularity Component—An Overview

The popularity component of a search engine algorithm consists of two subcomponents:

- Link popularity
- Click-through or click popularity

Attaining an optimal popularity component is not as simple as obtaining as many links as possible to a web site. The quality of the sites linking to your site holds more weight than the quantity of sites linking to your site. Because Yahoo! is one of the most frequently visited sites on the web, a link from Yahoo! to your web site carries far more weight than a link from a smaller, less visited site.

To develop effective link popularity to a site, the site should be listed in the most frequently visited directories. Yahoo!, LookSmart, and the Open Directory are examples of the most frequently visited directories.

More importantly, it can boost your search engine position if a directory that is associated with a search engine lists your site. For example, a site that is listed in LookSmart can be given higher visibility in an MSN Search.

Obtaining links from other sites is not enough to maintain optimal popularity. The major search engines and directories are measuring how often end users are clicking the links to your site and how long they are staying on your site and reading your web pages. They are also measuring how often end users return to your site. All these measurements constitute a site's click-through popularity.

The search engines and directories measure both link popularity (quality and quantity of links) and click-through popularity to determine the overall popularity component of a web site.

If a single page (web page 1) ranks well in the search engines and end users click the links to that web page and browse your site, web page 1's popularity level increases. If a different web page (web page 2) ranks well in the search engines for a different keyword phrase, web page 2's popularity level increases. The total page popularity of your site will increase your overall site's online visibility.

One of the reasons that a site's home page is more important than any other web page is that search engines assign a higher "weight" to it. In all likelihood, the home page is going to be the URL listed in the major directories, and the home page has more links to it from within the web site.

Figure 1.6 illustrates the popularity within a web site. Pages with more links pointing to them have a higher page popularity "weight."

Figure 1.7 illustrates the popularity of a web site, which search engines do not always measure. Search engines measure a web page's popularity; a web site owner also will measure a web site's popularity. Sites with more links pointing to them have a higher site popularity "weight."

Figure 1.6

How search engines measure web page popularity.

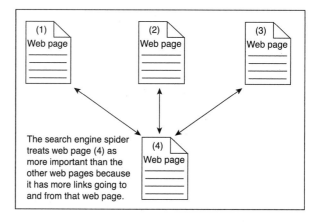

Figure 1.7

How web site owners measure web site popularity.

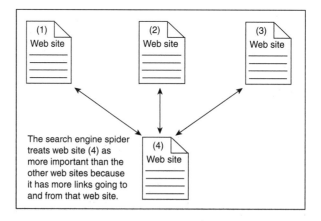

Because popularity consists of multiple subcomponents and these subcomponents are always fluctuating, the popularity measurement is dynamic and cumulative.

All search engine marketing campaigns should begin with the popularity component because all the major search engines measure popularity as a part of their search engine algorithms. The quickest way to achieve an initial, effective popularity component is to have your site listed in what search engines consider reliable sources: the major directories.

Web Directories

Web directories use human editors to create their listings. When you submit a site to be included in a directory, a human editor reviews your site and determines whether to include your site in the directory. Human editors also discover sites on their own through searching or browsing the web.

Every web page (or site) listed in a directory is categorized in some way. The categories are typically hierarchical in nature, branching off into different subcategories. Web searchers can find sites in directories by browsing categories, or they can perform a keyword search for information.

For example, a company that sells "organic teas" might be listed in this Yahoo! category: Business and Economy > Shopping and Services > Food and Drinks > Drinks > Tea > Organic. If we place the categories in a vertical hierarchy, it will look like this:

Business and Economy

    Shopping and Services

        Food and Drinks

            Drinks

                Tea

                    Organic

In this example, the top-level category is called "Business and Economy." A subcategory of "Business and Economy" is "Shopping and Services." A subcategory of "Shopping and Services" is "Food and Drinks," and so on. As we move down (drill down) the category structure, notice that the categories get more and more specific.

A company that sells "herbal teas" might be listed in a different Yahoo! category: Business and Economy > Shopping and Services > Food and Drinks > Drinks > Tea > Herbal. Let's place this categorization into a vertical hierarchy:

Business and Economy

    Shopping and Services

        Food and Drinks

            Drinks

                Tea

                    Herbal

A company that sells a variety of teas might be listed in a less specific Yahoo! category:

Business and Economy

    Shopping and Services

        Food and Drinks

            Drinks

                Tea

Directories are structured in this manner to make it easier for their end users to find sites.

Web pages are generally displayed in directories with a Title and a Description. The Title and Description originate either from the directory editors themselves (upon reviewing a site) or are adapted from site owner submissions. It is important to remember that directories do *not* necessarily use the HTML <title> tag or the description contained in your site's meta tags.

Because most web directories tend to be small, directory results are often supplemented with additional results from a search engine partner. These supplemental results are commonly referred to as *fall-through* results. In fact, many people mistakenly believe that their sites are listed in a directory when they are actually appearing in the fall-through results from a search engine.

Directories usually differentiate their directory listings and their fall-through listings. If you perform a keyword search on a directory, the directory results might appear under a heading titled "Web Site Matches" or "Reviewed Web Sites." Sites that are listed in directories generally have a category displayed with them.

When a web directory fails to return any results, fall-through results from a search engine partner are usually presented as the primary results. Fall-through results are typically labeled "Web Page Matches" or something similar.

One way you can tell if your site is listed in a directory is to perform a keyword search on your company name or URL. If you see a "Powered by Google" or "Powered by Inktomi" near your web site listing, then in all likelihood, your site is listed in the search engine fall-through results but not in the directory (see Figure 1.8).

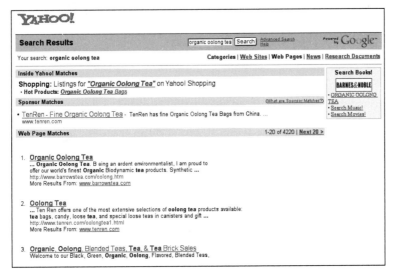

Figure 1.8

The "Powered by Google" image indicates that the search results came from the search engine (Google), not the directory (Yahoo!).

Finally, directories tend to list web sites, not individual web pages. A web site is a collection of web pages that generally focuses on a specific topic. In other words, a web page is part of a web site. A directory is most likely to list only your domain name (www.companyname.com), not individual web pages. In contrast, search engines can list all individual web pages from an entire web site, not just a single home page.

If a particular web page (or set of pages) within a site contains unique, valuable information about a particular topic, that page can be listed in a different directory category. Glossaries and how-to tips are examples of content-rich sections of web sites that can receive additional directory listings.

Paid Submission Programs

A search engine or directory that uses a paid submission program charges a submission fee to process a request to be included in its index. Payment of the submission fee guarantees that your site will be reviewed within a specified period of time (generally 48 hours to 1 week).

If you want to have individual, content-rich web pages included in separate categories, in most cases, you must pay an additional submission fee for another review. Some directories accept content-rich pages without payment, but directory editors generally do not review these pages as quickly as the paid submissions.

The main advantage of paid submission is speed. You know your web site is being reviewed quickly, and, if the editors find your site acceptable, your site is added to the directory database quickly. Furthermore, after your site is added to the directory, the listing gives your site a significant popularity boost in the search engines. Yahoo! is an example of a directory that has a paid submission program.

How Directories Rank Web Sites

When you perform a keyword search in a directory, the search results are displayed in order of importance. Top directory listings are based on the following criteria:

- The directory category

- The web site's title

- The web site's description

If the words you searched for appear in a category name, the category name appears at the top of a directory's search results. For example, if we searched for "organic teas" on Yahoo!, the category that has both the word "organic" and the word "tea" appears at the top of the search results, as shown in Figure 1.9.

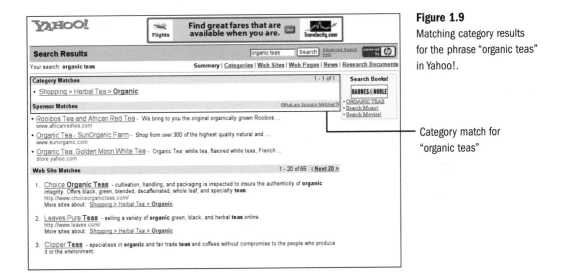

Figure 1.9

Matching category results for the phrase "organic teas" in Yahoo!.

Category match for "organic teas"

Immediately following the category listings are Sponsor Matches, which are pay-for-placement advertisements (see Figure 1.10).

If the words in a search query do not appear in a directory category, the search results display sites that use these words in their titles and descriptions. Figure 1.11 shows the results of scrolling down the Yahoo! search results page.

Sites that have keywords in the category name, title (company name), and description are displayed at the top of the page. Figure 1.11 shows how Yahoo! provides access to some web sites that it feels are directly relevant to the search.

Sites that have keywords in their company name and description appear next, and sites that have only keywords in the description appear after that.

Figure 1.10
Paid advertisements appearing in Yahoo! search results.

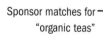

Sponsor matches for "organic teas"

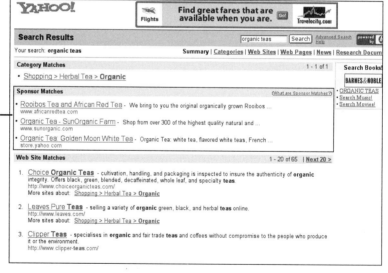

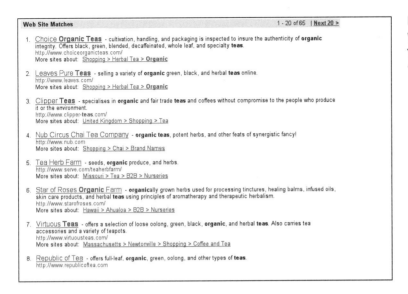

Figure 1.11

Web site matches in Yahoo! for the phrase "organic teas."

How Directory Editors Evaluate Web Sites

Directory editors look at a submitted web site to determine (a) whether unique, quality content is present on the web site, and (b) how this content is presented. Great content is the most important element of any web site, and that content needs to be delivered to your target audience in the most effective way possible. Figure 1.12 illustrates the directory submission process.

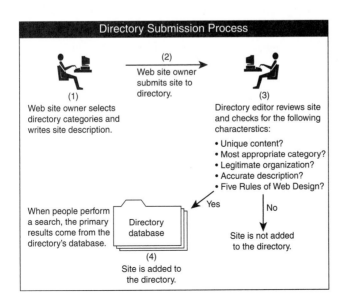

Figure 1.12

How directory editors evaluate a web site.

Directory editors are looking for particular characteristics before including a site in the directory. We discuss those characteristics next.

Unique Content

Directory editors do not want to place sites with identical information in the same category. Thus, before you submit your site to a directory, check out the other sites in your targeted category. Make sure your site contains unique information so that it will add value to that directory category.

You can point out any unique content to the directory editor using your description or the extra comments field in the submission form.

Most Appropriate Category

To select the most appropriate category (or categories) for your web site, type your selected keywords in the directory search box and study the results. If multiple categories appear, view many of the web sites listed under each category. Your site's actual content must accurately reflect the category or categories you wish to be listed under and be similar to the other sites listed in those categories.

You will probably be listed under the same categories your competitors are listed under, though it is important to understand that from directory editors' perspectives, your site belongs in a category that they deem appropriate, not necessarily in a category in which you believe your target audience is searching.

Legitimate Organization/Company

Editors want legitimate organizations and companies listed in their commercial categories. They do not want a small start-up company that will not be around next year. This would result in a dead link to a URL in the directory.

Having a virtual domain (www.companyname.com) is an indication that you are a legitimate organization or business. Having all your contact information (address, telephone number, fax number, and email address) readily available on your site is also an indication that you have a legitimate business. Directory editors will perform a WHOIS lookup (www.netsol.com/cgi-bin/whois/whois) to see if the information there matches the information you gave in your submission form.

If you have an e-commerce site, directory editors are looking for such items as secure credit card processing (for sites that accept credit cards), a return policy or a money-back guarantee (for sites the sell products), and a physical address, not a post office box.

Accurate Description

The description you submit to directory editors should accurately reflect the content of your web site. Directory editors should be able to determine that the description is accurate just by viewing your home page.

For example, if you sell organic tea on your web site and you specialize in three types of tea (oolong, black, and green teas), those three specialties should be obvious to an editor just by his viewing your home page. Furthermore, if directory editors navigate your site or perform a search on a site search engine, they should easily be able to find the pages that show the items used in your description.

Part 2 of this book, "How to Build Better Web Pages," details how to write effective directory descriptions.

Web Design Rules

The Five Basic Rules of Web Design state that a web site should be:

- Easy to read
- Easy to navigate
- Easy to find
- Consistent in layout and design
- Quick to download

In other words, your web site should be easy to use by your target audience.

To have a web site that your target audience will like and that directory editors will approve, these rules all need to be followed. The most successful web sites generally follow these guidelines. What is good about these rules is that they apply not only to directory submissions but also your target audience.

It is important to understand that these rules are interrelated. For example, let's say that your home page has a #1 position in one of the major search engines for your targeted keywords, and people click the link to your site. If your site designer has placed a considerable amount of graphic images, animations, and scripting on your home page, causing it to download slowly, most people will not wait for that page to download. Thus, a perfectly good #1 search engine position can be wasted if your site designer does not consider download time, or any of the other design rules.

Rule #1: Easy to Read

I hear people say all the time, "Of course my web site is easy to read. I'm looking at it right now and I can read it." It would be great if every single person in your target audience were using the exact same computer screen, the exact same browser, the exact same Internet connection, and the exact same computer you are using. In all likelihood, your target audience is using a variety of different computers, monitors, Internet connections, and browsers.

In fact, no one knows how directory editors are viewing your web site. They might be using a notebook computer. They might be using a dial-up connection or a high-speed connection. They might be using a Macintosh computer. Site designers need to accommodate as many platforms, browsers, and Internet connections as possible.

Thus, as a general rule, before you submit your site to the major directories, every single item on your web pages needs to be legible on both of the major browsers (Netscape and Explorer) and on the two types of computers (PCs and Macintosh).

All HTML text should be legible with the graphic images turned on and the graphic images turned off (for the visually impaired users). That means producing HTML text, background images, and text in graphic images with a high color contrast. (The highest color contrast comes from using black and white.) Your site designer should not use backgrounds that obscure your text or use colors that are hard to read.

Your site designer should not set your text size too small (too hard to read) or too large (it will appear to shout at your visitors). If a site is specifically designed for visually impaired users, the text size should be adjusted accordingly.

All text in graphic images should be legible. High color contrast and font/typeface selection are very important for legibility in graphic images. Generally, producing graphic images that use text in a sans serif ("without feet") typeface results in better legibility. See Figure 1.13 for examples.

Times and **Times New Roman** are serif typefaces.

Arial and **Helvetica** are sans serif typefaces.

Figure 1.13
Serif and sans serif typefaces.

Animations (both GIF and Flash animations) should not move so quickly that your target audience is unable to read them. If your target audience must watch the animation loop three or more times to view the full message, the animation is moving too fast.

When your site design or redesign is in the template stage, view it on different browsers, platforms, and Internet connections. Go to a library or a store (such as Kinko's) that has different computers than you have and view your site. Better yet, have other people view your site (they will probably be more objective) and tell you if everything is legible. Do not rely on your singular, personal perspective to determine your site's legibility.

Rule #2: Easy to Navigate

"Easy to navigate" means your target audience should know where they are at all times when they visit your web site. If they get lost, they should be able to go to a site map, a help section, a site search, or a home page from any page on your site to determine (a) where they are, (b) where they might want to go, and (c) where they have been.

Directory editors are always thinking about your target audience. If professional directory editors, who are generally seasoned web users, are having a difficult time navigating your site, your target audience is likely to have a difficult time navigating your site as well.

All your hyperlinks should be clear to both your target audience and to the directory editors. Graphic images, such as navigation buttons or file tabs, should be clearly labeled and easy to read. Just as indicated in the First Rule of Web Design, your site designer should select the colors, backgrounds, textures, and special effects on your web graphics so that they are legible on the major browsers, computer screens, and platforms.

Colors in your text links should be familiar to your target audience. Blue, underlined text usually indicates an unvisited link and purple/maroon, underlined text usually indicates a visited link. If you elect not to use these default colors, your text links should be emphasized in some other way (bold, a different color, different size, set between small vertical lines, or a combination of these effects).

Your hyperlink colors and effects should always be unique—they should not look the same as any other text on your web pages.

Many site designers like to take the underline out of hyperlinked text to be more creative. If you are designing a site that targets the more experienced web user, this design technique should not be problematic as long as the hyperlinked text is unique. However, if your target audience is not web savvy, it is best to keep the underline on the hyperlinked text.

Some directory editors are volunteer editors, and these editors are generally selected for a particular category because of their expertise. You do not know whether volunteer editors are web savvy. Thus, it is important to select your navigation scheme with great care.

Rule #3: Easy to Find

Rule #3 has multiple meanings. Your web site should be easy to find through the search engines. In addition, the individual products, services, and information that you offer should be easy to find after your target audience arrives at your site.

For maximum online visibility, your web site should be easy to find on the search engines, directories, and popular industry-specific web sites. For example, download.com is an industry-specific site for free software downloads. If your company offers a free demo of a 30-day trial of your software, having a link to your site from download.com can significantly increase your site's traffic. Other popular, industry-specific sites (in the fields of healthcare, finance, manufacturing, and so on) will link to your site.

Internally (within your web site), the products, services, and information you offer on your web pages should be easy to find after your target audience arrives at your site. Generally speaking, your target audience does not want to land on your home page and hunt around for information. People prefer to go directly to the web page that contains the information for which they are searching. If they cannot go directly to the web page(s) containing the specific information, they need to find that information within seven to eight clicks, preferably less. If they have to click more than that, they might get frustrated and leave your web site.

After your target audience finds the page that contains the information for which they are searching, they need to see that information "above the fold," or at the top part of the screen. Even if people can't immediately see your product/service on top of the screen, they need to know that what they are searching for is on a particular web page. People should not have to scroll to verify that the information for which they are searching is available on a web page.

A Frequently Asked Questions (FAQs) page is an example in which web site designers do not use the "above the fold" strategy particularly well (see Figure 1.14). Let's say you place ten questions on your FAQs page, and the information that your target audience is looking for is the answer to Question #4. Suppose your site designer formats your FAQs page in a Question 1–Answer 1, Question 2–Answer 2 format, as shown in Figure 1.14.

Figure 1.14
FAQs page with a Question-Answer, Question-Answer format.

Let's assume that the person viewing this page is a domestic violence victim with children. By looking at the top of this screen, this person is not able to determine whether parent/child interaction is allowed at the shelter. In other words, an answer to an important question might not be available on that web page or site.

However, if all your important questions are placed at the top of your screen, your target audience will know that the answer to a question is available on that web page or site, as shown in Figure 1.15.

All your FAQs pages should be formatted in this manner. Not only is this particular strategy beneficial for reaching your end users, but also it is beneficial because this format is a search engine–friendly layout.

Making your main products and services easy to find is important to directory editors. As stated, if your home page states that your firm specializes in three particular services, those three services need to be obvious on your home page, in terms of graphic images and HTML text. If directory editors, and ultimately your end users, have to hunt around too much to determine what your company specializes in, you did not make your services easy to find.

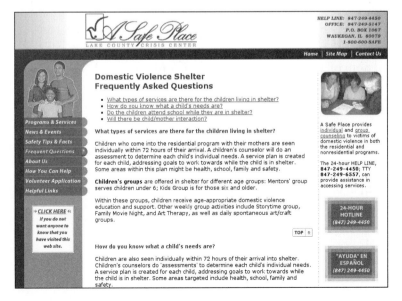

Figure 1.15

A properly formatted FAQs page makes important information about the web page available at the top of the screen.

If the information on your site is password protected or requires some kind of plug-in to get to, directory editors are unable to determine whether your site delivers the information you claim it does. Make sure some of the information available on your web site is not password protected so that directory editors (and your target audience) can see that your site delivers the content that you claim it does.

The last item that should be easy to find is your company's contact information (mailing or physical address, telephone number, fax number, and contact person's email address). Directory editors in particular will search for this information on your web site.

In general, your contact information should be in one of four places:

- A header or footer
- The About Us page or section
- The Contact Us page or section
- A Locations page or section

The most likely place directory editors are looking for your contact information and the correct spelling of your company name is your About Us page. Thus, even if you do provide contact information in other places, it is still a good idea to always place that information in your About Us section—especially if you place your contact information in a footer because many end users do not scroll to the bottom of a web page to view information.

Rule #4: Consistent in Layout and Design

Layout means the use of HTML code, scripting, and white space on your site. This is screen "real estate" where you place your text, graphic images, and navigation schemes. Consistency in layout design helps your target audience navigate your site and feel comfortable doing business with you.

Design means the use of graphic images, the special effects on your graphic images, fonts and typefaces, and the color on your site. Many aspects of the design should be repeated throughout a web site. The fonts, typefaces, and colors used in the main body text, hyperlinks, and headings should be the same on every page of your site.

If you are showing photos of the products you offer, the photo dimensions (length and width) should fall within a short range. Horizontal photos should have the same dimensions and vertical photos should have the same dimensions. If you use a drop shadow on your product photos, you should use drop shadows on all your product photos.

Graphic images and text should never be placed on a web page randomly or arbitrarily. Everything should have a visual connection with other items on a web page. Related items, such as a main navigation scheme and a secondary navigation scheme, should be grouped so that they are seen as a cohesive group rather than as unrelated items.

Making two navigation schemes visually different creates visual contrast but also shows how they are interrelated. For example, a main navigation scheme can be shown at the top of a page using a set of specific colors, and the secondary navigation scheme can open up on the left side of the screen with a different set of colors that blend well with the main navigation.

Figure 1.16 shows an example of a web page that shows visual contrast and connectivity. This is also a well-constructed web page for search engines, directories, and the target audience.

Figure 1.16

Sample of a well-constructed web page.

Subnavigation buttons   Main heading   Subheadings   File tabs

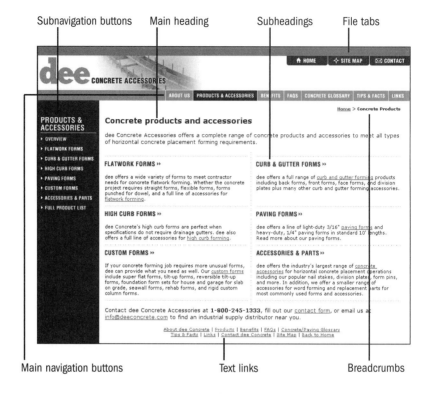

Main navigation buttons   Text links   Breadcrumbs

Note the following in Figure 1.16:

- File tab graphic images link to the home page and site map, in the event the target audience gets lost or needs to reorient themselves. This set of navigation images is in the same place on every web page.

- Main navigation buttons change color when end users are visiting that section of the web site.

- A secondary navigation scheme, or subnavigation, opens up when end users click the link from the main navigation. Text in the subnavigation repeats the text in the main navigation to further indicate that the navigation buttons on the left are a subset of the main navigation.

- Breadcrumbs indicate which page the end users are currently visiting.

- A main heading (which can also be a graphic image) indicates which page the end users are currently visiting.

- Subheadings (graphic images) highlight the main features of this section of the web site. Arrows on the subheadings give a subtle hint that they are hyperlinks.

- Text links at the bottom of the page correspond to the main navigation buttons. These links indicate which pages the target audience has already visited. The hypertext link colors remain similar to a browser's default colors because the target audience is not considered to be as web savvy as people who regularly work on the web.

Rule #5: Quick to Download

Directory editors look for web pages that download very quickly, preferably within 30 seconds on a standard dial-up connection. Of course, there are a few exceptions to this guideline, such as pages that specialize in online video games. Then it is understandable that a web page might take longer to download because plug-ins such as Flash or Shockwave must download first for the game to display.

Most pages do not fall in the "video game" category, so it is best to minimize your pages' download time, particularly your home page. The following are some general guidelines to follow that will decrease your pages' download time:

- **Use animation sparingly:** Animation should be used only to call attention to important sections of your web site. Graphic artists who specialize in animation can safely use animation on their pages as long as they are useful.

- **Follow the KISS rule:** Keep it simple, stupid. You want customers to notice the products, services, and information you offer on your web site, not your pretty site design. If your target audience notices your site design before they notice your content, the design is not effective. A person searching for "accounting software" does not type the words "pretty site design" in a search box when he or she is looking for information about accounting software.

- **Use smaller graphic images, called thumbnails, for product photos:** On your Products pages, a gallery of small photos will download more quickly than full-size photos. Give your target audience the choice to view the larger photos after they show interest.

- **To get a faster download time, always create separate, unique thumbnail-size graphic images from their larger versions:** All graphic images should be resized in graphic image software, not with HTML.

- **Use the same graphic images on multiple pages of your site whenever possible:** Using graphic images consistently also lends to continuity in your presentation. For example, placing your logo on every page of your site (with a hyperlink to your home page) helps with both navigation and branding, and it helps your target audience know whose site they are visiting at all times. The logo image will download only once because it will be saved in the browser's cache. Introducing new graphic images on each page requires time-consuming downloading as a visitor moves around your site.

- **Understand the variety of customers in your target audience:** Different customers will tolerate different download times. If you have graphic design or an online game site, your customers are more likely to wait for pages to download to experience your creative flair. However, if you are selling machine parts to busy manufacturers, ease of access to valuable information should be your primary concern.

Download time is not only important to your target audience. It is also important for search engine visibility. When a search engine spider requests a web page from your server, if the page takes too long to download, or if your server does not give the page to the spider quickly, the search engine might not add the page to the index.

Conclusion

To get the best search engine visibility, web designers should follow the Five Basic Rules of Web Design, which state that a web site should be:

- Easy to read

- Easy to navigate

- Easy to find

- Consistent in layout and design

- Quick to download

By following these rules, you are building your web site to satisfy your target audience. The added benefit of following these rules is that both directory editors and search engines are looking for these same characteristics.

The following design components help form the foundation of an effective search engine marketing program:

- Text component

- Link component

- Popularity component

Web pages that contain the words that your target audience is typing into search queries generally have greater search engine visibility than pages that contain little or no keywords.

The way your web pages are linked to each other also affects your site's search engine visibility. If search engine spiders can find your pages quickly and easily, your site has a much better chance of appearing at the top of search results.

If two web sites have the same text component and link component "weights," the site that end users click the most will usually rank higher. Sometimes, a popular web site will consistently rank higher than sites that use plenty of keywords. Therefore, building a site that appeals to both directory editors and your target audience is very important for maximum search engine visibility.

How to Build Better Web Pages

Introduction

The foundation of a successful search engine optimization program consists of three components: the text component, the link component, and the popularity component. Web sites that utilize these three building blocks, in synergy, gain far more search engine visibility than sites that do not use them.

This part provides details for building each component. The result? A web site that pleases your site's visitors, the search engine spiders, and directory editors.

Text Component

To obtain maximum search engine visibility, it is essential to understand how your target audience is searching for actual information on your web site. When your target audience uses a search engine to find the products and services you offer, they type a set of words or phrases into the search box. This set of words is commonly called your site's *keywords* or *keyword phrases*.

For your target audience to find your site on the search engines, your pages *must* contain keyword phrases that match the phrases your target audience is typing into search queries.

When a search engine spider analyzes a web page, it determines keyword relevancy based on an algorithm, which is a formula that calculates how web pages are ranked. The most important text for a search engine is the most important text for your target audience—the text your target audience is going to read when they arrive at your web site.

To best understand the most important text on a web page, the text should satisfy the following requirements:

- The text must be visible on a standard web browser without your target audience performing some type of action.

- You must be able to copy and paste the text directly from the web browser to a text editor (such as Notepad).

The two most important places to put keywords are in the title tag and in the visible-body text. Title-tag text and visible-body text are considered primary text by the search engines because all the search engines index this text and place significant weight on it. Most of your copywriting efforts should focus primarily on this text.

Meta-tag text and alternative text are considered secondary text by the search engines because not all search engines read and record this text.

For example, using the aforementioned criteria, your target audience must perform an action (View Source) to see meta-tag content (see Figure 2.1). However, I highly recommend that you write effective copy for these tags for the search engines that do read this text.

Title tag

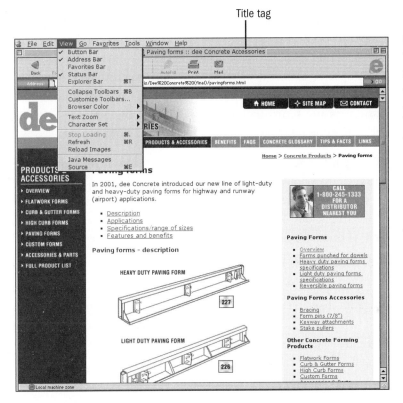

Figure 2.1

To view the meta-tag content on this web page, end users must perform an action. They must select View > Source on the drop-down menu in their browsers. Alternative text can be viewed in this manner as well as placing your mouse over a graphic image. Note that the title tag can be viewed without having to perform an action.

Keyword Selection

The foundation of an effective search engine marketing campaign is selecting the best keywords that your potential customers use to find your site. Selecting the right keywords requires research.

Pretend that someone has never heard of your business but is looking for your type of product or service. Remember that you must determine the keywords that your potential *customers* would type in a search box, not the words that *you* would type in a search box.

You probably have a decent list of keywords already. Review your company's printed materials. What words are used over and over? Remove all words used for sales and marketing hype from your printed materials. Many of the remaining words are possible keywords.

When you speak to new and current customers on the phone, what questions do they frequently ask and what words do they use? Do they mention a specific product or service? Do they frequently ask for a specific department? Ask your current customers how they would find you on the web. You might discover that your current customers use terms that you haven't even thought of. Consider including these unexpected terms in your keyword list.

When you prepare a potential list of keywords, you must determine the various word combinations your target audience is most likely to type to a search query. Singular and plural versions of your most important keywords, synonyms, misspellings, acronyms, and abbreviations (with and without periods) are all potential keywords. Begin by brainstorming.

For example, let's use a fictitious company called TranquiliTeas Organic Teas, Inc., which is a company that sells organic teas and tea sets. The TranquiliTeas site might have the following keyword list:

organic teas	organic tea	oolong tea
oolong teas	green tea	green teas
organic oolong tea sets	organic green tea	tea set
tea recipes	tea cups	teacups
herbal tea	organic tea recipes	herbal teas
decaffeinated tea	black teas	black teas
whole leaf tea	decaffeinated teas	decaffeinated tea
iced tea recipes	whole leaf teas	tea drinks
tea spoons	loose leaf teas	tea accessories
tea kettles	tea pots	tea pot
tea bags	tea kettle	what is organic tea
specialty teas	jasmine tea	gourmet tea
tea gifts	tea ceremony	china tea sets

chinese tea	tea mugs	porcelain tea sets
chinese oolong tea	japanese tea	indian tea
japanese tea ceremony	japanese green tea	indian black tea
whole leaf tea	herbal tea recipes	accessories

You might have noticed that all the keywords in the preceding list are in lowercase. Generally, when people type words in a search box, they tend to type the words all in lowercase. Initially creating your keyword list in lowercase makes this task easier.

Some search engines are case sensitive. This means that searching for "Chinese tea" might yield different search results than searching for "chinese tea." Later on when you narrow down your keyword list, you might determine that the uppercase version of a word is more frequently used than the lowercase version of a word.

When you create your keyword list, think up as many combinations as possible. When people are searching for something specific, they tend to use more than one word. For example, if a person is looking for "software," he or she might find a wide variety of software listed in the search results. That person might be looking for "accounting software" and not "graphic design software." If that person is running a small business, a more accurate search phrase might be "small business accounting software" or "accounting software for small businesses."

It is usually better to target longer keyword phrases because the people who type specific keyword phrases are more likely to be converted into customers. Three-, four-, or five-word keyword phrases often yield more accurate results in the search engines.

Targeting longer keyword phrases does not mean that you give up the chance to rank well for other keyword phrases or a single word. When you target the keyword phrase "organic herbal tea recipes," you are concurrently targeting all the following words and phrases:

- Organic tea recipes

- Herbal tea recipes

- Organic herbal tea

- Herbal tea

- Organic tea

- Tea recipes

- Herbal recipes

- Tea

- Recipes

After you have determined your initial keyword list, you can begin to narrow it down using many of the tools available online.

Tools, Techniques, and Tips

When you begin to analyze your keyword list, you are looking for trends. Whenever I prepare a keyword list, I always put the list into a spreadsheet. A spreadsheet can help you see the trends more quickly and easily.

The first set of data is your initial keyword list. After you have this keyword list, you need to determine which keyword combinations your target audience is most likely to type in search engine queries. Questions you need to ask yourself include the following:

- Did people tend to use the singular or plural version of a word?

- What three or four words appeared together most often?

- What was the word order?

If you have a new web site and do not have any statistics on keywords, you can use the major search engines and directories to assist you.

Related Searches

Many search engines and directories offer a "Related searches" or "Others searched for" or "Narrow your search" feature in their search results. For instance, after searching for "organic tea" at AltaVista, the search box on the results page displays "Refine your search with AltaVista Prisma," as shown in Figure 2.2.

The keyword phrases listed under the "People who did this search also searched for" heading are some of the most popular related searches conducted by HotBot's users. See Figure 2.3.

Notice that there are some words that have nothing to do with the tea business, such as the Texas Education Agency, whose abbreviation is T.E.A. You know you can safely ignore that keyword phrase. In this instance, you can see that the plural version of "tea" is popular along with the phrases "green tea" and "herbal tea."

Likewise, if you perform the same search on Yahoo!, you might get a different set of popular keyword phrases, as shown in Figure 2.4.

Notice that some of the keyword phrases are on your initial keyword list (Chinese tea, herbal tea, and green tea). In addition, a phrase that you might not have thought to target (English tea) is also on the list. What we are beginning to see is a possible pattern. Both "green tea" and "herbal tea" are popular searches. Therefore, when you are designing and writing your web site, you might want to have pages dedicated specifically to green teas and herbal teas.

Figure 2.2
"Refine your search" results for the keyword "organic tea" at AltaVista.

Figure 2.3
Related search results for the keyword "tea" at HotBot.

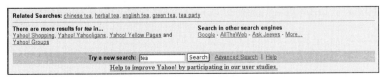

Figure 2.4
Related search results for the keyword "tea" at Yahoo!.

Other items you might want to keep track of are directory categories. Which directory categories appeared most often during a search? In your spreadsheet, keep track of the names of directory categories. Many directory categories contain keywords, and you might want to use some of these keywords on your pages.

Did some phrases not yield any related searches? This could mean that your targeted keyword phrase might not be a popular search phrase on the search services *but* it could be a popular search phrase by your target audience. Data from any site statistics program (such as WebTrends) and your site search engine, if you have one, can confirm the actual keyword phrases your target audience is actually using to find your site.

AlltheWeb.com (FAST Search), Lycos, AskJeeves, and Teoma offer a version of "Related searches." An online service called Word-Tracker can also assist you in your keyword research.

Overture

Overture is a pay-per-click search engine that enables you to easily check for what Overture users are searching. The "Search Term Suggestions" feature is an excellent tool for refining your keyword list. The current URL for this tool is http://inventory.overture.com/d/searchinventory/suggestion/.

Enter one of your keywords into the search box. The search results are a list of the most popular search terms containing your keyword. For instance, entering the term "herbal tea" generated the list of matches shown in Figure 2.5.

This list shows how many times people searched for the word "herbal tea" in May 2002. You can see that 6,812 people searched for the keyword phrase "herbal tea" in that month, "essiac tea" was the second-most-popular keyword phrase, and "herbal tea recipe" was the fourth-most-popular keyword phrase.

Perform as many searches as you can to get a thorough picture of what your target audience is searching for. Because the fictional tea site we are working on specifically sells organic teas, we can perform a search on Overture for "organic tea" (see Figure 2.6).

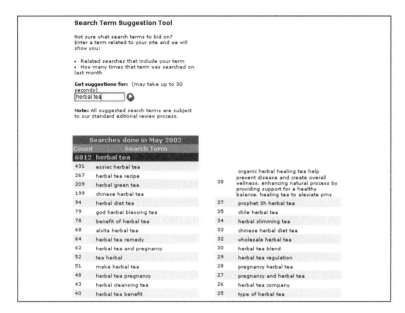

Figure 2.5
Search results for the keyword phrase "herbal tea" at Overture.

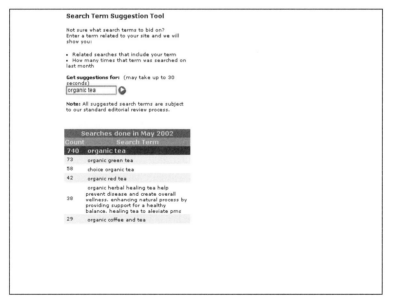

Figure 2.6
Search results for the keyword phrase "organic tea" at Overture.

Notice that the types of organic teas searched for are green and red teas. ("Choice" is a brand name.) The keyword phrase "herbal tea" might be a more popular search phrase, but the phrase "organic herbal tea" might yield better conversions.

Always perform multiple searches to get a clear picture of what your target audience is interested in reading. Search for single words, such as "tea" to see the variety of related searches. Based on that search, narrow down your list. Search for "herbal teas," "herbal tea recipes," and "tea recipes." Keep track of your search results in a spreadsheet.

Google AdWords

Google has its own research tool for its pay-per-click AdWords program. The current URL for this tool is https://adwords.google.com/select/main?cmd=KeywordSandbox.

For this tool, you can enter one keyword or keyword phrase per line in the query box, and Google presents you with a list of keyword phrases. For example, in Figure 2.7, if you enter the single keyword phrase "herbal tea" in the query box, only three search results display. Notice that the keyword phrase "herbal tea recipes" appeared in both Google and Overture. Therefore, the TranquiliTeas company might want to create a section of recipes on its site. When applicable, Google also suggests other keywords.

Figure 2.7

Search results for the keyword phrase "herbal tea" at Google.

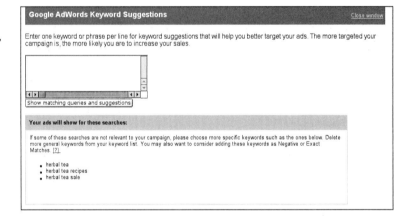

Both Google and Overture have created these tools for their paying customers. To keep these services free, do not perform exhaustive numbers of searches daily to determine your keyword list. Generally, you can figure out your keyword list within 10 searches or fewer on each engine. After you determine your keyword list, you can rely on other tools, such as your site statistics software and site search engines, to maintain your list.

The Truth About Misspelled Words

Many search engine marketers recommend using misspelled words as part of a keyword list. Sometimes this is a good keyword strategy and sometimes it is not a good strategy. It depends on the word(s) you are targeting.

For example, "oolong" is a commonly misspelled word. When you perform a search for the misspelled "olong" on Overture, only one keyword phrase each appears in the search results, as shown in Figure 2.8.

Figure 2.8
Search results for the misspelled word "oolong" at Overture.

Because this word does not appear to be a popular search, I would not be overly concerned with the misspelling. To minimally compensate for a misspelled keyword phrase, put the misspelling in the meta keywords tag.

Remember that for the search engines to consider a word important, you must use that word in your primary text: your title tag and your visible-body text. In all likelihood, you will not need to create a web page specifically for a misspelled word unless that word is a popular misspelling.

Word Stemming

Word stemming is the capability of a search to include the root or stem of words for multiple search results. For example, stemming enables a searcher to enter "marketing" in a search query and get search results for the stem word "market."

Not all search engines have stemming capabilities. Therefore, whenever possible, try to determine the most popular, targeted variation of a specific keyword. Quite often, the plural version of a keyword is more popular than the singular version of a keyword. If you believe multiple versions of a word (such as "market" and "marketing") are both important, then leave both words in your keyword list.

Stop Words and Filter Words

Filter words are common words (a, an, but, or, nor, for, the) that the search engines ignore during a search. Search engines filter out these words because the use of these words in a search query can slow down search results without improving their accuracy. Filtering out common words can save search engines enormous amounts of space in their indices.

Stop words are words that cause the search engine to stop recording all the text on a web page. In other words, when a search engine spider encounters a word or phrase from its list of stop words, it leaves the site without saving any of the site information to its index. Sites already in the search engine index can be removed and banned from resubmission if the search engine finds stop words on your web pages. Some search engines define "stop words" and "filter words" identically.

When preparing your keyword list, eliminate all filter words because they are ignored anyway. If you would like to determine whether a word is a filter word, perform a search on a search engine, such as Google. In the search results, Google tells you which words it ignores (see Figure 2.9).

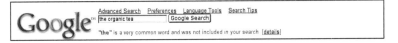

Figure 2.9
Google ignores the word "the" because it is a common word and filters it out of search queries.

Web Site Search Engines

If you have a search engine on your own web site, the words entered into site search queries can also be potential words for your keyword list.

Many times, when your target audience finds your site through a search engine, they want to find the information they are searching for within five to seven clicks. The best-case scenario for your potential customers would be to go from the search engine results directly to the page on your site that contains the exact information for which they are searching. However, this scenario is not always realistic. In all likelihood, your potential customers will browse your site if they do not see the information immediately available. If your visitors cannot find the relevant information by browsing, they might use your site's internal search engine.

Many usability experts report that people prefer to browse for information rather than to use a site search engine. Therefore, when you gather potential keywords from your site search engine, keep in mind that your potential customers probably cannot find that information from browsing your site.

What to Do with Your Keyword List

Based on the data gathered from various resources, you can narrow down your keyword list. The following is the keyword list I came up with for the fictional TranquiliTeas company:

organic teas	organic tea	oolong tea
oolong teas	organic oolong tea	organic oolong teas
green tea	green teas	organic green tea
organic green teas	black tea	black teas
organic black tea	organic black teas	herbal tea
herbal teas	organic herbal tea	organic herbal teas
tea recipes	organic tea recipes	decaffeinated tea

decaffeinated teas	herbal tea recipes	loose leaf teas
whole leaf teas	Japanese teas	Chinese teas
English tea sets	Indian black tea	Indian teas
porcelain tea sets	gourmet teas	tea sets
		tea accessories

Now the TranquiliTeas company knows how to build part of its web site based on this keyword list. They know that the company should create product pages about green, oolong, organic, herbal, black, English, Chinese, and Indian teas.

The web site owner can also create a section of tea recipes, because that appears to be a popular search. Are black tea recipes different from oolong tea recipes? Probably so, because they have considerably different flavors. Maybe they can have seasonal tea recipes—hot tea recipes for winter and cold tea recipes for summer.

This keyword list also sets up some possible Frequently Asked Questions (FAQs) pages. Many people do not know what organic tea is. Thus, some possible questions on a FAQs page might include the following:

- What is organic tea?

- What is the difference between organic and non-organic teas?

- What types of organic teas do you offer?

- Are your organic teas available in both loose leaf and whole leaf varieties?

If you look at this short set of questions, how many times was the word "tea" or "teas" mentioned? How many times was the keyword phrase "organic tea" or "organic teas" mentioned? Creating keyword-rich FAQs pages based on audience keyword preferences is a way to generate search engine traffic—something of which both search engines and directory editors approve.

The following list shows a possible layout of the TranquiliTeas Web site based on the keyword list:

Home Page

Organic Teas

- Organic green teas
  - Asian blend green tea
  - Jasmine green tea
  - Green Moroccan mint tea
  - Decaffeinated green tea with peach
  - Toasted green tea (Ban-cha)
- Organic black teas
  - Darjeeling tea
  - Earl Grey tea
  - Orange Pekoe tea
  - Celtic Breakfast tea
  - Mango Ceylon with vanilla tea
  - Lapsang Souchong
- Organic oolong teas
  - Hunan red oolong tea
  - Oolong orange blossom tea
  - Oolong tea
- Organic herbal teas
  - Peppermint herbal tea
  - Chamomile herbal tea
  - Roseberry herbal tea
  - Orange herbal tea
  - Ginger herbal tea
  - Licorice tea

- Loose leaf teas
  - English Breakfast
  - Irish Breakfast
  - Earl Grey
  - Jasmine green tea

Tea Sets and Accessories

- Japanese tea sets and accessories
- Chinese tea sets and accessories
- English tea sets and accessories
- Porcelain tea sets and accessories
- Tea pots
- Tea infusers
- Tea spoons
- Tea bag holders

Special Offers

- Tea samplers
  - Loose leaf teas
  - Whole leaf teas
  - Tea bags
- Gift baskets

Frequently Asked Questions

- Questions about organic tea
- Questions about Japanese or green tea
- Questions about Chinese or oolong tea
- Questions about Indian or black tea
- Questions about herbal tea
- How to order

Tea Facts

- Japanese teas
- Chinese teas
- Indian teas
- English teas
- History of tea
- Japanese tea ceremony

Tea Recipes

- Hot tea recipes
  - Green tea
  - Black tea
  - Oolong tea
  - Herbal tea
- Iced tea recipes
  - Chai tea
  - Herbal tea

About TranquiliTeas Organic Tea

- Company history
- In the news
- Money back guarantee
- Return policy
- Privacy policy

Links & Resources

Contact Us

Request Catalog

Site Map

Important

If you plan on selling products and services directly on your web site, create additional pages with a return policy, money back guarantee, and a privacy policy, when applicable.

Directory editors will be looking for this type of information on e-commerce sites.

Although this TranquiliTeas layout is by no means complete, you can see how all the keywords naturally appear in the site architecture. This type of site architecture is commonly referred to as a *hierarchical site architecture*.

Natural Themes

Themes are recurrent and consistent ideas presented throughout a web site. By narrowing your keyword list to approximately 20 to 50 targeted phrases, natural themes begin to emerge.

For example, for our fictional TranquiliTeas web site, the theme keyword that is consistently used throughout the site is "teas," and more specifically, "organic teas." These top words are the main theme of a web site. You know that when you land on any page of the TranquiliTeas web site, you are reading information about teas.

The secondary themes for this site might be green teas, oolong teas, black teas, and herbal teas. Various pages on the site can be created around these secondary themes. For example, a set of pages about green teas might be the following:

- Green teas (products) > Loose-leaf green teas
- Green teas (products) > Green tea in tea bags
- Green teas > Japanese tea sets and accessories
- Green teas > Recipes
- Green teas > History of green teas
- Green teas > Frequently asked questions about green teas

Likewise, a natural theme might emerge about oolong teas:

- Oolong teas (products) > Loose-leaf oolong teas
- Oolong teas (products) > Oolong tea in tea bags
- Oolong teas > Chinese tea sets and accessories
- Oolong teas > Recipes
- Oolong teas > History of oolong teas
- Oolong teas > Frequently asked questions about oolong teas

Based on these natural themes, the TranquiliTeas web site owner now knows how to cross-link related pages based on keywords.

A simple way to create natural themes on your site is to create a corresponding set of Frequently Asked Questions (FAQs) pages for each category of products or services. For the fictional TranquiliTeas site, the web site owner can create a set of FAQs for each main tea category: organic teas, green tea, oolong tea, black tea, and herbal teas. Likewise, since "tea recipes" is a popular search phrase, the TranquiliTeas web site owner can create various recipe pages for the different types of teas.

Whenever you create a FAQs page, make sure you link it to the related products or services page. If the FAQs page ranks well in the search engines, you want to encourage site visitors to view your products and services, not just to read your FAQs page.

Likewise, in terms of sales, if a potential customer is interested in purchasing loose leaf green tea, for example, maybe that customer might need a loose leaf tea spoon (to measure the loose tea) or a tea infuser. Maybe a customer interested in Japanese tea sets might also be interested in purchasing green tea. Carefully planned cross-linking encourages your site visitors to make more purchases and communicates to the search engines which pages are important on your web site.

Building your web pages based on keyword research and natural theming makes your content easier to find on the search engines for the following reasons:

- Most web pages on your site contain very specific content, keeping your pages tightly focused.

- Important pages are linked to each other, making it easier for your site visitors to find and purchase related products and services.

Important

It is not necessary to build a Frequently Asked Questions page for every product or service you offer, just the main categories. All FAQs pages should contain unique content and provide information that your target audience is generally interested in reading.

A general rule of thumb is to have at least 4 to 15 questions and answers on each FAQs page. If a FAQs page only contains three questions and answers, the FAQs page probably will not contain enough content on a specific topic.

After a FAQs page contains 16 questions and answers, specific information becomes more difficult to locate, and the download time of the page can significantly increase.

Keyword Placement

After you have gathered a list of your 20 to 50 most popular keyword phrases, you can begin to place them in various HTML tags on your web pages.

Writing Effective Title Tags

A title tag has a specific meaning when it comes to web site design and the search engines. A title tag is the text placed inside the <title> and </title> tags. From Figure 2.10, the title tag looks like this in an HTML editor:

<title>Valley Plastic Surgery Center - specializing in aesthetic and cosmetic surgery</title>

On an actual web page in a web browser, the title tag looks like what is shown in Figure 2.10.

Figure 2.10
The title-tag content displays on both Netscape and Explorer browsers at the very top of the screen. Notice the company name on this page (Valley Plastic Surgery Center) comes first because a popular keyword phrase is a part of the company name.

Title tag

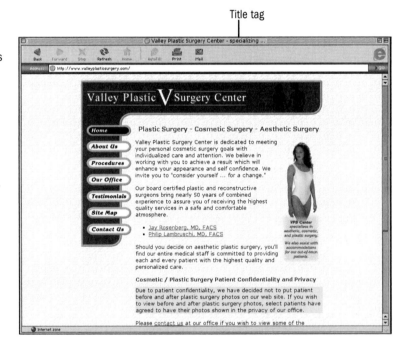

The title tag is very important in terms of search engine visibility because it serves multiple functions:

- Title-tag text is considered primary text by all the search engines, meaning that all the search engines record this text and place a considerable value on it.

- Title-tag text is the first text shown in search results. The text is highlighted in the search results as a hyperlink to your web site. This hyperlink is the call to action—it's letting your target audience know that there is a link to information pertaining to the words they entered in a search query.

- Title-tag text is the text shown in Bookmarks and Favorites.

Thus, a title tag serves two main functions. The first function is for search engine visibility. All the search engines consider title-tag text when calculating relevancy. The second title-tag function is a call to action. Your title-tag content should encourage your target audience to click the link to your site.

As a general rule, write a unique, descriptive title of 5 to 10 words for each page—or 69 to 75 characters. Remove as many filler words as possible from the title. Titles should contain your most important keywords and phrases and accurately reflect the content of your web pages.

All title-tag text should be unique because every page of your web site contains unique content. Does your About Us page contain the same information as your Products pages? Probably not, and your title tags need to reflect the differences in page content.

Unless your company name is well known and has excellent branding, it is best not to place your company name in the title tag. To get or maintain branding and to modify your site to accommodate your target audience, do *not* put your company name in the beginning of the title tag unless you have a keyword in your company name.

For example, the company name TranquiliTeas Organic Teas is a good company name for the search engines because the keyword phrase "organic teas" is part of the company name. Therefore, a good title tag for a page that sells organic green tea might be this:

<title>TranquiliTeas Organic Teas: green tea</title>

Some search engine marketers change an official company name to artificially inflate the keyword density inside the title tag. They might separate words that are normally put together. In the following example, a search engine marketer wanted the word "teas" to be more prominent in the title tag. Thus, he purposely misspelled the company name in the title tag:

<title>Tranquili Teas Organic Teas: green tea</title>

Rather than ruin some otherwise excellent branding, it would be better to put the singular version of the word tea at the end of the title tag because the plural version is already a part of the company name:

<title>TranquiliTeas Organic Teas: green tea</title>

An alternative title that can be equally as effective for both branding and search engine visibility is this:

<title>Green tea from TranquiliTeas Organic Teas</title>

Notice that I didn't include the abbreviations such as Inc., Ltd., or Co. Why? These are words that the target audience is not likely to type into a search engine query. Thus, placing these abbreviations in the title tag is not necessary.

Power Combination Strategy

The best way to write a title with targeted keywords is to utilize a strategy called the *power combination strategy*, or Power Combo. Whenever possible, the first three words in your title tag should consist of words that, when typed in any combination in a search query, can be a keyword phrase. For example:

<title>Organic green teas from TranquiliTeas Organic Teas</title>

The targeted keyword phrases contained in this title tag are as follows:

- Organic green teas

- Organic teas

- Green teas

It is not always possible to create your title tags utilizing the Power Combo strategy. For instance, if a three-word phrase seems very unnatural, don't use it.

Remember that your target audience is going to see your title-tag content in the search results. They don't want to see a list of keywords. They want to see a short phrase that clearly and accurately describes the contents of your web page.

The reason that you should place related keywords close to each other, whenever possible, is that search engines also measure *keyword proximity*. Keyword proximity is measured not only in the title tags, but also throughout the text of an entire web page.

Singular and Plural Strategy

Many businesses find that their target audiences use both the singular and plural version of a word to find their web site. Therefore, using both the singular and plural version of a keyword can be a good title-tag strategy.

For example, the following title tag contains both the singular and plural version of tea:

```
<title>Green tea from TranquiliTeas Organic Teas</title>
```

Keep a list of various titles so that when it comes time to resubmit a page to a search engine or to build another web page targeting the same keywords, you have a database of effective title-tag text. Sometimes, search engines show a preference for short title tags. Sometimes, they show a preference for longer ones. Test every single title and measure your audiences' responses to those titles. Use the titles and keywords that get the best response, and rewrite other web page titles based on your testing results.

The following is a short list of title tags that can go on a page with content about green tea:

- Green tea

- Green teas

- Organic green tea

- Organic green teas

- Organic green tea from TranquiliTeas Organic Teas

- Organic green teas from TranquiliTeas Organic Teas

- Green tea from TranquiliTeas Organic Teas

- Green teas from TranquiliTeas Organic Teas

- TranquiliTeas Organic Teas: green tea

- TranquiliTeas Organic Teas: green teas

- TranquiliTeas Organic Teas: organic green tea

- TranquiliTeas Organic Teas: organic green teas

Body Text

The visible-body text on a web page is the HTML text contained between the <body> and </body> tags that you can copy and paste directly from a web browser to a text editor. Text inside of headings, paragraphs, ordered lists, unordered lists, and tables are examples of visible-body text.

Search engines constantly change the tags on which they place emphasis. You never know if a search engine emphasizes meta-tag content one month and then ignores it the next month. One aspect about the search engine spiders does not change: They always index title tags and body text. For this reason, it is extremely important to place keywords throughout the visible-body text in your web pages to guarantee that search engines can find and record all your relevant keywords.

Keyword Prominence

All the search engines consider the words at the top of a web page, commonly referred to as *above the fold*, more important than the words on the rest of the web page. How high up a keyword is on a web page is called *keyword prominence*.

For example, the Elgin Area Chamber wanted an aesthetically pleasing home page that would help the Elgin community find the site. To be sure that the home page could be found in the search engines, they placed their most important keywords in prominent places, as shown in Figure 2.11.

One simple way to include your important keywords at the top of your web pages is to always include a heading or headline that contains keywords. Use a variation of the title-tag text for a headline. For example, the title tag might state the following:

<title>Green teas from TranquiliTeas Organic Teas</title>

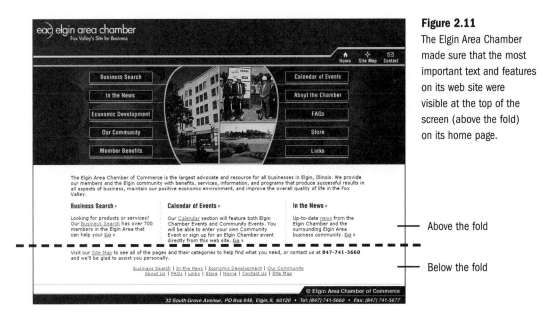

Figure 2.11

The Elgin Area Chamber made sure that the most important text and features on its web site were visible at the top of the screen (above the fold) on its home page.

A simple headline might state this text:

`<h1>Organic green tea</h1>`

If you want your headline to contain a call to action, you can change your headline to contain an action verb, such as the following:

`<h1>Order our organic green tea gift set</h1>`

The first paragraph on your web page should accurately describe the contents of that page, using your most targeted keywords. If your web page contains content that falls below the fold, the first set of text on your page should let your target audience know that the information they are searching for is available on that web page.

An effective way to optimize a long web page is to write multiple headlines using keywords (as shown in Figure 2.12). At the top of the web page, make sure that there are hyperlinks leading to those headlines. Figure 2.12 is an example of a long web page with headlines.

Although using keywords in your introductory paragraph is very important, web pages that contain keyword phrases used consistently throughout the body text often have greater search engine visibility.

Figure 2.12
A Safe Place offers multiple services for children. To be sure that its target audience knows of the different children's services available, the webmaster placed hyperlinks to each children's service at the top of the screen.

Another way to increase keyword density is to write conclusion paragraphs or sentences that can go on almost every single page of a site. Every conclusion sentence contains keywords and an appropriate call to action. For example, consider the following:

```
<p>If you would like more information about our organic green teas,
please email John Smith in our Japanese tea division.</p>
```

If you prefer that your target audience calls you instead of emailing, you can use this text:

```
<p>If you would like more information about our organic green teas and
the other organic teas we provide, please call John Smith at 1-800-xxx-
xxxx.</p>
```

Calls to Action

Obtaining top search engine visibility is only half the battle. To be victorious, you need to convince potential customers to click the link to your site, to purchase the items for sale on your site, or to perform whatever call to action you desire. What do you want people to do when they visit your site? Do you want them to subscribe to a newsletter? Pick up the phone and call you? Place an order using shopping cart software? Fill out an online form?

A search engine–friendly web page does not just satisfy the search engines. It must also satisfy your target audience and help you achieve your site's goals. Therefore, every page that you want listed in the search engines should also contain appropriate calls to action. One of the simplest calls to action is a hypertext link.

The benefits of hypertext links are as follows:

- Many search engines consider the text in and around the anchor tag to be important because you do not link to pages that are not important.

- Your target audience automatically understands that the blue, underlined word (or just the underlined word) should link directly to the information contained in that word. In other words, a hypertext link is a natural call to action.

For example, suppose you have a web page that summarizes the main types of products you have. Many web copywriters use the phrase "learn more" to indicate that there is more detailed information about a product. If there is more information about a specific product, why not add a specific keyword phrase to highlight it?

Thus, instead of this text:

`<a href="greenteas.html">`**Learn more**`</a>`

you could write this anchor text:

`<a href="greenteas.html">`**Learn more about our green teas**`</a>`

One way I like to remind myself to use more keywords is to ask this question:

What kind of ＿＿＿＿＿＿＿＿＿＿ ?

If you offer services, what kind of services do you offer? If you offer products, what kind of products do you offer? If you want your target audience to read more, about what should they read more? Your products? What kind of products do you want them to read more about?

By answering these questions, you can naturally come up with your own set of keywords that you can place within the body of your web pages.

Meta Tags

A *meta tag* is an HTML tag that gives information about the content of a web page, such as what HTML specifications a web page follows or a description of a web page's content. A meta tag, however, does not affect how a web page is displayed in a browser. For search engine visibility, the most common uses for meta tags are the keyword, description, and robots exclusion attributes.

One of the most widespread beliefs about meta tags is that they are the secret ingredient to obtaining optimal search engine rankings. In fact, only some major search engines use meta-tag content for relevancy. Some search engines use meta-tag content when they display the results of a search query. Others (and almost all directories) do not use meta-tag content at all. Thus, meta tags are not a secret ingredient at all. Rather, they are *secondary text* meant to enhance your site in the search results pages.

The Meta-Tag Description Attribute

When writing meta-tag content, spend more time writing a good description than writing a keyword list. In terms of search engine visibility, the description is far more important than the keywords list.

Some major search engines use meta-tag descriptions when displaying the results of a search query. Therefore, the meta-tag description must accomplish two goals:

- Help obtain a good search engine ranking in the search engines that use the meta-tag description for relevancy

- Elicit a call to action, such as encouraging people to click the link to your web site

A meta-tag description is placed between the <head> and </head> tags. The HTML code for a meta-tag description looks like this:

```
<meta name="description" content="Page description goes here.">
```

When writing your meta-tag descriptions, select the most important four to five keywords per page based on your keyword research. Write careful 200-to-250-character sentences and phrases, targeting the most important words contained on your web pages. When you are writing meta-tag descriptions, try to eliminate as many filler words as you can to make room for the keywords.

If you use words in your meta-tag description that you do not use on your web pages, most of the search engines consider it spam. As a rather extreme example, it is the equivalent of an adult/pornography site using the word Disney in its meta tag.

General guidelines to writing meta-tag descriptions include the following:

- Do not repeat your exact title-tag content in the meta-tag description. This sets off a red flag to the search engine spiders that you are keyword stacking.

- The most important keyword phrases should be placed at the beginning of your meta-tag description.

- Use the singular and plural version of your most important keywords, when applicable.

- Try not to separate important keyword phrases.

- Although the search engines do not give specific guidelines for keyword repetition, try to keep repetition to a minimum. I generally stop at three to four repetitions. Too much repetition sets off a red flag to the search engines that you are keyword stacking.

- Some search engines treat different words, such as the singular and plural version, as the same word. When writing your meta-tag descriptions, be aware of this.

- If you are going to repeat words, try not to put them right next to each other. Separate them with other words.

- You should be encouraging your target audience to click the link to your site. Ask your target audience to read more about or learn more about your targeted keywords.

- Placing a list of keywords in your meta-tag description is not an effective way of encouraging your target audience to click the links to your site. It also sets off a red flag to the search engine spiders for potential spam (keyword stuffing).

- Whenever possible, make sure your meta tag contains sentences or long phrases.

Here is an example of a simple but effective meta-tag description:

```
<meta name="description" content="Get gourmet herbal teas at
wholesale prices from TranquiliTeas.  Organic tea importer offers
decaffeinated herbal teas and other herbal blends. Black, oolong,
green, and iced teas available as loose tea or in tea bags.">
```

The preceding meta-tag description contains 183 characters without spaces and 217 characters with spaces. You can determine this in Microsoft Word using the Tools > Word Count function.

Simple ways to create similar meta-tag descriptions are discussed in the following sections.

Changing the Verb

In the aforementioned meta-tag description, you can remove the word "get":

```
<meta name="description" content="Gourmet herbal teas at wholesale
prices from TranquiliTeas.  Organic tea importer offers decaffeinated
herbal teas and other herbal blends. Black, oolong, green, and iced teas
available as loose tea or in tea bags.">
```

You can also change the word "get" to one of the following:

- …Providing gourmet herbal teas at wholesale prices…

- …Offers gourmet herbal teas at wholesale prices…

- …Select gourmet herbal teas at wholesale prices…

- …Buy gourmet herbal teas at wholesale prices…

- …Your online resource for gourmet herbal teas…

Adding a Call to Action at the End of the Meta Tag

Another way to add quality keywords to your meta-tag content is to add the phrase "Learn more about *keyword*." Other ways of stating this phrase are as follows:

- …Read details about our gourmet herbal teas…

- …Contact us for more information about our gourmet herbal teas…

You can also change the verb to a different verb tense. In the following example, we used the word "offering" instead of the word "offers":

```
<meta name="description" content="Gourmet herbal teas at wholesale
prices from TranquiliTeas.  Organic tea importer offering decaffeinated
herbal teas and other herbal blends. Available as loose tea or in tea
bags.  Also offering black, oolong, green, and iced teas.">
```

Changing the Word Order or Phrase Order

When you adjust phrases, be careful that you are not keyword stacking. Remember that all meta-tag descriptions should accurately reflect the body-text content of the web page.

<meta name=description content=Gourmet herbal teas at wholesale prices. Also offering black, oolong, green, and iced teas. Organic tea importer offering decaffeinated herbal teas and other herbal blends. Available as loose tea or in tea bags.>

If you do not have the time to write unique meta-tag descriptions for your web pages, copy and paste the first two sentences of your main HTML text into the meta-tag description. If you do not place text in the meta-tag description, the search engines (which use meta-tag descriptions) might come up with their own description based on the content of your web page. That description probably will not showcase your web pages in the best light, as shown in Figure 2.13.

Many search engine marketers use a list of keywords in the meta-tag description. Not only is this search engine marketing strategy borderline spam, but also it is a poor way to encourage visitors to click the link to your site. Take a look at Figure 2.14. Would you click this in a search result?

Figure 2.13

This web page obtained a #5 position in HotBot, but its description reads "Please turn on JavaScript in your web browser for QuickLinks." A meta-tag description with keywords and a call to action could yield more clicks.

5. Green tea,Sencha,Black tea,Kukicha,hot tea,Assam,iced tea,Ceylon tea,chai,herbal...
656 - TeaTeaTea triple the flavor. Selection of teas from green **tea** to oolong to **black tea**. Single estate,blended,**organic**,decaffeinated,flavored and scented.

Figure 2.14
A top search result from AlltheWeb.com. This search result is difficult to read and contains no call to action.

Using a Company Name in a Meta-Tag Description

Just as with the title tag, unless an official company name contains a keyword, either do not use it in a meta-tag description or move it to the end of the description. For example, "inc." is not a keyword unless the site is Inc. magazine.

The Meta-Tag Keywords Attribute

When selecting words to place in the meta-tag keywords attribute, it is best to select keywords that you actually use on the content of the web page. If a word appears in your meta tags that does not appear in your main body content, your web page very likely can receive a spam penalty from the search engines.

When selecting keywords and keyword phrases for the meta-tag keywords attribute, consider the following variations:

- **Singular versus plural.**

  When creating your keywords list, place the version of the keyword that your site visitors use the most at the beginning of your keyword list.

- **Uppercase versus lowercase.**

  Most search engines do not use case sensitivity as an element of their algorithms. Thus, using all versions (all uppercase, all lowercase, or all initial capitalization) of keywords and keyword phrases is probably a waste of time and can result in a spam penalty for keyword stacking.

  Consider this as well: When people type words and phrases in a search engine query, they tend to type words very quickly. The quickest way to type words is not to use any capitalization.

Important

The meta-tag keywords attribute is important for sites with an internal site search engine. It is not important for visibility in the major search engines. If you do not have the time to create unique content for this attribute, then you can safely skip this optimization procedure.

■ **Commas versus no commas.**

It makes no difference to the search engines that use the meta-tag keywords attribute whether you use commas or spaces to separate your keywords and keyword phrases. If it is easier for you to view your keyword phrases with commas, use them. Using commas does not affect your web page's relevancy.

■ **Misspelled keywords.**

Because some keywords (such as the word "millennium") are commonly misspelled, you might want to put a misspelled keyword in your meta-keywords tag. However, if that misspelled word does not appear in your main body text, this strategy is generally a waste of time.

Search engines use both keyword frequency and keyword placement in their algorithms. If you are putting a misspelled keyword in only one place, it's not helping your web page's relevancy because the keyword density for that one word is practically non-existent.

The Meta-Revisit Tag

The meta-revisit tag supposedly instructs a search engine spider to revisit a web page within a specified period of time. The HTML code for this tag looks like this:

```
<meta name="revisit-after" content="14 days">
```

According to the instructions in this meta tag, the search engine spiders are instructed to revisit this particular web page every 14 days. I like to use this particular meta tag to quiz potential search engine marketers to see how knowledgeable they really are. I know that this particular meta tag is useless.

No one can tell a search engine spider what to do. You cannot tell a search engine to revisit your site every 14 of days. You cannot tell a search engine the language in which to index your site. In fact, on their submission forms, search engines do not even guarantee that your web pages will be listed. So don't use this tag. It is useless.

The Meta-Robots Tag

Some web site owners do not want search engine spiders to index the content of a specific web page. Thus, they use the meta-tag robots exclusion attribute. The following shows the proper HTML coding for this meta tag:

```
<html>
<head>
<title>Green tea from TranquiliTeas Organic Teas</title>
<meta name="robots" content="noindex">
</head>
```

Not all search engines honor this type of meta tag. Instead, they indicate that you should use the robot.txt file, which is discussed in the section titled "The robots.txt File" later in this chapter.

Many search engine marketers like to instruct the search engines to index a page using this meta tag:

```
<html>
<head>
<title>Green tea from TranquiliTeas Organic Teas</title>
<meta name="robots" content="index, follow">
</head>
```

According to this meta tag, the search engines are supposed to index the text on the web page that contains this tag, and the search engines are supposed to follow the links on this web page. This is another useless meta tag. Search engines automatically index the text and follow links on a web page.

Alternative Text

Alternative text is the text that is placed inside graphic images in HTML code. Alternative text tells a browser that if this graphic image is not downloaded, show this text in its place.

The HTML code for alternative text looks like this:

```
<img src="images/home.gif" height="25" width="60" alt="TranquiliTeas
Organic Teas home">
```

Here are the elements that you see in the code:

- img is the HTML coding that tells the browser (Netscape or Explorer) to insert a graphic image into a web page.

- src is the attribute that indicates which filename or URL of the graphic image you want to place on the web page. In this example, the image name is a GIF called home.gif, which is stored in the directory called images on a particular web site. The filename or URL must be enclosed in quotation marks.

- width and height are your graphic image's dimensions, measured in pixels. Using the width and height attributes in your img src tag preserves the layout of your web pages. Also, web pages using the width and height attributes in their img src tags download faster than pages not using these attributes.

- alt stands for the alternative text attribute. Alternative text must also be enclosed in quotation marks.

Alternative text appears in the place of graphic images if your visitors are using a text-only browser. Furthermore, some people might use devices such as screen readers. These devices translate the contents of a web page into Braille or into speech. Therefore, the only way that graphic images can be "read" is by placing alternative text inside your site's graphic images.

Search engine marketers and web designers often overlook this attribute. Some search engines index alternative text, thus making your graphic images another place to strategically place keywords.

In addition, if you are using Explorer as your browser, when you position your cursor over a graphic image, Explorer displays the alternative text message in a little box next to the cursor (similar to pop-ups).

For example, let's say you have a web site that offers graphic design services. One of your navigation buttons has the word "Services" on it. The alternative text for that graphic image can be this:

```
<img src="images/services.gif" width="120" height="20"
alt="Services">
```

The word "Services" is not very descriptive of the type of services your site offers. Remember the question "What kind of _____?" Fill in the blank. What kind of services does your web site offer? If your site offers graphic design services, for example, a better phrase for the alternative text would be this:

```
<img src="images/services.gif" width="120" height="20" alt="Graphic
design services">
```

Many unethical search engine marketers try to stuff as many keywords as they can into a graphic image, a spam tactic called *keyword stuffing*. The following alternative text is an example of keyword stuffing:

```
<img src="images/services.gif" width="120" height="20" alt="Graphic
design – graphic designer – graphic designs – graphic designing
services">
```

The keywords and phrases must be relevant and accurately describe the graphic image. Keyword prominence also applies to graphic images. In other words, the graphic images (containing alternative text) that your target audience views at the top of the screen are more important than the graphic images at the bottom of a screen.

Transparent Images

Many web designers use a transparent 1×1-pixel transparent image, commonly called a blank.gif or a clear.gif, to get elements on a web page to line up correctly. Because of current browser incompatibilities, there still is a need to use these types of images.

However, according to the search engines, when you place alternative text inside a graphic image, that text must be relevant: (a) to the actual graphic image, and (b) to the web page on which the image is placed. Hiding keywords or links inside a graphic image is considered spam.

Thus, if you must use transparent images on your web pages, do not place any alternative text in the graphic image. You can also place just a punctuation mark (such as an asterisk) as the alternative text. Search engines do not read punctuation marks.

URL/Filenames

Many search engine marketers believe that placing keywords in your domain name and your filenames greatly affects search engine positioning. In other words, this domain name:

www.tranquiliteasorganic.com/

should get a significant boost in search engine visibility because the words "teas" and "tea" are in the domain name. This domain name:

www.tranquiliteasorganictea.com/

should get a stronger boost than the previous domain name because this domain name contains more keyword phrases. The best domain name of all for this site would be this:

www.tranquili-teas-organic-tea.com/

Therefore, a page on the TranquiliTeas site should name its green tea page greenteas.html, as follows:

www.tranquili-teas-organic-tea.com/green-teas.html

As stated, some search engine marketers believe that this strategy gives a significant boost whereas others believe that the boost is miniscule.

Simply placing keywords in a domain name and/or a filename is not going to make or break top search engine visibility. Remember that search engines index text and follow links. If a web page does not contain keywords and does not have a link architecture for the search engines to follow, changing the domain name to a keyword domain will not cause your site to magically appear at the top of search results.

Keywords in the domain names and filenames are not as important as people are led to believe. Unfortunately, as soon as people read that an item has an impact on search engine positioning, they place far too much importance on it. Why focus your energy on a strategy that has miniscule impact rather than strategies that have true impact, such as web copywriting, site architecture, and popularity?

Keywords in a domain name give miniscule boost when all other factors (text, link, and popularity components) are equal. A filename for a graphic image is important if you want your site's graphic images to appear in graphic image searches. Otherwise, do not obsess over file naming. Other items on your site are far more important.

Keyword Density

Keyword density is a measure of the number of times keywords occur within a web page's text, as shown in the following formula:

$$\frac{\text{Keyword phrase}}{\text{Total number of words on page}} = \text{Keyword density}$$

Search engine marketers calculate keyword density in different ways. Some marketers include all the words on a web page. Some marketers do not include stop words or filter words as part of the total word count. Regardless, you will hear many different numbers, depending on the search engine marketer with whom you speak.

A 250- to 800-word page (including stop words, but not including meta tags and alternative text) is a good benchmark because a page with this amount of text generally contains genuine content on a subject. When a page contains more than 800 words, your site's visitors have to scroll many times to view all your pages' content. In all likelihood, they will not read much farther down than the top of the screen.

Furthermore, if you cannot present sales copy in fewer than 800 words, you will probably lose audience interest. So make sure your pages contain high-quality, relevant content in as few words as possible.

Because keyword density can be artificially generated quite easily, search engines are placing less and less emphasis on it. Although it is important to use keywords on your web pages to show both the search engines and your target audience what your pages are about, I do not recommend spending a great deal of time on measuring the keyword density on every page of your site.

Foreign Languages

The major search engines tend to be U.S.-centric. Content from the United States tends to dominate the search results and highlighted news, even though the search engines do not officially have U.S. editions of their spiders. However, their search interfaces and search results are presented in English.

Generally speaking, if you have a U.S.-based company, your domain name should end in .com, .net, .edu, .gov, or .org. When you register your domain name, your official contact information should contain a U.S.-based address, phone number, fax number, and email address. In all likelihood, if you have a U.S.-based domain name, your company has a physical location in the United States.

If your site is written in English, it automatically is submitted to English-speaking, country-specific search engines. For example, U.S.-based sites show up in regional search engine results from Australia, United Kingdom (U.K.), and Canada.

If you feel that your target audience extends to non-English speaking countries, you will need to modify your web site to meet the needs of that target audience. To be successful in non-English search engines, you might need to purchase country-specific domain names and write the web pages in the appropriate language.

Having a domain name for a specific country is a key indicator that your site belongs in foreign search engines. If it is within your budget, I highly recommend creating unique web sites for each targeted country. If you do not want to create an entirely new web site for each country, you can create subdomains or subdirectories on a single main site.

For example, let's say our fictional TranquiliTeas company has a target audience in the United States, France, Germany, and the United Kingdom. This company might want to register the following domain names:

- www.tranquiliteasorganic.com (United States)

- www.tranquiliteas.fr (France)

- www.tranquiliteas.de (Germany)

- www.tranquiliteas.co.uk (United Kingdom)

These four domain names can all point to the same web site. On the home page, ask visitors to select a preferred language. When the appropriate language is selected, the link would go to a subdirectory (as shown in Figure 2.15) or a subdomain that is written in the appropriate language.

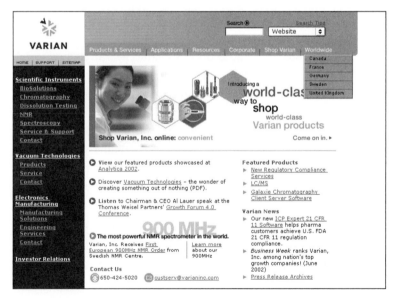

Figure 2.15
Varian, Inc. has a drop-down menu that enables site visitors to view pages in the language of their choice. Because Varian, Inc. has international offices, it is appropriate for them to have country-specific sections of their web site.

Country-specific web pages should always be written in the official language of the targeted country. Thus, if you are targeting France, your web pages should be written in French. Web pages written in French can be located in a subdirectory called France or français, like this:

http://www.tranquiliteasorganic.com/francais/

As an alternative, you can create a subdomain with pages written only in French. The subdomain can have this URL:

http://francais.tranquiliteasorganic.com/

When you submit your site to foreign search engines and directories, be sure to submit the appropriate domain name. For example, one of the most popular search engines in France is called Voilá. The TranquiliTeas company might want to submit www.tranquiliteas.fr to Voilá and any French-language directory. Likewise, www.tranquiliteas.co.uk can be submitted to U.K.-based search engines and directories.

Crawler-based search engines do not enable web designers to tell them what language is used on the web page. (Remember that no one can tell a search engine what to do.) Search engines can determine what language is used on a web page. Many major crawler-based search engines check pages for common words from specific languages. For example, if a search engine spider finds a common word used in the French language, the web page is tagged internally as being in the French language and will appear in French search results.

Special Characters

When writing for non-U.S. search engines, you often find that you use specialized HTML code to specify a letter in an alphabet. For example, in Spanish, if you want to write the word Olé in HTML, the code might look like this:

Olé

It could also look like this:

Olé

Currently, the crawler-based search engines do not translate many foreign-language characters neatly into search results. Until the search engines become more effective with languages other than English, do not use any special characters in your title tags and meta tags. If you are using Olé in your title tag, you want it to appear in the search results like this:

Ole

You do not want the word to appear in search results as this:

Olé

If you do plan to target non-U.S. search engines, write a set of targeted keywords and keyword phrases for each language, even for English-language search engines. For example, in the United States, we commonly refer to wireless telephones as cellular phones or cell phones. In the U.K. and most of Europe, these phones are referred to as mobile phones. Therefore, if you know you are targeting different countries, all keyword research should be country-specific.

Link Component

One of the most important components of a successful search engine marketing campaign is the link component, also referred to as site architecture. Site architecture refers to a web site's navigation scheme, individual page layout, and how directories are set up on your web server.

Site architecture is very important because the search engine spiders must be able to find and record the keyword-rich text on your web pages. Therefore, the way your pages are linked to each other, and the way your web site is linked to other web sites, has a major impact on your site's search engine visibility. Without an effective site architecture, web site marketers must pay for search engine visibility through paid inclusion or pay-per-click programs.

Navigation Schemes

Web site designers should always consider their target audience first when they create a site's navigation scheme. Navigation schemes should enable visitors to find what they are searching for as quickly and as easily as possible.

Many web sites use multiple navigation schemes. For example, a site might have a series of navigation buttons down the left side of a screen and have corresponding text links at the bottom of a screen (see Figure 2.16).

Common navigation schemes include the following:

- Hypertext links
- Navigation buttons
- Image maps
- Drop-down/pull-down menus
- Animation/Flash buttons
- Dynamically generated URLs, such as those generated by a site search

Figure 2.16
Dee Concrete has multiple navigation schemes to ensure that the target audience can find the concrete form or accessory for which they are searching. Dee placed text links at the top and the bottom of the screen, and it has navigation buttons at the top and the left side of the screen. For usability purposes, Dee also placed text links within the actual body content.

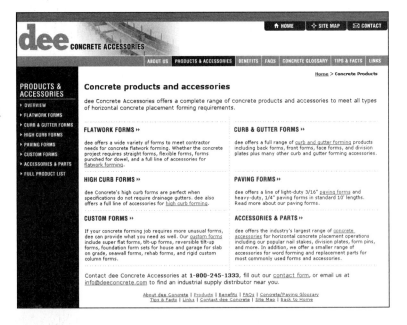

In the following sections, I go over each type of navigation scheme, its advantages and disadvantages, and how the navigation scheme you select can impact your site's search engine visibility.

Hypertext Links

A *hypertext link* is a word or set of words placed inside an anchor tag. Hypertext is the text placed between the <a> and </a> tags. Consider the following HTML code for a simple hypertext link:

```
<a href="oolongtea.html">Oolong tea</a>
```

- <a begins the anchor tag.

- href is the attribute of this anchor tag. This refers to the target location of a web document. In this example, the location of the web document is a web page named oolongtea.html. It is *very* important that the location of the web page in a hyper-text link be enclosed in quotation marks.

- Oolong tea is the anchor text.

- </a> closes the anchor tag and hypertext link.

All search engine spiders love text links because they can record the text in and around the link and follow these links from web page to web page. In fact, search engine marketers use a specific term that refers to the HTML text inside a hyperlink: anchor text.

Many search engines consider anchor text relevant because webmasters generally link to pages that contain information in which their target audiences are interested. Therefore, anchor text is deemed as important.

Usability experts also like text links because they provide the target audience with valuable information about visited and unvisited pages. Your target audience automatically understands that a blue, underlined word (or just an underlined word) indicates an unvisited link and that a purple or faded color indicates a visited link.

Furthermore, usability experts often recommend breadcrumb links. *Breadcrumbs* are text link schematics on every web page that let people know where they are and where they have been. Breadcrumbs are commonly used at the top of a web page and are hierarchical in nature. Figure 2.17 shows how breadcrumbs typically look on a web page.

Many directories, including Yahoo!, use breadcrumbs as a navigation scheme, as shown in Figure 2.18.

Figure 2.17
Evolution Design Systems uses breadcrumb links as part of its navigation scheme.

Breadcrumb links

Figure 2.18
Yahoo!'s breadcrumb links are shown at the top of the screen. Home > Business and Economy > Shopping and Services > Food and Drink > Drinks > Tea > Organic are all breadcrumb links.

Because breadcrumbs are generally placed at the top of web pages, search engines consider the text placed inside the breadcrumb links important. Therefore, if you have a site that uses breadcrumbs as a navigation scheme, try to use keywords consistently in them.

Absolute and Relative Links

In general, there are two types of links: absolute and relative. An *absolute link* defines a specific location of the web file or document. The location information includes the protocol to use to get the document, the server from which to get it, the directory in which it is located, and the name of the document itself.

The following is an example of an absolute link:

```
<a href="http://www.tranquiliteasorganic.com/oolongtea.html">Oolong
tea</a>
```

- <a begins the anchor tag.

- href is the attribute of this anchor tag that is referring to the target location. The URL enclosed in quotation marks gives the location of the web file when you click the link. In this example, if you click the text link, you go to the Oolong Tea page on the TranquiliTeas web site.

- http:// is the protocol (Hypertext Transfer Protocol).

- www.tranquiliteasorganic.com is the domain name, which has a specific address on a web server.

- oolongtea.html is the name of the HTML document on TranquiliTeas' web server.

- Oolong tea is the anchor text.

- </a> closes the anchor tag and hypertext link.

With a *relative link*, the search engine spider or browser already knows where the current document is on a server. Thus, if you link to another document in the same directory, you don't need to write out the full URL. Only the filename is necessary. The following is HTML code for a relative link:

```
<a href="oolongtea.html">Oolong tea</a>
```

Because it makes no difference to the search engine spiders whether you use an absolute link or a relative link, use the type of link with which you are most comfortable. All search engine spiders can follow both types of links.

Best and Worst Places to Use Text Links

Because all search engines can index the text and follow the links in a hypertext link, for maximum search engine visibility, I highly recommend using them as either the primary or secondary navigation for a web site design.

Figure 2.19 highlights the best and worst places to put text links, using a page from my own web site as an example.

The top of a web page is not always the best place to put text links because this is often the first text that the search engines see. As long as the text is short, it should not interfere with search engine visibility.

Breadcrumb text links at the top of a web page generally are not problematic because they tend to be short. For this text to be effective for search engine visibility, be sure to use keywords whenever appropriate.

Figure 2.19
Various places on a web page where you can place navigation schemes.

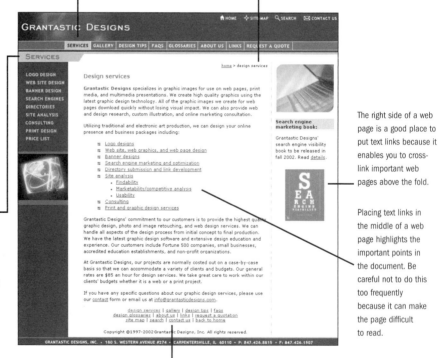

The right side of a web page is a good place to put text links because it enables you to cross-link important web pages above the fold.

The left side of a web page is not always the best place to put text links because this is also the first text that the search engines see.

If the amount of text inside the text links is too long, the search engines often use this text in their snippets in the search results. In addition, the web page might not appear to be focused on a specific topic.

Placing text links in the middle of a web page highlights the important points in the document. Be careful not to do this too frequently because it can make the page difficult to read.

The bottom of a web page is a good place to put text links. These text links can correspond to the graphic images (navigation buttons or image maps) at the top of the screen.

Potential Problems with Hypertext Links

On the surface, a text-link navigation scheme might seem like an ideal solution because all the search engines prefer this type of link. Additionally, a web page full of text links tends to download much faster than a web page full of graphic images. Thus, using text links as a main navigation scheme can satisfy both the search engines and your target audience.

However, too many text links can interfere with keyword density. If you find that you have more words in your text links than you do in the main body content, you might want to consider using graphic images as part of your navigation scheme. The web design team at About.com uses a text-link navigation scheme at the top of the page and in the sidebar (see Figure 2.20).

Figure 2.20

The web design team at About.com uses a text link navigation scheme at the top of the page and in the sidebar. Because there are so many text links on this page, they can dilute the keyword density and interfere with keyword prominence. One way About.com retains keyword prominence throughout their site is the use of breadcrumb links at the top of the page.

Another disadvantage of using text links as the primary navigation scheme is that they are often the first body of text that the search engines read. Because this text tends to be the same on many web pages, the first text introduced (in this particular layout) to the search engine spiders is not unique.

Furthermore, if a search engine does not use the meta-tag description to display in the search results, it generally takes the first text found at the top of a web page. Generally speaking, a series of text links does not accurately describe the contents of a unique web page, and they usually don't have an effective call to action. To your target audience, the description can appear as a bunch of unrelated words.

Too many text links on a single page can also interfere with a page's legibility. The whole point of writing a web page is to have your target audience read it and perform a desired action. People like simplicity and ease of navigation. Thus, find ways to make your text links more visually distinct, easy to find, and legible, such as placing them in a colored table cell or a colored sidebar.

If you find that your text links are interfering with search engine visibility and page legibility, consider using graphic images as an alternative means of navigation. See Figure 2.21.

Figure 2.21
Evolution Design Systems uses text links as the primary means of navigation. Because the text links do not dominate the site's main content and utilize targeted keywords, this is an effective, search engine-friendly navigation scheme.

Navigation Buttons

A navigation button is a graphic image, generally in a GIF or a JPEG format, that links to a single URL. Corrugated Metals, Inc. utilizes navigation buttons as its main navigation scheme. The webmaster chose to place navigation buttons at the top of the screen and along the right side of the screen (see Figure 2.22).

Navigation buttons give your visitors a visual representation of how to navigate your site right away, especially if the navigation buttons are visible on the top part of the computer screen. They are visually appealing and can easily draw attention to important parts of your web pages. Peoples' eyes are naturally drawn to a splash of color or a change in dimension. ARCH Venture Partners' web designer used contrasting colors to highlight the on and off buttons on the site (see Figure 2.23).

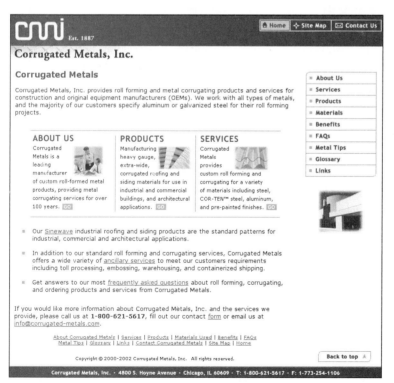

Figure 2.22

Corrugated Metals, Inc. utilizes navigation buttons as its main navigation scheme. The webmaster chose to place navigation buttons at the top and along the right side of the screen. Even though the navigation buttons appear to be a single graphic image, when you right click and select the Open Image in New Window option, you will see that there is one navigation button per link.

Figure 2.23
ARCH Venture Partners' web designer used contrasting colors to highlight the "on" and "off" buttons on the site. This use of color draws attention to the navigation scheme and lets site visitors know what page they are on, visually.

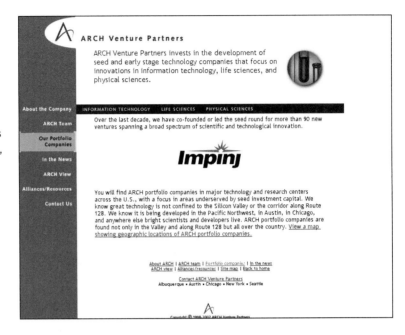

Web designers and graphic designers, in particular, like to use navigation buttons because they know that a site's target audience is viewing the font/typeface exactly as intended. With graphic images, fonts do not need to be installed on the end users' computers to view them as the web designer intended.

Navigation buttons should always contain alternative text in the event your target audience cannot or chooses not to view your graphic images. As long as the navigation buttons have alternative text in the HTML code, visitors can click that text to navigate your site. The Corrugated Metals site utilizes alternative text (see Figure 2.24).

Figure 2.24
The Corrugated Metals site utilizes alternative text. The Materials button is not loading. In its place is the alternative text. Site visitors will still be able to click on the alternative text and go to the Materials page.

Potential Problems with Navigation Buttons

All the search engines can follow the link surrounding a navigation button, as long as the navigation button does not contain JavaScript within the anchor tag. JavaScript can pose problems with search engine spiders; therefore, not all search engines follow this type of link.

This type of link is search engine friendly:

```
<a href="oolongteas.html"><img src="images/oolong.gif" width=
"60" height="20" alt="Oolong organic teas"></a>
```

- <a begins the anchor tag.

- href is the attribute of this anchor tag referring to the target location, which is the web page called oolongteas.html.

- The greater than sign (>) closes the anchor tag.

- <img begins the image tag.

- src is an attribute of the img tag. This attribute is often called "source." The source of the image tag can be found in a directory called images. Inside the images directory is a GIF image named oolong.gif.

- The width and height attributes tell the browser the dimensions of the graphic image. Always use the height and width attributes because they greatly decrease the download time of a web page.

- alt is the alternative text attribute. The alternative text in this example is Oolong organic teas.

- The greater than sign (>) closes the img tag.

- </a> closes the link to the Oolong Teas page.

This type of link, a navigation button with a rollover effect, is not as search engine friendly:

```
<a href="oolongteas.html" onMouseOut="MM_swapImgRestore()"
onMouseOver="MM_swapImage('images/oolongon.gif','','images/
oolong.gif',1)"><img src="images/oolong.gif" width="60" height=
"20" alt="Oolong organic teas"></a>
```

When you look at this code, what is the primary difference you see? There is additional code inside the anchor tag:

onMouseOut="MM_swapImgRestore()" onMouseOver="MM_swapImage ('images/oolongon.gif','','images/oolong.gif',1)"

When you begin to add too many attributes to the anchor tag, such as a rollover script, the attributes can make links less search engine friendly—though some rollover scripts are more search engine friendly than others. Currently, the major search engines prefer straightforward link coding without any type of script. Thus, if you know your site is utilizing rollover effects on navigation buttons, it is best to include an alternative navigation scheme that the search engine spiders can follow.

One effective search engine–friendly layout is to use navigation buttons (with or without JavaScript rollovers) and corresponding hypertext links at the bottom of a web page. With this layout, designers can place keywords in multiple places: both within the hypertext links and in the alternative text of the navigation buttons. Many search engine marketers recommend this combination because of the dual benefit.

Image Maps

An *image map* is a single graphic image that enables users to access different web pages by clicking different areas of the image. Figure 2.25 shows an example of an image map.

Many search engines do not follow the links inside an image map because of the possibility of image spam. Thus, if you choose to use an image map as part of your site's navigation scheme, always use text links or navigation buttons elsewhere on your web pages.

Many search engine marketers mistakenly believe that because many search engines do not follow the links inside image maps, they should never use image maps in site navigation. This belief is not always a credible conclusion because in many situations, a single graphic image downloads much more quickly than multiple graphic images.

Figure 2.25
The Tesko Enterprises Web site uses image maps as a main navigation scheme. On this page, there are two image maps: the side navigation and the graphic image in the middle of the screen.

For example, if a site has 16 navigation buttons that are 2K each in file size, the total for these graphic images is 32K. A single image map might only be 8–10K in size, much smaller than the set of navigation buttons. With the image map, there is only one call to the server, as opposed to 16, which speeds things up regardless of file sizes.

Furthermore, sometimes search engine spiders have an easier time accessing the main body text on a web page if the navigation scheme is a single graphic image rather than multiple ones. Some of the HTML code for an image map can go at the bottom of a web page, below the main body text, rather than at the top.

Important

Browsers download graphic images on a web page. Search engines do not download your graphic images when they request a page from your server. Remember that search engines index text and follow links. They are not looking for graphic images on your web pages. They are looking for a web page's HTML text and links to follow within that text.

Only search engines that crawl the web for graphic images store information about your graphic images.

For example, some of the HTML code for the image map can be placed at the bottom of a web page, right before the </body> tag, as shown in the following code for the Tesko Enterprises site:

```
<map name="imagemap">
 <area shape="rect" coords="0,180,164,194" href=
"metalcomponents.html">
 <area shape="rect" coords="0,195,164,208" href=
"laserfabrication.html">
 <area shape="rect" coords="0,164,164,179" href="conceptart.html">
 <area shape="rect" coords="0,150,164,163" href="interiors.html">
 <area shape="rect" coords="0,133,164,149" href="exteriors.html">
 <area shape="rect" coords="0,111,164,132" href="gallery.html">
 <area shape="rect" coords="0,288,164,312" href="contact.html">
 <area shape="rect" coords="0,263,164,287" href="links.html">
 <area shape="rect" coords="0,238,164,262" href="tips.html">
 <area shape="rect" coords="0,213,164,237" href="faqs.html">
 <area shape="rect" coords="0,86,164,110" href="benefits.html">
 <area shape="rect" coords="0,61,164,85" href="services.html">
 <area shape="rect" coords="0,36,164,60" href="about.html">
 <area shape="rect" coords="0,4,164,35" href="index.html">
</map>
</body>
</html>
```

For web designers who use Macromedia products, particularly Dreamweaver, the HTML code for image maps is automatically placed at the bottom of a web page.

When is it not a good idea to use an image map? If the only navigation scheme on your web site is graphic images, it is best to use navigation buttons because all the search engines can follow the links surrounding navigation buttons. However, if you are using both graphic images and text links as a navigation scheme, consider the pages' download times. If the image map downloads more quickly than a set of navigation buttons, the image map might be a better choice.

Remember that an image map is a graphic image. Always place alternative text in the HTML code of an image map, especially if the image map is at the top of a web page.

Drop-Down and Pull-Down Menus

Figures 2.26 and 2.27 show examples of two types of drop-down menus: an HTML and a DHTML menu.

Figure 2.26

An example of an HTML form drop-down menu on the Sure Fit Slipcovers site. Two HTML drop-down menus are located in the left navigation. Any HTML editor can automatically generate drop-down menus.

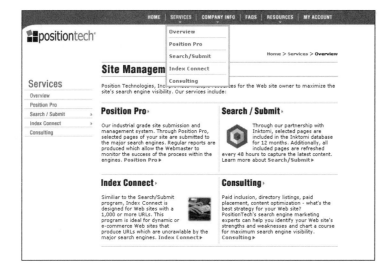

Figure 2.27

A DHTML drop-down menu, which was coded using JavaScript and Cascading Style Sheets (CSS).

The main advantage of using drop-down menus in a navigation scheme is screen real estate. Drop-down menus do not initially take up as much screen space as a series of navigation buttons or text links. Furthermore, by freeing up screen space, web site owners are able to place more content that their target audience wishes to read above the fold.

Potential Problems with Menus

Drop-down menus are generally not search engine friendly because they require either JavaScript or a CGI program to work. Because search engines generally do not follow these types of links, you should always have an alternative form of navigation for the search engines to follow.

Additionally, usability experts do not always recommend drop-down menus as a navigation scheme because people decide what they are going to click before they view the contents of the menus.

Web designers can use a combination of drop-down menus with corresponding text links at the bottom of a web page for search engine visibility.

Dynamically Generated URLs

Dynamically generated web pages are usually created using a technology such as Active Server Pages (.asp), Cold Fusion (.cfm), Hypertext PreProcessor (.php), Java Server Pages (.jsp), or Perl. Often, search engine marketers state that search engines cannot follow the links inside dynamically generated web pages. This statement is partially true. A more accurate statement is that search engines might not like the URL used to retrieve web pages.

If a URL contains a question mark (?), search engines do not automatically reject the URL. Rather, the question mark is seen as an indicator of dynamic content. Other symbols also act as indicators of dynamically delivered content. These symbols include &, $, =, +, and %.

Why don't search engines like these characters in URLs? Basically, there are three reasons:

- **Search engines do not want the same content delivered to them over and over again, which is often a problem with dynamic URLs:** In addition, end users do not want to see identical pages dominating search results. By stopping at the question mark, search engines can prevent some identical content from being listed in search results.

For example, on Danny Sullivan's Search Engine Watch site, these two URLs deliver the same content (the subscriber page shown in Figure 2.28):

www.searchenginewatch.com/about/subscribe.html?source=home
www.searchenginewatch.com/about/subscribe.html?source=wgtse

The search engines do not want to include both these URLs because both contain the same content. One of the ways they can prevent mirror page delivery is to stop recording the URL at the question mark:

www.searchenginewatch.com/about/subscribe.html

Because the page loads in a browser (Explorer or Netscape) even though the characters after the question mark are deleted, this single URL can be indexed by the search engines (see Figure 2.28).

Sites that generate session IDs in the URLs also have the same problem. For example, if the TranquiliTeas web site had the following URLs:

www.tranquiliteasorganic.com/products.jsp?BV_SessionID=
0532038767

www.tranquiliteasorganic.com/products.jsp?BV_SessionID=
0235426067

these pages would not be considered search engine friendly due to the question mark (?) and the equals sign (=). These URLs have the same content but different URLs. However, if the following URL loads into a browser:

www.tranquiliteasorganic.com/products.jsp

the search engines should be able to list the page.

Figure 2.28

Because the Search Engine Watch Subscribe page loads without all the content after the question mark, the URL is search engine friendly.

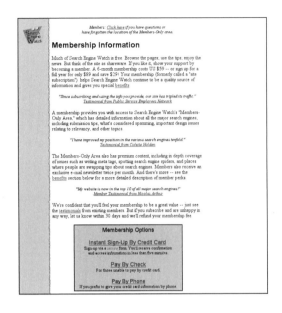

■ **Search engines want their search results to be accurate:** Search engines update their indices every four to eight weeks. If they include dynamically generated URLs in their search results, the content might change between the time they recorded the URL and the time the URL appears in the search results. The possible outcome? The search results might not be accurate. For example, let's say a search engine accepts this URL:

www.tranquiliteasorganic.com/cgi-bin/gt/recipe.html?recipe=2489

The content of recipe #2489 is a hot oolong tea recipe for the winter. But suppose it is July, and the web site owner decides to change recipe #2489 to an iced tea recipe because it is summertime. It is a very simple change to make in a database.

In the search results, if someone searches for a hot oolong tea recipe and this URL appears in the search results, the content delivered will be a recipe for iced tea, which is not what the end user was searching for.

Thus, by not enabling some dynamically generated URLs in the search results, search engines are helping preserve the accuracy of their search results.

■ **Some dynamically generated URLs can trap a search engine spider and cause it to crash:** In some cases, a search engine spider might come upon a dynamic web page where the database program or CGI process feeds it an infinite number of URLs. Programmers who fail to close their if or while statements on web pages can crash a search engine spider.

Search engines are progressing in their capability to spider dynamic URLs. In the meantime, web designers should focus their efforts on delivering web pages to the search engines that do not contain stop characters in their URLs.

Robots Exclusion Protocol

The Robots Exclusion Protocol is a text file that you place on your server to instruct search engine spiders *not* to record the information in specified areas of your web site. In other words, the protocol tells the search engine spiders which sections of your site are off limits.

With the Robots Exclusion Protocol, web site owners can instruct search engine spiders not to index individual web pages, subdirectories, or even an entire site. Instructions can also be tailored for individual search engines.

For example, Google and FAST Search currently are the only search engines that index Flash sites. A web site owner can use the Robots Exclusion Protocol to instruct Google to index the Flash site and tell the other search engines not to index the Flash site.

When to Use the Robots Exclusion Protocol

Some web files, such as items in a cgi-bin directory, are not important to the search engines. When your target audience searches for
information, they are not interested in the programs that generate
your forms or your drop-down menus. They also are not interested
in a web page that is under construction. Your target audience
is interested in the products and services you are offering on your
web site.

Using the Robots Exclusion Protocol ensures that unnecessary
pieces of information, such as pages that are under construction,
are not shown in search results. Be sure that the Robots Exclusion
Protocol is placed on your server before you place any excluded
content. Why? Sometimes, the search engine spiders come to your
web server before you have had a chance to place the Robots
Exclusion Protocol. It only takes seconds for a search engine to
gather information about your web pages.

Dynamically generated pages that could present a spider trap are
also good candidates for the Robots Exclusion Protocol.

The Meta-Tag Robots Exclusion

One way to instruct the search engines not to index the content of
a specific web page is to use the meta-tag robots exclusion on every
page that you do not want the search engine to index. The proper
HTML coding for this meta tag is as follows:

```
<html>
<head>
<title>Page title goes here.</title>
<meta name="robots" content="noindex, nofollow">
</head>
```

Some web developers like to place the following robots exclusion
meta tag on web pages:

```
<html>
<head>
<title>Page title goes here.</title>
<meta name="robots" content="index, follow">
</head>
```

Actually, this meta tag is a waste of time because this is the default setting. Furthermore, not all search engines honor this type of meta tag. Thus, it is best to use the robots.txt file.

The robots.txt File

The robots.txt file is a simple text document that instructs the search engines not to index parts of your web site. You can easily build this file in Notepad (PC) or SimpleText (Mac).

The robots.txt standard should be placed in your server's root directory. In other words, put your robots.txt file in the same place that you put your home page, as shown in Figure 2.29. The URL for all robots.txt files looks like the following:

www.companyname.com/robots.txt.

A search engine respecting the robots.txt file asks for the file before trying to index any page within your site. For example, if your entire web site is under construction and you do not want the search engines to record any of the information on the site until you are finished, type the following text into a text editor:

User-agent: *
Disallow: /

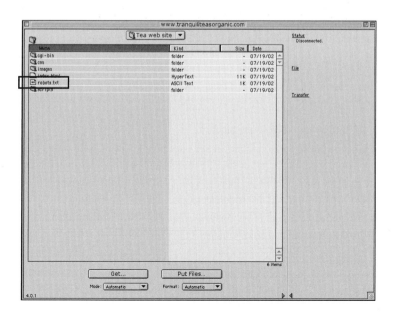

Figure 2.29
The robots.txt file is always placed in the same directory as your site's home page. In this example, the home page is named index.html.

Be sure to name the file robots.txt and to not use any other file extension. If you save the file as a Word document and call it robots.doc, the search engines ignore the instructions in the file.

In the preceding example, User-agent enables you to specify the search engine engines or browsers that should follow the directions on the second line. The way to exclude all search engines is to use the asterisk symbol (*), as shown.

The Disallow portion enables you to specify the directories and filenames on your server that you do not want the search engines to index. In the example, the forward slash (/) instructs the search engines to ignore everything in your root directory. In other words, the search engines will not index the pages in your entire web site.

Generally, most web site owners do not want the search engines to ignore an entire site. Instead, they want specific sections of a web site ignored. For example, sites that use drop-down menus commonly use a cgi script or a JavaScript in the menu. Because this is the type of information in which search engines are not interested, you can create a robots.txt file that instructs the search engines to ignore the contents of the directories that contain these scripts. To create this type of file, type the following text into a text editor:

```
User-agent: *
Disallow: /cgi-bin/
Disallow: /scripts/
```

Be sure that all your JavaScript is placed in the /scripts/ subdirectory. The search engines respecting the robots.txt file do not index anything in the site with these URLs:

```
www.companyname.com/cgi-bin/
www.companyname.com/scripts/
```

Pages that are under construction or pages that might present spider traps, such as a Calendar page, are also good pages to place in the robots.txt file. To exclude an individual web page, type the following text into a text editor:

```
User-agent: *
Disallow: /calendar.html
```

In this example, search engines respecting the robots.txt file do not index anything in the site with this URL:

www.companyname.com/calendar.html.

Details on how to further use the robots.txt file are discussed in Part 3, "Page Design Workarounds."

Internal and External Search Engine Optimization

If you have site search engine or some kind of search function, how well your own pages show up in your own search results indicates how effective your *internal* search engine optimization is.

How well your pages show up in the search engines outside your site (Google, Inktomi, FAST Search, AltaVista, and so on) indicate how effective your *external* search engine optimization is. By comparing the two sets of data, you can determine the total effectiveness of your site optimization strategies.

Site search engines are a valuable place to collect keyword data because you can compare (a) what people are typing into the search engines to find your type of site and (b) what people are typing into your site search engine after they have arrived.

For example, if you find that your end users are able to find a popular product or service using your internal site search engine but are not able to find that information using the major search engines, it might be a good idea to place a dynamic URL into a paid inclusion program. If your site has its own search engine, the following is a list of terms that marketers should track:

- Most popular searches (top search words)

- Least popular searches

- Searches that yielded no results (the top not-found words)

- Percentage of searches that yielded no results

- Searches that yielded results but no click-throughs (the top not-clicked words)

If you find that the most popular searches on your site search engine yield little or no results, you know you should be adding web pages that give your target audience what they are searching for. In fact, according to *User Interface Engineering* in a report titled "Getting Them to What They Want," top usability expert Jared Spool determined that users who found content were far more successful when they navigated by using categories and text links than by using a site search engine. Users were far more likely to find their target content when they didn't use the site's search engine than when they did use it. Thus, if your site's visitors are using your site search engine too much, it is an indication that they are having difficulty finding information using the site's normal navigation scheme.

Another good item to check is your meta-tag description. If the meta-tag description is displayed in Inktomi's search results, and your site ranks well in Inktomi, you know that you probably have written an effective meta-tag description for the external search engines.

Compare that data to your site's search engine data. Many site search engines use the meta-tag description for display on search results. If a site search yields targeted pages in the search results but very few people click those links in the search results, the meta-tag description and the title-tag content might not be effective for your target audience.

Popularity Component

Popularity has become increasingly important among the search engines. A web site's popularity component provides the search engines with feedback about a site's usefulness to a target audience. In other words, sites that more users find useful are more relevant to a particular search.

If two web sites have similar text and spider-friendly link architectures, the site with greater popularity consistently ranks higher over time because of the following reasons:

- Credible web sites usually link to pages with valuable information.

- A site's end users tend to use the same web site over and over again because the information is relevant.

Therefore, building a site that appeals to both directory editors and your target audience is very important for getting and maintaining maximum search engine visibility.

As mentioned in Part 1, "Before You Build." the popularity component of a search engine algorithm consists of multiple subcomponents:

- Link popularity

- Click-through popularity

Link Popularity

The *link popularity* of a web page is the number and quality of links pointing to that web page. Link popularity is not as simple as obtaining as many links as possible to a web page. The quality of the sites linking to a web page holds far more weight than the quantity of sites.

The major search engines have gone beyond measuring the number of links to a web site. Some links are more credible than others, especially because many unethical search engine marketers have created free-for-all link farms in the attempt to boost link popularity. For this reason, sites with high-quality, credible links pointing to them gain more popularity than sites with low-quality links.

Therefore, sites with three high-quality links pointing to them (from Yahoo!, LookSmart, and Open Directory) often rank higher than sites with hundreds of low-quality links pointing to them. Thus, before beginning a link-building campaign, carefully select the places from which you want to obtain links, beginning with the most credible.

Directories

Let's say the fictional TranquiliTeas company created an online store that sells organic teas. On this site, they might sell organic teas, and they might also might have a series of web pages providing recipes for spiced tea. To get maximum link popularity from the major directories, the site can be listed in multiple categories. On LookSmart, the home page can be submitted to this category:

Shopping > Online Stores > Food & Wine > Beverages > Tea >
Specialty Teas

The page that shows the various spiced tea recipes can be submitted to a completely different category:

Lifestyle > Food/Wine > Beverages > Tea > Tea Recipes > Spiced Tea

Not all web sites can have multiple pages listed in the major directories. However, if a web page's individual content offers unique, substantial information (such as tips, advice, definitions, and how-to articles), *and* the individual page is submitted to a completely different branch of the directory structure, the chances of getting multiple directory listings are favorable.

Industry-Specific Web Sites

Some credible web sites offer information on very specific topics. For example, if you were looking for information on health-related issues, WebMd.com might be a good place to search for information. A link from WebMd.com to a health-related site can increase the site's link popularity. If you offer a free software demo on your web site, you can request a link from shareware.com or download.com. If you offer marketing tips, find a web site that publishes marketing tips and offer to write an article for them.

Professional Associations

Many professional associations offer links to member web sites. This is another way to help your site gain link popularity because professional associations are generally considered credible sources of information. A Chamber of Commerce site also can be a good place to obtain additional listings.

Educational Institutions

Many grade schools, colleges, and universities look for web sites that relate to the specific subject they teach. A religion professor might look for a site about the history of Japanese Buddhism. An art professor might look for sites that discuss the psychology of color. Links from educational institutions are valuable not only for popularity but also for branding purposes. Many students remember your site after they become professionals.

Requesting Links

To find credible, industry-specific web sites, use the major search engines and directories. If sites are consistently appearing at the top of the search results and are listed in the major directories, the search engines consider those sites important.

Go to the search engines and type your major keyword phrases and analyze the search results. Determine the best non-competing sites and see if they have a Links or a Resources page. These are sites from which you can request links. To get the best popularity boost, make sure that the sites linking to you are also listed in the three major directories.

When requesting that your site be added to an industry-specific or a non-competing site, do not waste the web site owner's time. Make your link request as easy as possible for the web site owner to process. Send the owner a polite email, complimenting him or her on site characteristics or specific pages with excellent content (to make sure the web site owner knows that you have read the site), the exact URL and description that you would like added to the Links page, and why you believe your web page is beneficial to the particular web site.

An even better way might be to add targeted web sites (that you like) to your Links or Resources page. When you email the web site owner, you can tell him or her that you have linked to his or her site. You then can ask the owner to review the title and description you

Important

Just because a site is listed in Yahoo!, LookSmart, and Open Directory does not mean it is a legitimate site. Directories are subject to spam as well as the search engines.

have written on your Links page. Give the web site owner the opportunity to edit the title and description. If the web site owner likes your site, he or she is very likely to provide a reciprocal link.

Be Careful Who You Link To!

Important

Web rings, in and of themselves, aren't automatically considered "bad neighborhoods." For example, if all of the domestic violence shelters (with web sites) in the state of New York linked to each other, that would be an effective web ring.

All the search engines make it very clear that linking to "bad neighborhoods" can get your site penalized. Though no one can control which web sites link to you, you have total control over the sites to which you link. Thus, do not participate in any free-for-all (FFA) web sites or participate in web rings to artificially boost your site's link popularity.

Always make sure that your Links page is part of your web site and is hosted on your web server. If your Links page is not a part of your web site, your site might be penalized for artificial link building. For example, one of the best URLs for the TranquiliTeas site looks like the following: www.tranquiliteasorganic.com/links.html. Thus, it is best to link to credible sites.

Click-Through Popularity

Getting other web sites to link to your web site is not enough to obtain long-term search engine visibility. Your target audience must be able to find the information they are searching for when they arrive at your web site. Hopefully, your target audience can perform a search on a search engine, click the link to your site, and go directly to the web page with the information for which they are searching. However, this often is not the case. Sometimes, your target audience navigates your site a bit, usually between five and seven clicks, to be sure the information on your site is credible.

If your target audience cannot find the information for which they are searching, they will click the Back button to return to the search results. The search engines are able to measure whether your end users are returning to the search results or staying on your web site. This measurement constitutes a page's *click-through popularity*.

Many search engines can measure the following:

- The number of times end users click links to your site

- How long end users visit your site

- How often end users return to your site

If your target audience members continually click the links from the search engines to your site *and* they stay on your site to gather information, your site popularity increases. If your target audience members click links to your site and do not find the information for which they are searching, your site's popularity decreases. In other words, your target audience influences how visible your site is among the search engines.

Off-the-Page Criteria

Some aspects of link popularity are examples of *off-the-page criteria*, which are factors that web site owners cannot influence to increase search engine visibility.

Web designers have complete control over what words they place on their pages and where they place these words. They have control over how pages link to each other. In fact, on-the-page factors can be computer-generated for search engine visibility, which is one reason why *doorway pages* came to be a popular search engine marketing strategy.

Because items such as keyword density and keyword prominence can easily be created, search engines are relying more and more on off-the-page criteria to determine relevancy. Link popularity and click-through popularity are just two types of off-the-page criteria. However, unethical search engine marketers have discovered ways to artificially generate popularity through FFA link farms, affiliate programs, and domain spamming. Therefore, search engines are continuing to find other off-the-page criteria to determine which web pages receive top positions.

Compromising Between Marketing and Design

Some of the most beautiful web pages are created entirely in Flash or with graphic images to preserve the aesthetics of the colors, uncommon typefaces, and movement. These web pages, by virtue of effective offline and online advertising campaigns, get plenty of traffic and sales conversions.

To make pages like these more search engine friendly, search engine marketers might recommend that visible HTML text be added to the pages. They might recommend placing text links at the bottom of the screen or using a series of breadcrumb links at the top of the screen. They might recommend placing a 250-word paragraph on each page. However, these items, though essential for search engine visibility, can interfere with the overall look and feel of a web site. What should a web site owner do when faced with this dilemma?

Web sites should be constructed primarily for your target audience. Your customers are the ones who purchase your products and services, not the search engines. So, if your target audience prefers a Flash site and your other marketing efforts are providing effective sales leads and conversions, a pay-for-placement search engine strategy is the best solution. Always build a site based on what your target audience prefers. Testing your audience preferences is imperative for a successful web site.

Do not assume that your marketing departments or design teams know what your target audience prefers without testing the effectiveness of your web pages. If you have a Flash site, create an HTML version of your site. Measure the traffic on each site. You might find that your target audience, overall, uses the HTML version of the site more frequently but that the Flash version generates more targeted sales leads.

On the other hand, you might find that your target audience does not mind a set of text links at the bottom of your web pages, especially if those links fall below the fold. Those text links can help increase your site's search engine visibility and higher search engine visibility can increase sales.

Search engines do not change their rules based on a designer or marketer's personal preferences. Sometimes, aesthetic preferences conflict with search engine visibility. Ultimately, web site owners must decide which is more important: personal aesthetics or increased search engine visibility?

Conclusion

The foundation of an effective, long-term search engine marketing campaign contains three building blocks:

- Text component
- Link component
- Popularity component

Building a search engine–friendly web site is also building a customer-friendly web site because you are building the site based on words your audience types into search queries. Web pages that contain the words that your target audience is typing into search queries generally have greater search engine visibility than pages that contain few or no keywords.

The way your web pages are linked to each other, the way your web site is linked to other web sites, and the way other sites link to your site affects your site's search engine visibility. If search engine spiders can crawl your web pages quickly and easily, the pages stand a much better chance of appearing at the top of search results. Furthermore, your target audience is more likely to land on the pages that contain the exact information for which they are searching.

If two web sites have similar copywriting, spider-friendly navigation schemes, and site architectures, the site with greater popularity usually ranks higher. Therefore, building a site that appeals to your target audience is imperative for maximum search engine visibility.

part 3

Page Design Workarounds

Introduction

Most companies already have existing web sites or are in the middle of redesigning their sites. Thus, building a completely new search engine–friendly web site can be cost prohibitive. If you have an existing web site and have problems being listed well in the search engines, this section can help you modify your site to make it more search engine friendly.

Bells and Whistles That Can Hurt More Than Help

Flash, DHTML, JavaScript rollovers, style sheets, and animation can add style and pizzazz to a web site. They can help your site visitors understand the navigation scheme better and make a site easier to read. Thus, "bells and whistles" are not necessarily bad items to add to a site—if they enhance the user experience.

However, bells and whistles can interfere with a search engine marketing campaign. Search engines always look for text on a web page, and some web site designs present the search engines with no text to index, as is the case with many Flash designs. Some site designs contain keyword-rich text, but some design and navigation choices do not give the search engine spiders easy access to that text.

Technical choices or methods for building a web site can also interfere with how well a search engine can spider a site. In other words, the design of Flash navigation buttons is not problematic for the search engines, but the actual Flash technology used to produce the navigation buttons *is*.

The best design solution involves planning. If you know your company is going to use search engine marketing as part of its online marketing strategy, creating search engine–friendly design templates can save your company considerable time and expense. However, if you already have a site and do not wish to modify its design too much, this section offers some simple page design workarounds that can help your site attain greater search engine visibility.

JavaScript and Search Engine Visibility

JavaScript is a programming language that enables web site designers to add flair and interactivity to their web sites. Some of the most common uses for JavaScript include rollovers/mouseovers, pop-up windows, form validation, and drop-down navigation menus. In fact, the use of JavaScript rollovers has become so widespread that they are now considered a standard part of web site design packages.

When a web designer uses JavaScript on a site's navigation scheme, the scripts can greatly decrease the crawlability of the links. Currently, most search engines do not follow the links embedded inside JavaScript code (including rollovers and menus), or they greatly limit the types of JavaScript-embedded links they crawl.

Some JavaScript code is more search engine friendly than other code. As a general rule of thumb, the simpler the script, the more likely a search engine spider can crawl the link.

Listing 3.1 shows a simple rollover script that is more search engine friendly than other scripts I have encountered. Though this script is not 100 percent search engine friendly, it is better than most of the scripts you find on web design software.

Web designers can put JavaScript in one of two places on a web page: between the <head> and </head> tags or between the <body> and </body> tags. In Listing 3.1, I am placing the script between the <head> and </head> tags.

Listing 3.1 Mouseover/Rollover JavaScript Placed Between the <head> and </head> Tags

```
<html>

<head>

<title>Organic green, oolong, and herbal tea from TranquiliTeas Organic
Teas</title>
```

continues

Listing 3.1 Continued

```
<meta name="description" content="Get gourmet herbal, green,
and oolong teas at wholesale prices from TranquiliTeas.  Organic tea
importer offers decaffeinated herbal teas and other herbal blends.
Black, oolong, green, and iced teas available as loose tea or in tea
bags.">

<meta name="keywords" content="organic teas green oolong tea herbal
blends decaffeinated loose tea bags">

<script language="JavaScript" type="text/javascript">

// begin mouseover script

if (document.images) {

  imageon1 = new Image
  imageoff1 = new Image

  imageon1.src = "images/homeon.gif"
  imageoff1.src = "images/homeoff.gif"

  imageon2 = new Image
  imageoff2 = new Image

  imageon2.src = "images/sitemapon.gif"
  imageoff2.src = "images/sitemapoff.gif"

  imageon3 = new Image
  imageoff3 = new Image

  imageon3.src = "images/contacton.gif"
  imageoff3.src = "images/contactoff.gif"
}

else {

  imageon1 = ""
  imageoff1 = ""
  document.image1 = ""

  imageon2 = ""
  imageoff2 = ""
  document.image2 = ""

  imageon3 = ""
  imageoff3 = ""
  document.image3 = ""
```

```
    }
// end mouseover script
// end hiding script from old browsers -->

</script>

</head>
```

This script defines the "on" and "off" buttons in a JavaScript rollover. In Listing 3.1, if you place your cursor over the navigation button named homeoff.gif, the script changes that button to display the "on" button named homeon.gif. In Figure 3.1, on the ARCH Venture Partners site, the cursor is placed over the Our Portfolio Companies button; therefore, the "on" button is highlighted.

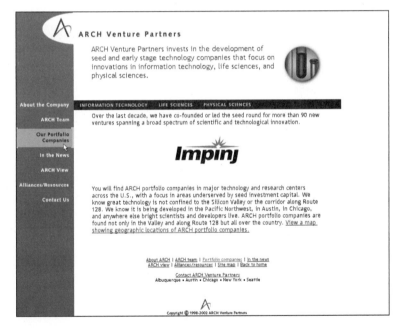

Figure 3.1

With a rollover or a mouseover, a graphic image is highlighted whenever the cursor is placed over it.

Many search engine marketing experts recommend placing the JavaScript within the body tags, specifically at the bottom of a web page right before the </body> tag. On the surface, this might seem to be a great solution because within the HTML code, the search engines have faster access to the text at the top of the page. Why? The spiders do not have to sort through all the JavaScript code before finding the code—the body text and links—that is most important to them. However, placing the JavaScript code at the bottom of a web page still can increase a page's download time, especially if the JavaScript code is longer than the actual HTML code and the page uses multiple scripts. So, what would be a better solution?

The External JavaScript File

Because search engine spiders are interested only in the visible body text on your web pages and the links that they can follow, they have no interest in a site's JavaScript code (unless you are using it to spam the search engines). Therefore, to decrease a page's download time for both the search engines and your site's visitors, do not place your JavaScripts on a web page. Instead, place all your JavaScript files in an external file whenever possible.

To do this, take all the content between the <script> and </script> tags and copy it into a text editor. In the aforementioned TranquiliTeas web page, resulting HTML code on the web page now looks like Listing 3.2.

Listing 3.2   The HTML Code from TranquiliTeas

```
<html>

<head>

<title>Organic green, oolong, and herbal tea from TranquiliTeas Organic
Teas</title>

<meta name="description" content="Get gourmet herbal, green,
and oolong teas at wholesale prices from TranquiliTeas.  Organic tea
importer offers decaffeinated herbal teas and other herbal blends.
Black, oolong, green, and iced teas available as loose tea or in tea
bags.">
```

```
<meta name="keywords" content="organic teas green oolong tea herbal
blends TranquiliTeas decaffeinated loose tea bags">

<script language="JavaScript" src="scripts/mouseover.js"
type="text/javascript">

</script>

</head>
```

In the text editor, the mouseover/rollover script looks like
the following:

```
// begin mouseover script

if (document.images) {

  imageon1 = new Image
  imageoff1 = new Image

  imageon1.src = "images/homeon.gif"
  imageoff1.src = "images/homeoff.gif"

  imageon2 = new Image
  imageoff2 = new Image

  imageon2.src = "images/sitemapon.gif"
  imageoff2.src = "images/sitemapoff.gif"

  imageon3 = new Image
  imageoff3 = new Image

  imageon3.src = "images/contacton.gif"
  imageoff3.src = "images/contactoff.gif"
}

else {

  imageon1 = ""
  imageoff1 = ""
  document.image1 = ""

  imageon2 = ""
  imageoff2 = ""
  document.image2 = ""

  imageon3 = ""
  imageoff3 = ""
  document.image3 = ""
```

continues

```
}
// end mouseover script
        // end hiding script from old browsers -->
```

Save this file with a name that is easy for you to remember, such
as mouseover.js or rollover.js. Place this file and all other scripts
in a subdirectory called scripts on your web server, as shown in
Figures 3.2 and 3.3.

Figure 3.2

Create a subdirectory called
scripts on your web server.

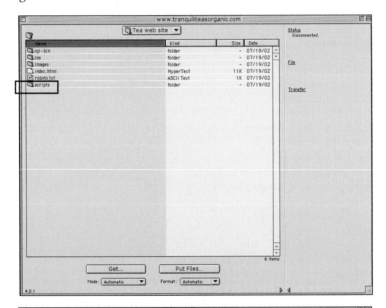

Figure 3.3

Place all your JavaScript
files in this directory. In this
example, the mouseover
script is placed in the
directory.

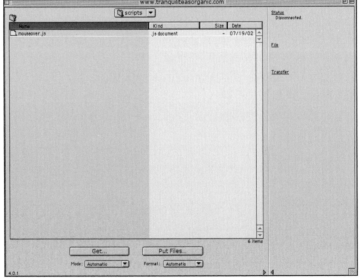

The next step is to instruct the search engine spiders not to crawl the contents of your JavaScript files, which you do using the Robots Exclusion Protocol. To do this, type the following into a text editor:

User-agent: *
Disallow: /scripts/

Name the file robots.txt, and place this file in the root directory, as was shown in Figure 3.2.

Using Multiple Scripts on a Single Web Page

This search engine strategy works for all the scripts on a web page. For example, using the TranquiliTeas site, let's say the web site owner wants to have a mouseover effect and pop-up windows on the home page. The resulting HTML would look like Listing 3.3.

Listing 3.3   Mouseover Effect and Pop-Up Windows for TranquiliTeas

```
<html>

<head>

<title>Organic green, oolong, and herbal tea from TranquiliTeas Organic
Teas</title>

<meta name="description" content="Get gourmet herbal, green,
and oolong teas at wholesale prices from TranquiliTeas.  Organic tea
importer offers decaffeinated herbal teas and other herbal blends.
Black, oolong, green, and iced teas available as loose tea or in tea
bags.">

<meta name="keywords" content="organic teas green oolong tea herbal
blends decaffeinated loose tea bags">

<script language="JavaScript" src="scripts/mouseover.js"
type="text/javascript">

</script>

<script language="JavaScript" src="scripts/popups.js"
type="text/javascript">

</script>

</head>
```

Then place the pop-up JavaScript in a text file and name it some-thing easy to remember, such as popup.js. Place this file in the scripts subdirectory on your web server, as shown in Figure 3.4.

Figure 3.4

The mouseover and pop-up scripts are placed in the scripts subdirectory on your web server.

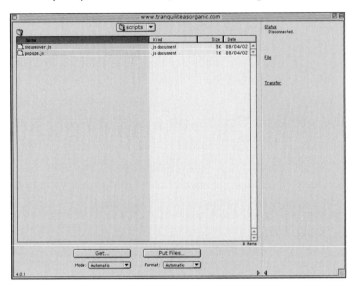

Because you have already placed instructions in the robots.txt file to exclude all files in the scripts subdirectory, there is no need to modify the robots.txt file every time you add a new script to your web pages.

Benefits of External .js Files

Using external JavaScript files benefits three different groups:

- The external files decrease the download time for your site visitors because the scripts are downloaded only once and cached in your browser. After your visitors have the scripts cached, they do not have to download them again whenever they visit other pages on your site that use the same scripts.

- The download time for your web pages decreases when a search engine spider requests web pages from your server. After the Robots Exclusion Protocol is placed on all the external JavaScript files, the search engines access only the text and links on your web pages. They ignore the JavaScript in the external files.

Many search engine marketers do not take into account download time when designing and marketing web sites. Search engine spiders do not wait for huge pages to download on web servers. A long download time often indicates spam or the database feeding the spider an infinite number of URLs, thus crashing the spider. Thus, the faster your pages download, the more spider friendly they are.

■ The external files benefit your design team because if they need to modify a script, they need only modify the script in a single document as opposed to every page on your site, saving them time and money.

Therefore, using external JavaScript files makes your site more search engine friendly and user friendly.

Specifying Alternative Content with the *<noscript>* Tag

The <noscript> tag provides alternative content for browsers that do not support JavaScript and for visitors who have disabled JavaScript while surfing the web. The <noscript> tag, if used, is placed between the <head> and </head> tags. The HTML code in Listing 3.4 shows the proper coding for the <noscript> tag in the fictional TranquiliTeas web site.

Listing 3.4   Coding for the *<noscript>* Tag

```
<noscript>

<h1>Organic green, oolong, and herbal tea</h1>

TranquiliTeas Organic Teas offers a wide range of gourmet organic teas
at wholesale prices.

To view our selection of choice organic teas, please select one of the
links below:

<ul>

<li><a href="herbalteas.html>Herbal teas</a></li>
<li><a href="greenteas.html>Green teas</a></li>
```

continues

Listing 3.4 Continued

```
<li><a href="oolongteas.html>Oolong teas</a></li>
<li><a href="blackteas.html>Black teas</a></li>
<li><a href="teasets.html>Tea sets and accessories</a></li>
<li><a href="teas.html>teas</a></li>

</ul>
```

If you would like more information about our organic teas or would like to order one of our catalogs, please fill out our <a href="contact.html">contact</a> form or call us at 1-800-XXX-XXXX.

```
</noscript>
```

The *<noscript>* Tag and Spam

Unfortunately, many unethical search engine marketers discovered that they could hide text on a web page by using the <noscript> tag, even though the actual web page does not contain any JavaScript. Some search engine marketers abuse the <noscript> tag in an attempt to boost rankings. Never use this tag to hide any unrelated content or links that you would not otherwise show to your end users.

Because of the widespread abuse of this tag, most of the search engines either ignore or decrease the relevancy of the text inside the <noscript> tag. Additionally, most end users never see the content inside the <noscript> tag. Except for the title tag (which is not really hidden), the search engines ignore all hidden tags—or at least do not use them to determine relevancy.

Adding all this extra HTML code inside the <noscript> tags can significantly increase the download time of your web pages. Therefore, before adding any type of JavaScript and <noscript> tags to your site, determine whether the extra code is necessary. If JavaScript is written well, the <noscript> tag is unnecessary. Many sites get plenty of qualified traffic from the search engines without any JavaScript in the site design.

Cascading Style Sheets (CSS)

Cascading Style Sheets (CSS) are a feature of HTML developed by the World Wide Web Consortium (W3C). With style sheets, web site designers and end users can create style templates that specify how different text elements appear on a web page—all without affecting its structure.

Using CSS in web site designs enhances the end-user experience as well as search engine visibility. Style sheets can help reduce code bloat and the overall file size of a web page. Style sheets also enable web designers to customize the properties of individual HTML tags. For example, CSS enables web designers to display fonts and type-faces exactly as they intended instead of relying on browser default settings. The result? Site visitors find web pages much easier to read.

One way CSS benefits web pages is in headings. Heading tags—especially the <h1> tag—can be more attractive when using CSS. Without any font specifications, the appearance of the <h1> tag depends on the settings of your site visitors' browsers. Figure 3.5 shows how various heading tags might look like on a standard browser.

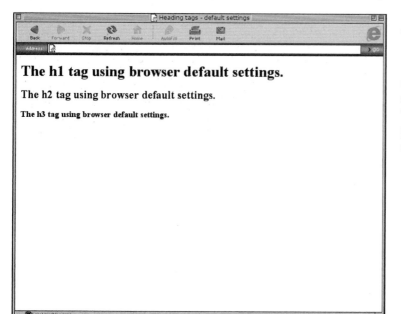

Figure 3.5
The appearance of various heading tags in Internet Explorer on a Macintosh computer. The default font setting for this browser is Times New Roman. On a PC platform, the text appears much larger.

Notice how large the headings appear and how they dominate the web page. If you are trying to place the most important information at the top of your web pages, using <h1> and <h2> tags can crowd important information farther down the computer screen, and your site visitors might not be able to view that information. For maximum search engine visibility and sales conversions, a page's most important keywords should be visible at the top of the computer screen. Web designers can display the most important information at the top of the screen more easily and efficiently using CSS than with standard HTML tags.

Figure 3.6 shows the same type of page designed with an external style sheet.

The smaller, more legible heading tags are easier on the eyes and enable greater use of screen real estate.

Figure 3.6

The appearance of various heading tags in Internet Explorer, on a Macintosh computer, using HTML settings.

Creating External CSS Files

In terms of search engine visibility, external CSS files have the same benefits as external JavaScript files. Because search engines have no interest in a site's style sheets (unless you are using them to spam), you can place all style sheets in an external text file and place the Robots Exclusion Protocol in those files.

For ease of use, web designers can create the code for the style sheets using HTML software. The HTML code for the TranquiliTeas page in Listing 3.5 was generated using Dreamweaver. Notice that the style sheet code is placed between the <head> and </head> tags.

Listing 3.5   Code Generated in Dreamweaver

```
<html>

<head>

<title>Organic green, oolong, and herbal tea from TranquiliTeas Organic
Teas</title>

<meta name="description" content="Get gourmet herbal, green, and
oolong teas at wholesale prices from TranquiliTeas.  Organic tea
importer offers decaffeinated herbal teas and other herbal blends.
Black, oolong, green, and iced teas available as loose tea or in tea
bags.">

<meta name="keywords" content="organic teas green oolong tea herbal
blends TranquiliTeas decaffeinated loose tea bags">

<style type="text/css">
<!--

body {
font-family: Verdana, Arial, Helvetica, sans-serif;
font-size: 13px;
text-align: left
}

h1 {
font-family: Verdana, Arial, Helvetica, sans-serif; font-size: 18px;
font-weight: bold;
text-align: center
}
```

continues

Listing 3.5 Continued

```
h2 {
font-family: Verdana, Arial, Helvetica, sans-serif;
font-size: 16px;
font-weight: bold;
text-align: center
}

h3 {
font-family: Verdana, Arial, Helvetica, sans-serif;
font-size: 14px;
font-weight: bold;
text-align: center
}

p {
font-family: Verdana, Arial, Helvetica, sans-serif;
font-size: 13px;
text-align: left
}
-->
</style>

</head>
```

To create an external style sheet, take all the content between the <style> and </style> tags and copy it into a text editor. In the aforementioned TranquiliTeas web page, resulting HTML code on the web page now looks like the following:

```
<html>

<head>

<title>Organic green, oolong, and herbal tea from TranquiliTeas Organic
Teas</title>

<meta name="description" content="Get gourmet herbal, green, and
oolong teas at wholesale prices from TranquiliTeas. Organic tea importer
offers decaffeinated herbal teas and other herbal blends. Black, oolong,
green, and iced teas available as loose tea or in tea bags.">

<meta name="keywords" content="organic teas green oolong tea herbal
blends TranquiliTeas decaffeinated loose tea bags">

<link rel="STYLESHEET" type="text/css" href="css/style1.css">
<style type="text/css"></style>

</head>
```

In the text editor, the style sheet code looks like the following:

```
body {
font-family: Verdana, Arial, Helvetica, sans-serif;
font-size: 13px;
text-align: left
}

h1 {
font-family: Verdana, Arial, Helvetica, sans-serif; font-size: 18px;
font-weight: bold;
text-align: center
}

h2 {
font-family: Verdana, Arial, Helvetica, sans-serif;
font-size: 16px;
font-weight: bold;
text-align: center
}

h3 {
font-family: Verdana, Arial, Helvetica, sans-serif;
font-size: 14px;
font-weight: bold;
text-align: center
}

p {
font-family: Verdana, Arial, Helvetica, sans-serif;
font-size: 13px;
text-align: left
}
```

Save this file with a name that is easy for you to remember, such as style1.css. Place this file and all other style sheets in a subdirectory called css on your web server, as shown in Figures 3.7 and 3.8.

Figure 3.7

Create a subdirectory in your web server called css.

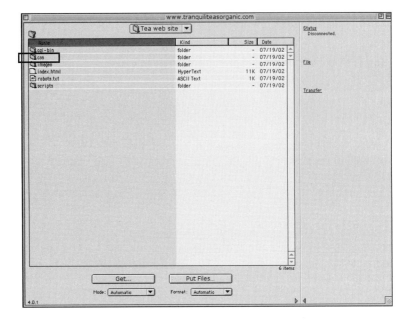

Figure 3.8

Place all your style sheets in the css subdirectory.

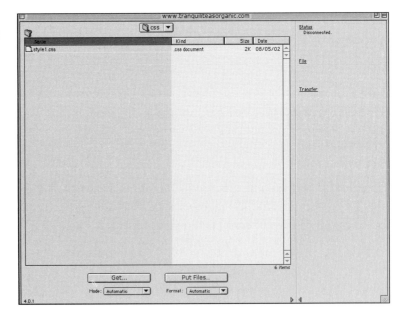

Benefits of CSS

Using external CSS files are beneficial to your site visitors, the search engines, and your design team for the same reasons that external JavaScript files are beneficial. First, the external files decrease the download time for your site visitors because the style sheets are downloaded only once and cached in your browser. After your visitors have the scripts cached, they do not have to download them again whenever they visit other pages on your site that use the same scripts. Additionally, style sheets can help reduce code bloat and the overall file size of web pages, further decreasing the download time.

The external files also benefit your design team because if they need to modify the look and feel of an entire web site, they need only modify the style sheets and not the entire web site.

Therefore, using external style sheets makes your site more user friendly and can help increase a site's search engine visibility.

Warning

Do *not* place the robots exclusion protocol on your external style sheets. Too many unethical search engine marketers have been using style sheets to artificially boost keyword density by hiding text. Because of this rampant abuse, some search engines are beginning to penalize sites that do not enable spiders to access style sheets.

Frames and Search Engine Visibility

Whether web site designers should use frames in web site design has been hotly debated. Usability experts do not recommend the use of frames because people are not able to properly bookmark a framed page and because the URL appearing in the browser does not match the content. End user opinions are divided as well. They either love them or hate them. Newbie web users often get confused with the navigation scheme. Savvy web users opt to view pages without the frameset. Overall, most people prefer not to navigate a framed site when given the choice.

If you are creating a new web site or modifying an existing design, I highly recommend not designing with frames. In terms of search engine visibility, the search engine spiders might not be able to find keyword-rich web pages on a site if the pages are not coded properly. In addition, search engine results can send visitors to web pages with no navigation schemes. However, with proper planning, framed sites can be search engine friendly. This section addresses design workarounds that can help a framed site.

Understanding Frames and the Search Engines

Because search engine spiders index text and follow links, the main problem with the initial frameset code is that it does not present search engine spiders with keyword-rich text to index and set links to follow. Listing 3.6 shows some standard HTML code for a basic frameset page for the fictional TranquiliTeas site.

Listing 3.6 HTML Code for a Basic Frameset Page

```
<html>

<head>

<title>Organic green, oolong, and herbal tea from TranquiliTeas Organic
Teas</title>

<meta name="description" content="Get gourmet herbal, green, and
oolong teas at wholesale prices from TranquiliTeas.  Organic tea
importer offers decaffeinated herbal teas and other herbal blends.
Black, oolong, green, and iced teas available as loose tea or in tea
bags.">

<meta name="keywords" content="organic teas green oolong tea herbal
blends TranquiliTeas decaffeinated loose tea bags">

</head>

<frameset cols="120,*" border="0" framespacing="0"
frameborder="no" marginheight="0" marginwidth="0">

<frame src="buttons.html" name="navigation" noresize scrolling="no"
border="0" marginheight="0" marginwidth="0">

<frame src ="content.html" name="content" noresize scrolling="auto"
border="0" marginheight="0" marginwidth="0">

</frameset>

<body>
</body>

</html>
```

If you analyze this code, you can see why many framed sites do not rank well in the search engines. There is virtually no content on this web page except for the title-tag and meta-tag content. If a search engine, such as Google, does not use meta-tag content for relevancy, the only content on this web page is the title-tag text. A single keyword phrase hardly communicates quality content to your target audience.

The *<noframes>* Tag

Conceptually, with a framed site, the browser displays one of two types of pages. If a browser can read frames, it is served the frameset content. If a browser cannot read frames, it displays the content between the <noframes></noframes> tags.

If your site uses a frames design, always include keyword-rich content and links to the most important pages within your site within these tags. That way, the search engine spiders record your most important text.

Listing 3.7 shows a short example of how to properly code an initial frameset page. If I were to create actual content inside the <noframes> tags, I would write at least 200–300 words of quality information to indicate to both the search engines and site visitors that this text is quality content. Also note that in the following code, I added the style sheet inside the <head> tags so that the <noframes> content matches the site design.

Listing 3.7   Sample HTML Code Illustrating the *<noframes>* Tag

```
<html>

<head>

<title>Organic green, oolong, and herbal tea from TranquiliTeas Organic
Teas</title>

<meta name="description" content="Get gourmet herbal, green, and
oolong teas at wholesale prices from TranquiliTeas.  Organic tea
importer offers decaffeinated herbal teas and other herbal blends.
Black, oolong, green, and iced teas available as loose tea or in tea
bags.">

<meta name="keywords" content="organic teas green oolong tea herbal
blends TranquiliTeas decaffeinated loose tea bags">
```

continues

Listing 3.7 Continued

```
<link rel="STYLESHEET" type="text/css" href="css/style1.css"><style
type="text/css"></style>

</head>

<frameset cols="120,*" border="0" framespacing="0"
frameborder="no" marginheight="0" marginwidth="0">

<frame src="buttons.html" name="navigation" noresize scrolling="no"
border="0" marginheight="0" marginwidth="0">

<frame src ="content.html" name="content" noresize scrolling="auto"
border="0" marginheight="0" marginwidth="0">

</frameset>

<body>

<noframes>

<h1>Organic green, oolong, and herbal tea</h1>

TranquiliTeas Organic Teas offers a wide range of gourmet organic teas
at wholesale prices.

To view our selection of choice organic teas, please select one of the
links below:

<ul>

<li><a href="herbalteas.html>Herbal teas</a></li>
<li><a href="greenteas.html>Green teas</a></li>
<li><a href="oolongteas.html>Oolong teas</a></li>
<li><a href="blackteas.html>Black teas</a></li>
<li><a href="teasets.html>Tea sets and accessories</a></li>
<li><a href="teas.html>teas</a></li>

</ul>

If you would like more information about our organic teas or would like
to order one of our catalogs, please fill out our <a
href="contact.html">contact</a> form or call us at 1-800-XXX-XXXX.

</noframes>

</body>

</html>
```

The *<noframes>* Tag and Spam

Unfortunately, a long time ago, unethical search engine marketers discovered that they could hide text on a web page by using the <noframes> tag, even though the actual web page did not contain a frameset.

Because of the widespread, blatant abuse of this tag, most of the search engines either ignore or decrease the relevancy of the text inside the <noframes> tag.

Navigation and Frames

As stated in Part 2, "How to Build Better Web Pages," a search engine design and user-friendly design have at least two forms of navigation: one that site visitors can follow and one that search engines can follow. A framed design is no exception, especially when it comes to search engine visibility.

The simplest way to make the main content of a framed site search engine friendly is to add a set of text links at the bottom of every web page.

For example, one Dee Concrete sample design was formatted in a frameset with two frames: The left frame contains navigation buttons, and the right frame contains the main content. Site visitors can access the Products & Accessories page from the home page, and the page appears in a browser, as shown in Figure 3.9.

However, if the page appeared in search engine results, and if visitors clicked the link from the search engine results directly to the Products & Accessories page, the page would not appear in the frameset. It would appear as shown in Figure 3.10.

Warning

Do not place a second grouping of meta-tag or title-tag content inside the <noframes> tag. Why? Meta-tag or title-tag content belongs between the <head></head> tags, not between the <body></body> tags.

Placing extra titles and meta tags on your web pages can result in a spam penalty because this technique is clearly used to artificially inflate keyword density, not to benefit your site visitors.

Main or content frame: This frame contains the
main content that the search engines index

Figure 3.9
The Dee Concrete Products
& Accessories page as it
would appear in a framed
site design.

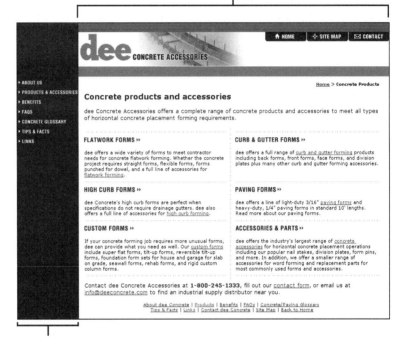

Buttons frame: This frame contains the navigation buttons

Figure 3.10
The Dee Concrete Products
& Accessories page as it
might appear after clicking a
link from the search
engines.

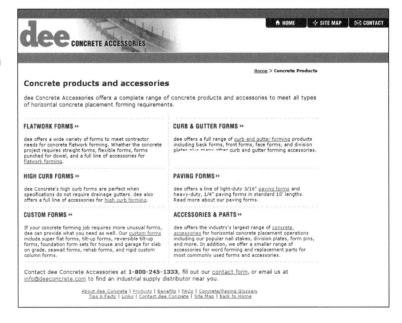

Even though this page does not appear within a frameset, the search engines can still spider this page and the other important pages in the Dee Concrete web site because of the following facts:

- The text links at the bottom of the page
- The breadcrumb links at the top of the page
- The text links embedded in the main body text

Therefore, whenever creating a web site with frames, always be sure the main content frame has a set of links the search engines can follow. The search engine spiders also have to, somehow, find the interior pages. If (a) there are no links to the internal pages from the frameset, (b) the actual interior pages are not submitted to the search engines, and (c) there are no links from other sites to the interior pages, the search engines cannot index the interior pages.

Frames and JavaScript

If you prefer that the web pages on your site always remain within the frames design, you can insert JavaScript on all your pages so that browsers automatically load the frames design. Place the JavaScript between the <head></head> tags, as shown in Listing 3.8 for the fictional TranquiliTeas site.

Listing 3.8 JavaScript *<head></head>* Tags

```
<html>

<head>

<title>Organic green, oolong, and herbal tea from TranquiliTeas Organic
Teas</title>

<meta name="description" content="Get gourmet herbal, green, and
oolong teas at wholesale prices from TranquiliTeas.  Organic tea
importer offers decaffeinated herbal teas and other herbal blends.
Black, oolong, green, and iced teas available as loose tea or in tea
bags.">

<meta name="keywords" content="organic teas green oolong tea herbal
blends TranquiliTeas decaffeinated loose tea bags">
```

continues

Listing 3.8   Continued

```
<script language="JavaScript">
<!--
if (top == self) self.location.href = "framesetname.html";
// -->

</script>

</head>
```

Important

Although other scripts exist to enable framed pages to be bookmarked and to load specific pages within the frameset, it is best to let your site visitors select their preference. Many people just do not like frames designs, and they greatly appreciate the option to turn the frames off.

This script does not load the most appropriate content page in the frameset. The script loads only the frameset you specify, which is generally the home page. Additionally, site visitors cannot use the Back button because each page on your site automatically loads the frameset page.

The best solution is to create a home page that gives site visitors the option to view a site both with and without a frames design. After analyzing your site's traffic logs for a period of at least three months, determine which design your visitors prefer. You might find that your site visitors greatly prefer the unframed version of your site because unframed sites are generally easier to navigate. If your visitors prefer the unframed version of your site, use that site design template for all future web site designs. Extra bonus? Qualified search engine traffic tends to increase after frames are no longer a part of a site design.

Flash Sites and Search Engine Visibility

Flash is a wonderful way of creating web sites with visual flair. Web designers love to use Flash because Flash provides a way to deliver vector images—as opposed to bitmap images—over the web. Vector graphics are scalable, which means that when site visitors resize a browser window, web pages designed in Flash stay in proportion no matter how large or small the browser window becomes. Furthermore, Flash movies are streaming, meaning that when part of a vector image downloads, that part of the image displays on the browser screen although the rest of the movie downloads. Thus, Flash designs have benefits for both web designers and site visitors.

In terms of search engine visibility, however, Flash sites are not an ideal choice. Although a few of the major search engines can crawl the links embedded inside a Flash navigation scheme, the main problem with Flash sites is that they contain very little text for the search engines to index.

Splash Pages

One of the main uses of Flash movies is to use them on a splash page. A splash page is a web page that consists either of (a) a large graphic image and a link instructing visitors to enter a web site or (b) a Flash animation, a link to skip the Flash animation (Skip Intro), and a redirect to a new page after the animation is completed. Many web sites use splash pages as their home page.

Generally speaking, both end users and the search engines do not like splash pages because they contain very little quality content, even though the page design might be outstanding. Using a splash page as a home page is like trying to force all people that visit a supermarket to watch a 30-second commercial before entering a store. For example, Figure 3.11 shows a beautifully designed splash page with a Flash movie.

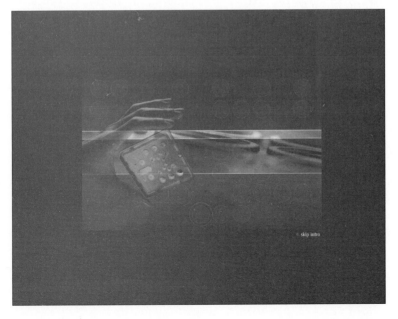

Figure 3.11
A splash page for the Caliper Technologies site. Even the only text on the page (skip intro) is an image. Note that there is no text for the search engines to index and no links for them to follow.

Viewing this page, you can immediately see multiple reasons why splash pages are not search engine friendly:

- **A splash page contains little or no text for the search engines to index:** Remember that the most important text on a web page is title-tag text and visible body text that can be copied and pasted into a text editor. This splash page contains no visible body text.

- **A splash page contains few or no links for the search engine spiders to follow:** Most splash pages link to a single page, which communicates to the search engines that you consider only one page on your site to be important. If JavaScript surrounds a link to an internal page, many search engines will not follow that link.

- **Most splash pages contain a redirect after the Flash animation is complete:** All the search engines consider redirects to be spam. In fact, most search engines do not include splash pages in their indices because of the lack of content and the redirect.

Important

Always remove the redirect from splash pages. Most search engines do not include in their search engine indices web pages that contain redirects.

One workaround is to add keyword-rich text and links to the splash page. If you want to keep the flair and ambiance of the Flash movie, place the text and links below the fold so that your site visitors have to scroll to view the text. In all likelihood, site visitors will click the Enter Site or Skip Intro button rather than scroll to the bottom of the web page. However, if your site visitors do scroll, the page contains quality content and important links.

One way to determine if a splash page is effective is to design two different home pages:

- A splash page as outlined in Figure 3.12, showing a large Flash movie and keyword-rich text below the fold

- A home page that presents site visitors with keyword-rich text above the fold, without the Flash movie

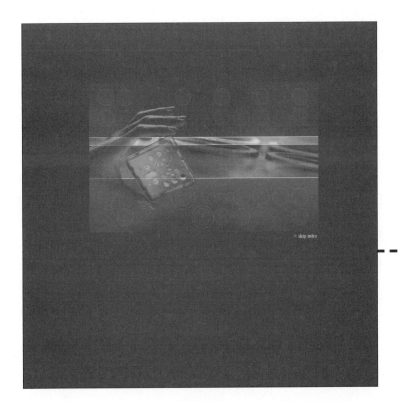

Figure 3.12
By adding keyword-rich text and important links to a splash page, the page becomes more search engine friendly without losing the impact of the Flash movie.

Above the fold

Below the fold

Place important keyword-rich text and important links, especially a link to a site map, below the fold

After analyzing your site's traffic logs for a period of at least three to six months, determine which home page design your visitors prefer. If you find that your target audience prefers the splash page with the Flash movie, keep the Flash movie and the quality content below the fold. If your site visitors do not prefer a less animated home page, continue using the non-Flash page as your home page. Both page designs can attain search engine visibility, but one design probably has a much higher conversion rate than the other.

Regardless of what your target audience prefers, a search engine–friendly splash page must contain keyword-rich content.

Important

Because the search engines are relatively new at indexing Flash sites, I'll be monitoring the progress of our Flash designs on the search engines and keeping that information posted on this book's companion site at www.searchenginesbook.com/flash.html.

Flash Sites

Some search engines have been able to follow the links inside Flash sites since 2001, and they have become increasingly better at it. In August 2002, FAST Search announced that its spider could index the contents inside a Flash site and follow the links as well, which is great news for Flash designers.

Because Flash sites rarely contain keyword-rich content, enable your site visitors to communicate their preferences by creating both a Flash and HTML version of your web site. On the home page, let your visitors select their preferred design, as SiteLab has done on its home page shown in Figure 3.13.

The main benefit of this type of layout is that the HTML version of the site can attain maximum search engine visibility until all the search engines can support Flash.

Figure 3.13
SiteLab's home page contains keyword-rich text for the search engines to index and gives site visitors the choice to view the Flash version or HTML version of the web site.

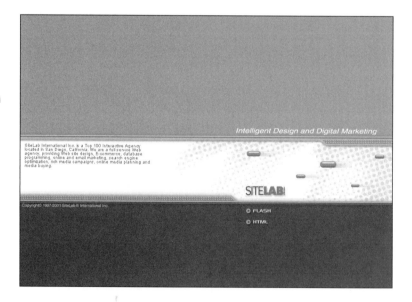

Dynamic Web Pages

Many dynamic web pages are pages that are generated using a database. Dynamic web pages are usually created with Active Server Pages (.asp), Cold Fusion (.cfm), Hypertext PreProcessor (.php), Java Server Pages (.jsp), and other technologies.

Search engines have problems indexing dynamic web pages, but not because they are driven by databases. The main problem is the URL that is generated.

Let's compare a static web page URL and a dynamic web page URL. A typical static web site is comprised of a series of web pages that end in an .html or .htm extension. Each page is a unique file and has unique content, and the URL has no stop symbols such as a ?, &, $, =, +, or %. For example, on the fictional TranquiliTeas web site, a static web page for the oolong tea page has the following URL:

www.tranquiliteasorganic.com/oolongteas.html

In contrast, a dynamic web site has very few files that contain original content. The files from a dynamic web site are comprised of templates that give instructions on how to present content, but the templates actually contain little or no unique content. The main content of dynamic web sites is stored in a database. When a page is viewed on a dynamic web site, the template loads content from the database. To tell the template to load specific content, parameters (or variables) are added to the URL. For example, if the TranquiliTeas site uses a database to showcase different products, the URL might look like the following:

www.tranquiliteasorganic.com/products.asp?product_no=25

The name of the template page is products.asp, the question mark (?) communicates to the search engines that the URL is dynamic, the product_no is the name of a variable or parameter, and 25 is the value assigned to the variable. In this example, the number 25 corresponds to the oolong tea content in the database.

The preceding URL is generally search engine friendly because there is only one parameter in the URL, and many search engines—especially Google and FAST Search—do not have any problems indexing dynamic URLs with a single parameter. However, when the URL contains multiple parameters, it becomes increasingly difficult for the search engines to determine if the resulting web page contains unique content.

For example, in a dynamic URL, you can display a single web page with multiple parameters by separating each parameter with an ampersand (&). A URL with two parameters can look like the following:

www.tranquiliteasorganic.com/products.asp?product_no=25&product_sortorder=asc

This URL is much more difficult for the search engines to index because they have no way of knowing what parameters identify a new web page and what parameters are just a means of sorting content, a navigation scheme, or anything else that is not a new and unique web page.

Thus, one way to make dynamic sites more search engine friendly is to minimize the number of parameters in the URL. Other ways to make dynamic sites search engine friendly are adding static information pages, modifying the stop characters in the URL, utilizing pay-for-inclusion (PFI) programs, and participating in pay-for-placement (PFP) advertising.

Static Information Pages

One of the simplest solutions for dynamic web sites is to create static HTML pages that the search engines can index. Not all web pages on a site need to be dynamically generated, especially pages whose content does not need to be updated frequently. In fact, many web sites naturally contain information pages. Does your site have a FAQs section, a glossary of industry-related terms, or a page with tips and facts related to your products and services? Figures 3.14 and 3.15 show examples of content that can be included on information pages.

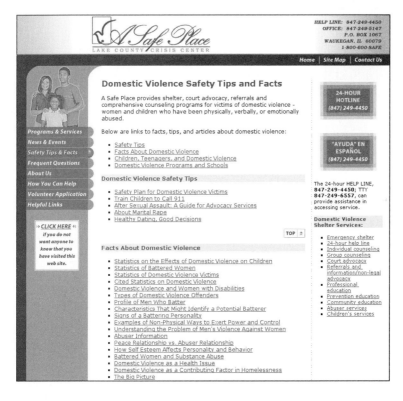

Figure 3.14
A Safe Place has a large set of information pages containing quality information about domestic violence safety tips and facts.

Figure 3.15
Koch Group, Inc., which provides industrial marketing solutions for manufacturers, has a set of tips that are tailored specifically for manufacturers.

Information Pages Versus Doorway Pages

Many people confuse information pages with doorway pages. The two types of search engine strategies are completely different. Doorway pages are a form of spam whereas information pages are acceptable to both search engines and directories.

Doorway pages are web pages created specifically for search engine positions. They are not created to benefit end users. Typically, the copy on doorway pages is computer-generated, *not* written by professional copywriters or content providers. Doorway page companies typically create thousands of computer-generated pages for a single keyword or keyword phrase. All these pages are fed to the search engines through free Add URL forms, polluting their indices with unnecessary and repetitive information. Doorway pages are not pleasant to look at, and they often contain so much gibberish they must be cloaked. End users would not continue visiting a web site if they viewed these pages.

Information pages, on the other hand, are specifically created to benefit site visitors because they provide information in which visitors are interested. Because information pages are always a part of a web site, they can help a site gain more popularity in the search engines *and* the directories.

Table 3.1 compares the characteristics of information and doorway pages.

Table 3.1   Characteristics of Information and Doorway Pages

Information Page Characteristics	Doorway Page Characteristics
■ Designed and written primarily for site visitors	■ Designed and written for positioning only
■ Visually match the appearance of your web site	■ Typically text-only pages
■ Never computer-generated web pages; always designed for human viewing	■ Typically computer-generated web pages
■ Always hosted on the same server as the main web site to help boost popularity	■ Often hosted on a server separate from the main web site
■ Pages with extraordinary content can be submitted and accepted into directories	■ Never accepted in major, reputable directories
■ Site visitors and search engine spiders always view the same page	■ Site visitors and search engine spiders often do not view the same page
■ Contain no spam techniques (redirects, hidden text, keyword stacking, and so forth)	■ Often contain spam techniques, especially redirects, which is why many doorway pages must be cloaked

Modifying Stop Characters in the URL

Search engines are becoming increasingly adept at spidering dynamic web pages. If you view the search results in many search engines, you can see URLs appearing with question marks (?) and equal signs (=).

One way to increase the search engine visibility of dynamic URLs is to convert the troublesome symbols in the URL into symbols, such as a comma or a forward slash, that are more search engine friendly. For example, this dynamic URL:

www.tranquiliteasorganic.com/products.asp?product_no=25

can be modified to be this URL:

www.tranquiliteasorganic.com/products.asp/product_no/25

so that the search engines include the pages in their indices.

Software and workarounds exist on the web that present web developers with solutions for Active Server Pages (ASP), Cold Fusion pages (CFP), CGI/Perl, and Apache servers. The most updated information is available on the subscribers-only section of Danny Sullivan's Search Engine Watch:

www.searchenginewatch.com/subscribers/more/dynamic.html

This information is also available on the companion web site for this book.

Pay-for-Inclusion (PFI) Programs

One strategy to consider for dynamic web sites is PFI programs. With a PFI model, a search engine guarantees to include pages from a web site in its index in exchange for payment. The PFI model is beneficial to search engine marketers and web site owners because of the following two reasons:

- They know their web pages will not be dropped from a search engine index.

- The pages are re-spidered very quickly.

This type of program guarantees that your submitted web pages are not dropped from the search engine index for a specified period of time, generally six months or a year. To keep your guaranteed inclusion in the search engine's index, you must renew your payment. This guarantee saves web site owners considerable time and expenses. With a PFI program, web site owners do not have to continually monitor each search engine to see whether a page has been dropped from an index.

Submitting web pages in a PFI program does *not* guarantee that the pages will appear in top positions. Thus, all pages submitted through such programs should be optimized.

Search engine marketers find that PFI programs save them considerable time and expense because a web page cannot rank if it is not included in the search engine index. Furthermore, PFI programs enable dynamic web pages to be included in the search engine index without having to implement costly redesigns and workarounds.

The seven steps to PFI success are described in the following sections.

Always Optimize the Pages That You Enroll in a PFI Program

PFI programs do not guarantee top placement. The same ranking algorithms apply to web pages in a PFI program that apply to web pages found through the natural spidering process. Therefore, if you want your pages to rank well, place keywords throughout your web pages as outlined in Part 2 of this book.

Use a PFI Program for Dynamic Web Pages That Search Engine Spiders Have a Difficult Time Crawling

One of the main reasons PFI programs were created was to make valuable information contained on dynamic web pages accessible to spiders. URLs with only one parameter are probably picked up by natural spidering. However, if you find that many dynamic pages on your site are not being picked up by the natural spidering process, enroll URLs with multiple parameters in a PFI program.

Learn How to Use PFI Programs Effectively for Your Most Frequently Modified Pages

A big advantage to using a PFI program is that the contents on submitted pages are updated in the search engine results within days. Thus, if you have pages whose contents are updated daily or weekly, such as sites with News sections and Products pages with featured discounts, enrolling those pages in a PFI program delivers that information to your target audience more quickly in the search engine results.

Enroll the Most Important Pages on Your Site in PFI Programs

If you are a small business and have a limited budget, submit only your most important pages into a PFI program. Many sites get an outstanding return on investment by enrolling only 10 or 20 optimized pages in a PFI program.

Enroll in PFI Programs That Offer Excellent Reporting

Many PFI programs offer detailed reporting on the actual keywords used to find each web page and the number of times your target audience clicked a link to your site from search results. All trusted feed programs (for sites with over 1,000 pages) offer this reporting feature, but very few PFI programs offer this type of reporting for smaller sites. One exception is Position Technologies, which offers click-through and keyword reporting for both Inktomi and FAST Search PFI programs. The URL for Position Technologies is available in the "Resources" appendix.

Test Different PFI Programs and Determine Which Search Engine Your Target Audience Is Using

Some PFI programs are more effective than others, depending on your industry. For example, many Teoma/AskJeeves users come from educational institutions, particularly grade schools. Therefore, enrolling pages in the Teoma PFI program might be good for web sites that are targeting educational institutions.

Do Not Submit Spam Pages in PFI Programs

The same spam guidelines that apply to pages submitted for free apply to web pages submitted to PFI programs. Spam pages found in a PFI program are immediately removed from a search engine index.

Session IDs and the Search Engines

Unfortunately, URLs that contain session IDs are often the "kiss of death" in the search engines. The problem with session IDs is that the same content is delivered over and over in the search results with a different URL. To counter mirror content being displayed in search results, many search engines do not include web pages with session IDs.

If a web site owner finds that session IDs are essential for delivering timely, quality content to site visitors, search engines offer PFP advertising programs.

Pay-for-Placement (PFP) Search Engine Advertising

Many web site owners find that it saves considerable time to participate in PFP search engine programs, such as those offered by Overture, instead of dealing with potentially costly workarounds. PFP search engine programs guarantee something that paid inclusion programs do not guarantee: top positions. As long as you bid the top two or three positions, your advertisement is guaranteed to be displayed in the top of the results for the search engine and its partners.

The seven steps to PFP success are described in the following sections.

Do Extensive Keyword Research Before Making a Purchase

Some keywords and keyword phrases are more expensive to purchase than others. Many keyword selections generate clicks but are of little value after visitors come to a site. For example, using the word "free" in a PFP advertisement often generates a lot of clicks and little or no sales.

Additionally, browse the search engines and directories to see which sites cater to your target audience. Some PFP search programs deliver more value than others. Prepare a series of text ads for each product or service you are advertising.

Microsoft does not show the same commercial year after year after year because people get bored after viewing the same commercial. Likewise, people viewing your PFP ads do not want to view the same ad month after month after month. Thus, be sure to regularly update your ads after they cease to be effective.

Give People an Incentive for Clicking Your Advertisement

Your target audience should understand what type of site they will be visiting as a result of clicking your ad. If they see no clear benefit from clicking, they are not as likely to visit your site.

One simple way to encourage clicks is to ask a question such as the following: "Do you want more traffic to your web site?" or "Need help with taxes?" The answer to that question can be on your destination page.

Prepare a Set of Destination Pages, or Landing Pages, for Each Product or Service You Are Advertising

When people click an advertisement, they want to go directly to the page that contains the "benefit" for clicking the advertisement. They do not want to go to a home page and hunt around for information.

Be Prepared to Do a Lot of Testing

PFP advertising involves a great deal of monitoring and testing. Advertisers need to determine which words generate the most qualified clicks, which destination-page designs and content generate the most sales, and which PFP program reaches a target audience.

The amount of work involved in maintaining this type of program can be overwhelming, especially if a site offers thousands of different products and services. Search engine marketers specialize in keyword research and monitoring statistics. Thus, if you find that your in-house staff does not have the time to continually create effective ads and destination pages, consider outsourcing this aspect of search engine marketing.

All Destination Pages Should Contain Quality Content and at Least One Call to Action

What do you want your site visitors to do when they arrive at your site? Do you want them to place an order, subscribe to a newsletter, or perhaps fill out a form? Give your site visitors enough information on your destination pages to help them make the desired call to action.

Place the Robots Exclusion Protocol on Destination Pages That Have Identical or Nearly Identical Content

Because many destination pages contain identical content with very slight variations in design and different calls to action, the spidering search engines often find these pages and include them in their indices. Because the search engines have no way to determine whether these pages are spam pages, be safe. Place the Robots Exclusion Protocol on pages designed and written for PFP search engines.

Understand That First Position Is Not Always the Best Choice

People are programmed to believe that the first position is always the best. In PFP programs, the best site is not necessarily in the first position. Many outstanding sites do not participate in PFP programs, and savvy web searchers understand that positions can be bought.

Also, review the distribution network of the PFP search engines. Bidding for and maintaining a third position in a PFP search engine is often more cost effective than bidding and maintaining a first position. An ad displaying in the third position often displays across the PFP network, as shown in Figure 3.16.

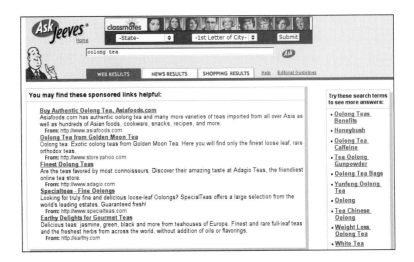

Server-Side Includes (SSI)

A Server-Side Include (SSI) is a type of HTML comment that instructs a web server to dynamically generate elements of a web page before it sends the web page to a browser or a search engine spider. The key item to remember is that a web server constructs a web page before it sends the web page to the search engines. Therefore, any page built with SSIs must contain the most important elements of a search engine–friendly page: keyword-rich text and a navigation scheme that the search engine spiders can follow.

Figure 3.17 outlines how web pages with SSI comments are presented to the search engines.

Web designers can place any type of element inside an include file. The most common items to use as include files are mastheads, navigation elements, and content.

To make SSI web pages search engine friendly, the fully constructed pages should contain keyword-rich text in the title tags, meta tags, visible body text, and alternative text. If a web developer inserts a navigation scheme through SSI, make sure the navigation scheme is spider friendly. When in doubt, create two forms of navigation: one for your target audience and one that the search engine spiders can follow. A set of text links at the bottom of every page can increase a site's search engine visibility.

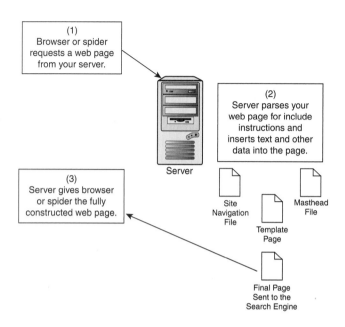

Figure 3.17
Web pages constructed
using SSIs are created in
the web server first, then
presented to the search
engines. As long as fully
constructed pages are
optimized, they can appear
at the top of search engine
results.

Web pages that use SSIs generally have a file extension of .shml
or .shtm. For example, if the fictional TranquiliTeas site used a SSI
as part of its design, the oolong tea page URL would look like
the following:

www.tranquiliteasorganic.com/oolongtea.shtml

Because this URL contains none of the stop characters that a
typical dynamic URL contains (?, &, $, =, +, or %), the URL is
search engine friendly.

Optimizing PDF Documents

Search engines have become increasingly efficient at indexing
different types of documents. Google, for example, can index
12 types of documents, including Microsoft Word, Microsoft Excel,
Microsoft PowerPoint, RTF (rich text format), and Adobe PDF
documents. Many other search engines can index PDF documents
as well.

Warning

One of the main
problems with a web
page that uses multiple
SSIs is download time.
When a search engine
spider requests a page
from a server, the server
should be able to present
the spider with a fully
constructed web page as
quickly as possible. Quite
often, a server can take a
considerable amount of
time to construct a page.
As a result, the spider
might "time out" and
leave the server without
recording the information
on a web page. This is
one of the technical rea-
sons that search engines
do not include all web
pages in their indices.

PDF stands for *portable document format*, which is a universal file format that preserves fonts, colors, graphic images, and formatting of any source document. Many web site owners like to create marketing brochures, media kits, and how-to manuals in PDF format and make them available on the web. Figure 3.18 shows a typical web page highlighting media kits.

Many web site owners like to have PDF documents on their web sites because they want to preserve the exact and look and feel of a printed piece. For example, let's say you would like your online brochure text to display in the typeface Avant Garde. In order for the online brochure to actually appear in this typeface, your site's visitors must have the Avant Garde typeface installed on their computers. If your visitors do not have this typeface installed, your online brochure will look completely different than what you intended. Therefore, many online brochures are formatted as PDF documents.

PDF documents can achieve top search engine visibility when formatted correctly. In fact, some top search engine results are PDF documents, as shown in Figure 3.19.

Figure 3.18
Position Technologies created its media kit documents in PDF format.

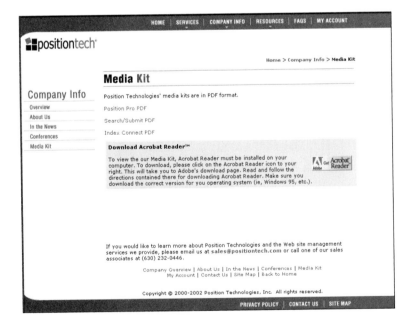

Figure 3.19
A PDF document displays
in the top search result in
Google for the keyword
phrase "chromatography
manuals."

To make your PDF documents search friendly, the documents must contain actual text, not a picture of text. One way to determine if a PDF document contains text the search engines can index is to check the Document Properties dialog box. If no fonts are displayed in the Document Properties dialog box, the PDF document does not contain any text.

To check for fonts in your PDF files, follow these steps:

1. Open the PDF document in Acrobat 5.0.

2. Select File > Document Properties > Fonts. The Document Fonts dialog box should appear, as shown in Figure 3.20. If any fonts appear in this dialog box, the PDF document contains text the search engines can index.

To see the specific text the search engines are able to index, use the Text Select tool, which is highlighted in Figure 3.21.

Try to highlight the text in the PDF document, as shown in Figure 3.22. The text you are able to highlight is the text that the search engines can index.

Figure 3.20

The Document Fonts dialog box for this PDF document displays four fonts, which means that search engines are able to index the text in this document.

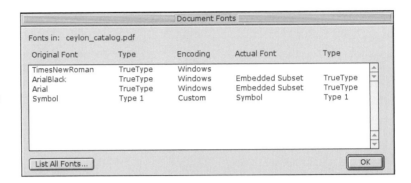

Figure 3.21

The Text Select tool in Adobe Acrobat 5.0.

Figure 3.22

In this PDF example, the text in the main paragraphs can be highlighted, but the text in the logo cannot. Therefore, the search engines are not able to index the text in this logo.

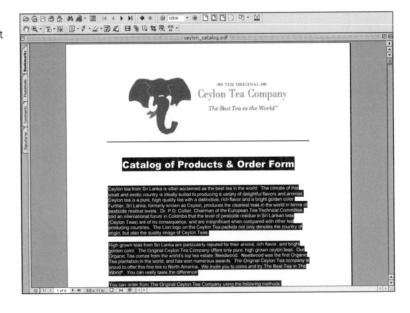

General Guidelines

The same optimization guidelines apply to PDF documents that apply to HTML documents.

- **Make sure your PDF documents contain text that the search engines can index.**

  Search engines are unable to index Image Only PDF documents. So if you create a PDF document by using a flatbed scanner, the search engines will not be able to extract that text.

- **Use keyword-rich text in your PDF documents.**

- **For PDF documents with multiple pages, the most important text is on the first page of your PDF document.**

  Be sure that the titles, headlines, and text on the first page of your PDF documents contain your most important keywords.

- **Minimize download time.**

  In general, search engine representatives recommend keeping document file size to less than 100K. If you find that your PDF documents are larger than 100K, consider creating abstracts.

- **Create optimized HTML pages with abstracts of PDF documents.**

  If your PDF documents are considerably large, such as a manual or a catalog, consider creating HTML pages that summarize PDF files. The abstract pages should contain at least 200 to 250 words of quality content within the <body> and </body> tags. Title tags and meta tags should also contain keywords.

  Whenever possible, the anchor text to the PDF file should contain keywords. Be sure to have links to your PDF documents on your Site Map page as well.

Important

Site visitors find it useful to know they will be viewing a PDF document before they click on a link. Since many PDF documents tend to be greater than 100K in file size, visitors like to know the file size information as well.

For example, on the fictional TranquiliTeas web site, a simple way to let visitors know they will be viewing a PDF document is to make the hypertext link look like the following:

View the TranquiliTeas Organic Tea Brochure— PDF (360K)

Conclusion

Pages with dynamic content and visual flair can attain excellent search engine visibility as long as web designers plan ahead. If a web site owner knows that he or she is going to utilize search engine marketing as part of an online marketing strategy, creating search engine–friendly design templates can save considerable time and expenses.

However, web sites should be designed primarily for your site's visitors, not the search engines. Thus, if a web site owner determines that his or her target audience prefers a design that is not search engine friendly, he or she should go with audience preference. Search engine spiders are not going to spend thousands or millions of dollars purchasing your products and services. Your target audience is making the purchases. Always design with your target audience in mind.

The search engines offer PFI programs and PFP advertising programs for sites that are not created with a search engine–friendly design template.

Nonetheless, a search engine–friendly design can be a more cost-effective use of time and resources than paid advertising. A carefully optimized site with a spider-friendly navigation scheme often delivers long-term results, often reaping a return on investment that lasts for years. Search engine advertising results frequently deliver short-term results, resulting in the continual development of new advertisements and destination pages.

Web site owners might also find that a combination of search engine marketing and search engine advertising delivers the best results. Ultimately, web site owners have to decide which form of search engine marketing delivers the best return on investment for their businesses.

part 4

After Your Site
Is Built

Introduction

When your web site is ready, you can submit it to the search engines and directories. However, submission is not the end of the optimization, design, and marketing process. Individual web page effectiveness must be monitored as well.

Directory Submission

When submitting to directories, there is no magic formula. All directories are unique, generally having different categories and different rules for submission. Directory submission can be quite time consuming because each submission must be tailored for a specific directory. Some directories permit 15-word descriptions, some permit 30 words, and some permit up to 200 words. Therefore, when submitting your site to the most popular directories, always keep their unique characteristics in mind.

Planning an effective directory submission campaign is crucial to your site's search engine visibility. In addition, in some ways, directory submission is even more important than search engine submission because, with directories, you basically have one chance to submit your site correctly. As long as a web site's directory listing is factually accurate, directory editors have no reason to modify the listing. Directory editors' main concern is not how web site owners market their web sites. Directory editors care that the information in their directory is unique, timely, and accurate.

Some directory results come from human editors who find sites through their own research and surfing. Although this is not a common occurrence, most companies prefer the opportunity to write their own titles and descriptions. So rather than risk a directory editor finding your site and writing a title and description you don't like, plan and implement your unique directory submission campaign.

Planning a Directory Submission Campaign

Before submitting your site to the directories, create a log file to keep track of your submissions. Directories keep records of all submissions and can verify this information very quickly. In the event your submission is rejected or the current listing must be modified due to factual errors, careful record keeping helps your directory submission campaign run more smoothly. Directory editors appreciate your careful record keeping as well.

In this log file, keep records of the following information:

- Name of the directory

- Name of the person submitting the web site

- Email address of the person submitting the web site

- URL submitted

- Date(s) of submission

- Categories selected

- Web site title

- Web site description

- Any additional information entered in a Comments field

- Relevant contact information of the company and organization, including physical address, telephone number, and fax number

- If using a paid submission process, a copy of the receipt and the tracking or order number

Directories generally rank web sites by category, title, and site description. In other words, if your title, description, and category contain keywords that people are typing into search queries, your site might appear at the top of directory results. Therefore, an effective directory submission campaign involves keyword research and copywriting.

How many of you truly and honestly spend hours researching the most appropriate directory categories and writing the best descriptions so that both the directories and your site can benefit? Does your site really have unique content or does it contain the same content that all the other sites contain? Web site owners tend to write the descriptions that benefit them most.

If you plan on using the directories as part of your online marketing plan, try not to think solely about your web site. Try to imagine how a directory might benefit from your information. That is what directory editors are thinking about when they evaluate your submission. Directories do not benefit from keyword-stuffed titles and descriptions. They benefit from sites with unique, quality content placed in the appropriate categories. Thus, help directory editors reach their goals. Build a good web site and do your research before you submit.

Selecting the Best Category

One of the biggest mistakes web site owners make during directory submission is not doing the necessary research on each directory.

To select the most appropriate category for your web site, type your selected keywords in each directory's search box, and study the results. Remember the 20- to 30-word keyword list you came up with in Part 2, "How to Build Better Web Pages?" These are the words that you should be entering in the directory search boxes.

Let's look at the fictional TranquiliTeas site. From our keyword list, we know that we must perform a search in each directory using the following keywords:

organic teas	organic tea	oolong tea
green tea	organic oolong tea	organic green tea
herbal green tea	organic tea recipes	herbal teas
tea recipes	herbal tea recipes	black tea
decaffeinated tea	decaffeinated teas	loose leaf teas
whole leaf teas	tea accessories	Chinese teas
English teas	Indian black tea	tea sets
porcelain tea sets	gourmet teas	

You might want to begin with the most generic search term, such as the word "tea." When you begin with a generic search term, categories might appear at the top of the search results. In all likelihood, your site belongs in one of the categories that appear at the top of the search results.

Sometimes, you can search for your top keyword phrases and discover that no categories appear in the search results, only web sites. If this happens, look underneath the descriptions of each web site. You can find different directory categories listed there, as shown in Figure 4.1.

Do not automatically select the category that appears at the very top of the search results. Your web site must truly be suited to a category to be accepted. Are your competitors listed in that same category? Is the type of information you are offering on your web site similar to the information offered by other web sites in that category? You might find that your site can easily fit in multiple categories. If this is the case, you can select the category that appears at the top of the list.

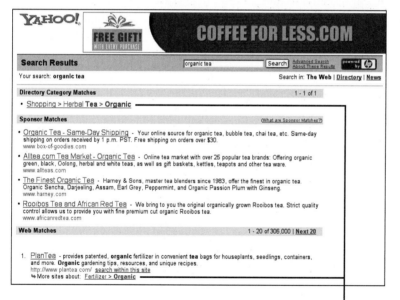

Figure 4.1

When you perform a search on Yahoo! for the keyword phrase "organic tea," a single category appears at the top of the screen. If you scroll down to the web site matches, you can see the different categories available for an organic tea site.

Categories appear underneath web site matches

For the TranquiliTeas web site, the most appropriate category in Yahoo! is the following:

Business and Economy > Shopping and Services > Food and Drinks > Drinks > Tea > Organic

The Open Directory displayed multiple categories that might be appropriate for the TranquiliTeas site:

Business > Industries > Food and Related Products > Beverages > Tea
Shopping > Food > Beverages > Coffee and Tea > Tea
Recreation > Food > Drink > Tea
Home > Cooking > Beverages > Tea

The first two categories contain a large number of tea sites, and the TranquiliTeas site probably will be buried in the search results. It might be better to find less-populated categories. However, based on the types of sites listed in these categories, a submission to either category might be appropriate.

The fourth category is not the best category for home page submission because most of the listings specifically mention recipes. Although the TranquiliTeas site contains recipes, the majority of its content is geared toward selling tea.

The third category is interesting because when you click the link to this category, the subcategories in Figure 4.2 appear.

Figure 4.2
Open Directory page after clicking the Recreation > Food > Drink > Tea link.

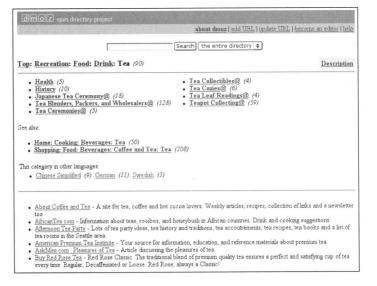

Because the TranquiliTeas site is a wholesale distributor of organic teas, "Tea Blenders, Packers, and Wholesalers" appears to be a more appropriate category for this site. After clicking that link, a completely new category appears at the top of the web page (see Figure 4.3).

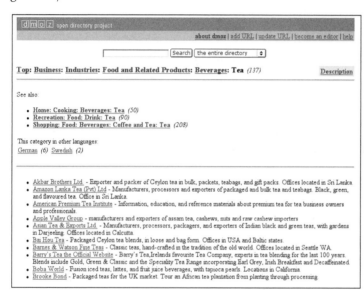

Figure 4.3

Open Directory page after clicking the Tea Blenders, Packers, and Wholesalers link. Notice that a completely new category appears.

Interestingly, the category that appears at the top of this page is the first category in our initial category list. Therefore, the TranquiliTeas web site should be submitted to the first category in the Open Directory:

Business > Industries > Food and Related Products > Beverages > Tea

Suggesting a New Category

Sometimes, after performing several searches, you might not find a directory category that accurately reflects the content of your web site. In this situation, you can suggest an additional category to the directory editors. To be safe, suggest a category that is similar to other categories in the directory.

For example, a particular state in the United States might display a specific category, but a different state might not. This situation arose when I submitted a web site from a domestic violence shelter located in Waukegan, Illinois. A domestic violence shelter listing belongs in a directory's regional section. In all likelihood, a person who is seeking domestic violence help in Connecticut is not going to travel to Illinois to seek an emergency shelter.

When I performed a search on Yahoo!, I found that there was a category in Woodstock, Illinois, for domestic violence shelters (see Figure 4.4).

However, there was no domestic violence shelter category in Waukegan, Illinois. In this situation, it was safe for me to suggest an additional category to Yahoo! because there were similar categories in other regions. To be sure that my additional category would be accepted, I also checked other states. I found the same categories existed in Texas, California, Minnesota, and North Dakota regional listings. I even found domestic violence shelter listings for other countries.

Figure 4.4

Regional domestic violence shelter category in Yahoo!.

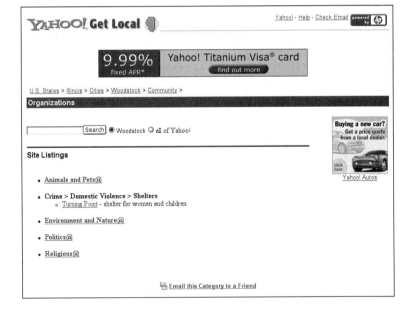

Types of web sites that belong in regional categories are physician sites, hospitals, landscaping firms, real estate offices, restaurants, local government offices, Chambers of Commerce, and any other organization that does business in a specific area. If you do not see the appropriate category for your type of business and organization, check out categories for other states.

In the submission form for Yahoo!, you can suggest an additional category in a field called Additional Information. Other directories might not have this field. If you find yourself in that situation, feel free to suggest an additional category in the Comments field in the submission form, if such a field is provided (see Figure 4.5).

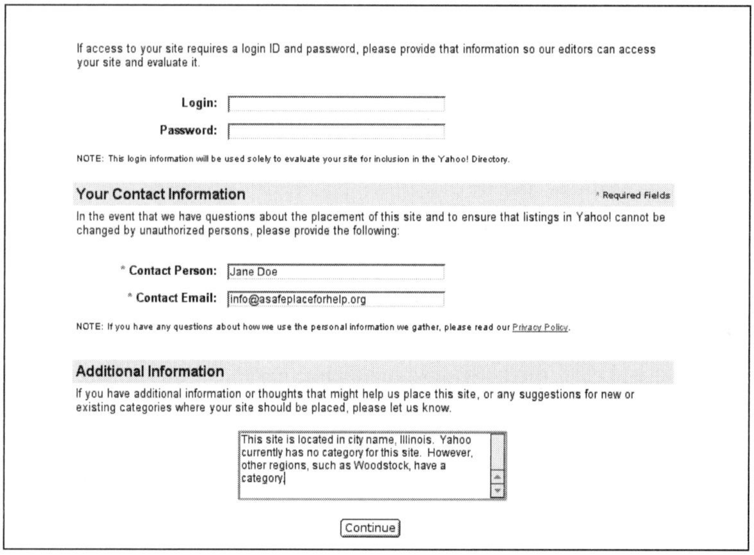
If access to your site requires a login ID and password, please provide that information so our editors can access your site and evaluate it.

Login:

Password:

NOTE: This login information will be used solely to evaluate your site for inclusion in the Yahoo! Directory.

Your Contact Information * Required Fields

In the event that we have questions about the placement of this site and to ensure that listings in Yahoo! cannot be changed by unauthorized persons, please provide the following:

* **Contact Person:** Jane Doe

* **Contact Email:** info@asafeplaceforhelp.org

NOTE: If you have any questions about how we use the personal information we gather, please read our Privacy Policy.

Additional Information

If you have additional information or thoughts that might help us place this site, or any suggestions for new or existing categories where your site should be placed, please let us know.

This site is located in city name, Illinois. Yahoo currently has no category for this site. However, other regions, such as Woodstock, have a category.

Continue

Figure 4.5
Yahoo!'s Additional Information field in the submission form.

Writing an Effective Web Site Title

Most of the time, a web site's title is the official company name, and, as mentioned in Part 1, "Before You Build," directory editors are looking for the official company name in one of four places:

- A header or footer

- The About Us page

- The Contact Us page

- The Locations page

The About Us page should always contain the correct spelling of your company name. Even if you use your official company name in other places throughout your web site, it is still a good idea to always make that information available in your About Us section.

Do not try to trick directory editors into using a company name that contains keywords if the official spelling of your company name does not contain keywords. For example, suppose the official company name of the TranquiliTeas site is Tranquili Teas Organic Tea, Inc. An unethical search engine marketer might not like the official company name and try to modify it. Why? Because the company name does not contain the plural version of "tea." He or she might change the official company name in the submission form to this:

Tranquili Teas Organic Tea, Inc.

Directory editors are aware of all the tricks unethical search engine marketers do to artificially inflate directory positions. Not only do they check that you use the correct spelling of the company name throughout your site, but also they check your domain name registration to be sure that your company's information (company name, physical address, and other contact information) matches the information that you typed into the submission form.

If you are submitting a page that is not your home page, your title can be a bit more descriptive. Let's say, for example, that the TranquiliTeas site contains information on the history of the

Japanese tea ceremony. If site owners were to submit this particular page (or set of pages to Yahoo!), the title might be this:

History of the Japanese tea ceremony

Notice that the titles in the previous examples are factual and contain no sales and marketing hype. The keywords "organic" and "tea" are in the home page title submission. The keywords "Japanese" and "tea" are in the individual web page submission. Even if your keyword research showed that your target audience typed "teas" more often, the acceptable titles do not use that form of the word.

Writing an Effective Web Site Description

At first, it might seem that directory editors and web site owners have conflicting interests. Directory editors want to preserve the quality of their directory results. They want descriptions to accurately describe the contents of a web site without any sales and marketing hype. Web site owners do not necessarily want their description to be objective. If a slogan or a set of keywords has worked for their businesses over the years, they want to preserve that branding and marketing strategy. With these seemingly conflicting goals, how can web site owners have their web sites displayed in directories in the best way possible?

In reality, directory editors and web site owners actually have the same goals. As a web site owner, you have complete control over how your pages are displayed and the content that you place on your pages. You would not like it if a complete stranger ordered you to change the content on your site because he or she did not agree with what you had to say or the manner in which you stated the information. No stranger should control the content of your web site.

Likewise, directory editors must deal with thousands of strangers telling them, every day, how they should display the contents of their web sites. Directory editors have a tough job. Viewing hundreds of submissions a day for hundreds or thousands of different categories while preserving the quality of the directories is a daunting task.

You should be aware that directory editors must deal with thousands of submissions every week. Directory editors are trying to preserve the quality of the information they deliver. By following their guidelines and examples, your submission is less likely to be modified or rejected.

After you have determined the most appropriate category for your web site, review all the descriptions listed in that category. How many words, on average, does the directory editor allow on the page? If you notice that most of the descriptions contain 12–15 words, you know that the directory editor prefers a 15-word description to a 25-word description, even though the guidelines might state that you can submit a description of up to 25 words.

What appears to be the writing style within the descriptions that are listed? Even though your description should resemble the description style of other sites listed in your targeted category, your description should be unique. Thus, if your company specializes in three types of services, mention those three services in your description. If your company targets a specific audience, mention the audience in your description as well.

Do not write a description that is identical to other descriptions in your targeted category. Directory editors understand that their end users do not want the same information delivered to them over and over again in search results. Editors want to know that with each web site they accept, there is unique and valuable information available. Thus, make sure that one of your unique selling propositions (USPs) is somehow shown in your description.

In addition, do not try to stuff too many keywords into the description. Directory editors and people who view search results do not want to read a list of keywords.

I tend to follow a basic description format and tailor the description based on directory research. This description format appears to satisfy the needs of both directory editors and web site owners:

(Keyword phrase 1) firm specializing in (keyword phrase 2), (keyword phrase 3), and (keyword phrase 4)

Using this format, a possible description for TranquiliTeas might be the following:

Wholesale organic tea distributor specializing in oolong, green, herbal, decaffeinated, and black teas. (13 words)

This description does the following: (a) objectively and accurately describes the contents of the web site, making the directory editors happy, and (b) contains targeted keywords.

This 13-word description contains the following keyword phrases:

Tea	Green tea	Organic green tea
Teas	Green teas	Organic green teas
Organic tea	Herbal tea	Organic herbal tea
Organic teas	Herbal teas	Organic herbal teas
Wholesale tea	Decaffeinated tea	Organic decaffeinated tea
Wholesale teas	Decaffeinated teas	Organic decaffeinated teas
Wholesale organic tea	Black tea	Organic black tea
Wholesale organic teas	Black teas	Organic black teas
Oolong tea	Organic oolong tea	
Oolong teas	Organic oolong teas	

If you have a specific target audience, you can include that information at the end of a description, as in the following example:

Wholesale organic tea distributor specializing in oolong, green, herbal, decaffeinated, and black teas for stores and restaurants. (17 words)

Sometimes, you might have more keywords that you would like to target. For example, the TranquiliTeas site might offer its teas as loose tea or in tea bags. This information is important to the target audience of store and restaurant owners. So, another possible description might be this:

Wholesale organic tea distributor specializing in oolong, green, herbal, decaffeinated, and black teas. Choose from loose tea or tea bags. (20 words)

This 20-word description contains an even longer list of keyword phrases:

Tea bags	Green loose tea	Organic oolong tea
Teas	Green loose teas	Organic green tea
Loose tea	Green tea bags	Organic green teas
Loose teas	Herbal tea	Loose organic green tea
Organic tea	Herbal teas	Loose organic green teas
Organic teas	Herbal loose tea	Organic green tea bags
Loose organic tea	Herbal loose teas	Organic herbal tea
Loose organic teas	Herbal tea bags	Organic herbal teas
Wholesale tea	Decaffeinated tea	Loose herbal green tea
Wholesale teas	Decaffeinated teas	Loose herbal green teas
Wholesale organic tea	Decaffeinated loose tea	Organic herbal tea bags
Wholesale organic teas	Decaffeinated loose teas	Organic decaffeinated tea
Wholesale loose tea	Decaffeinated tea bags	Organic decaffeinated teas
Wholesale loose teas	Black tea	Loose decaffeinated green tea
Wholesale tea bags	Black teas	Loose decaffeinated green teas
Oolong tea	Black loose tea	Organic decaffeinated tea bags
Oolong teas	Black loose teas	Organic black tea bags
Oolong loose tea	Black tea bags	Organic black tea
Oolong loose teas	Organic oolong tea	Organic black teas
Oolong tea bags	Organic oolong teas	Loose black green tea
Green tea	Loose organic oolong tea	Loose black green teas
Green teas	Loose organic oolong teas	Organic black tea bags

Notice that the target audience was eliminated from the 20-word description. If the words used to describe the target audience (stores and restaurants) are targeted keywords, why should they be eliminated from the description? Many directories allow 25-word descriptions. A longer description still follows directory guidelines.

When submitting your site to a directory, remember to *always* follow the lead of the editor. If the current listings in the directory have a shorter description, you know that a longer description has a higher chance of being modified—and you might not like the way the editor modifies your longer description, especially if the editor eliminates one of your most important keywords. Because I recognized that "stores and restaurants" was not one of the keyword phrases on the keyword list I came up with in Part 2 of this book, I eliminated that phrase to make the description as concise as possible.

Because all directories are different and vary in the number of words they accept in their submission forms, you should write descriptions of varying lengths. Write 7-, 10-, 15-, 20-, 25-, 30-, and 50-word descriptions and save them in a text file. When you begin the directory submission process, you can easily cut and paste the appropriate description into the submission form.

Paid Submission

If your budget allows it, use the paid/expedited submission programs whenever possible. Because most of the major search engines measure popularity, the faster your site can be listed in the directories, the faster your site can receive the popularity boost.

Paid submission does not guarantee that your site will be accepted into the directory. Rather, the fee guarantees that your site will be reviewed within a specified period of time, generally within 48 hours to one week. The fee pays for the time it takes for a directory editor to evaluate your title, description, and web site plus the time it takes to add your site to the database—if your site is accepted.

Important

When writing your descriptions for directory submissions, remember that editors are most likely to view your home page first. Therefore, on your home page, directory editors should be able to see the products or services you highlighted in your description. If editors are unable to determine that your site specializes in the very services that you claim to offer in your description, in all likelihood, they will modify your description.

Multiple Listings from a Single Web Site

Getting multiple listings from a single web site in a directory is the exception rather than the rule. Again, web site owners and directory editors appear to have conflicting interests. Web site owners desire multiple listings to increase their site's popularity and overall search engine visibility. Directory editors want to list URLs with unique, quality content. Web site owners' ultimate goal is to sell their products and services. Directory editors' ultimate goal is to find sites that provide information.

One way to determine whether a site can be successfully submitted for an additional listing is to ask yourself whether people can benefit from visiting your site without spending money. If your site provides information such as free tips, a how-to section, recipes, a dictionary, or a glossary, your site provides information for the clear benefit of your target audience. Both directory editors and end users like to see this type of information.

If your web site has been approved for admission into a directory, your specialized topic web page stands a better chance of being selected for a different category. When your main site is accepted, you know that your site has met the directory's rules and guidelines. The editors found your site's content easy to read and informative.

You have to go through the same submission process as outlined for your main site. You have to suggest an additional category and write a unique title and description for each additional URL you submit.

A general guideline to follow is not to submit multiple pages from the same site in the same branch of a directory. For example, in the Open Directory, the category selected for the TranquiliTeas main site was this:

Business > Industries > Food and Related Products > Beverages > Tea

Suppose TranquiliTeas site owners had a collection of unique organic tea recipes and wanted to submit their main Recipes page to additional categories. First, they would have to find the most appropriate category. After performing multiple keyword searches in the Open Directory, the most appropriate categories might be the following:

Home > Cooking > Beverages > Tea

or

Recreation > Food > Drink > Tea

Notice that both categories are not in the Business or Business > Industries branch of the Open Directory. Because the sites in the first category contain tea recipes in their descriptions, the first category is probably the better selection.

Before submitting the Recipes page, the TranquiliTeas site owner should verify that the following is true: (a) its recipes are unique, and (b) the content is substantial. Some of the sites listed in this category have a single tea recipe that is unique. Other sites have collections of tea recipes. Therefore, if the TranquiliTeas site has a collection of unique organic tea recipes, in all likelihood, the Recipes URL will be accepted into this category.

Assuming that the TranquiliTeas site does have a collection of unique organic tea recipes, the site owners can write a unique title and description for this submission. Many of the sites listed in this category mention the company name. Thus, it might be appropriate to submit a title such as this:

Organic tea recipes from TranquiliTeas Organic Tea

Note that a directory editor might not like that title because of the repetition of the keyword phrase "organic tea." Thus, a better title might be this:

Organic tea recipes from TranquiliTeas

This title is more concise but still accurately conveys the necessary information. If site owners want to keep the full company name intact without giving the appearance of keyword stacking, another appropriate title might be this:

TranquiliTeas Organic Tea recipes

Additionally, no web sites in this category specifically highlight organic teas. Thus, another appropriate title might be this:

Organic tea recipes

Because the sites (in the targeted category) that contain a collection of tea recipes mention the company name in the title, follow the directory editor's lead. Submit one of the titles containing the company name.

Now that both the title and category are selected, it is time to write an appropriate description. Notice that in the initial TranquiliTeas site submission that the word "recipes" was not mentioned:

Wholesale organic tea distributor specializing in oolong, green, herbal, decaffeinated, and black teas. Choose from loose tea or tea bags.

Search engine and directory users do not want the same sites appearing over and over again in the search results. In general, end users and directory editors do not want to see both the TranquiliTeas main site and the individual Recipes section appearing together in search results.

Keeping the words "recipe" or "recipes" out of the initial description was a strategic move. If a search engine marketer kept the word "recipes" in this description, the main site might show up in search results for the search query "organic tea recipes," and the additional listing might be rejected.

Remember, when people perform searches, they do not necessarily want to go to your home page. Rather, they would prefer to go straight to the information for which they are searching without having to surf for that information. By keeping the word "recipes" out of the main site submission and using that word in the additional submission, the TranquiliTeas site owners are thinking about their target audience by delivering them directly to the Recipe section of their site.

Additionally, the site owners are helping to preserve the quality of the directory category. If the TranquiliTeas site offers a unique collection of organic tea recipes, the site provides free information for visitors without forcing them to go to the home page first. There-fore, the additional listing benefits everyone. End users are delivered directly to the appropriate page. The directory has unique and accurate information, and the site owners have an additional listing.

Before you submit your site to a major directory, review your entire site using the following checklist to be sure that the site is ready for submission. This avoids rejections from the editors.

Directory Submission Checklist

To save the time and costs involved in directory submissions, use the following checklist to ensure that your site is ready for directory editors to review:

❏ Yes	❏ No	Did you read the Terms and Conditions on each individual directory before submitting your site to ensure that you are following its guidelines?
❏ Yes	❏ No	Does your site contain unique content? Have you researched your targeted categories to ensure that your site contains unique content?
❏ Yes	❏ No	Is all the text on your web site legible, both the HTML text and the text within graphic images?
❏ Yes	❏ No	Does your site have any broken links? Any type of broken link, be it an Error 404 page or a graphic image that does not load, is reason for a site to be rejected.
❏ Yes	❏ No	Is the site legible on Netscape and Explorer?
❏ Yes	❏ No	Is all of your contact information (physical address, telephone number, fax number, and email address) easily found on your site?
❏ Yes	❏ No	Is the correct spelling of your official company or organization name on an About Us, Contact Us, or Locations page, even if this information is available in a header or footer on your web site?

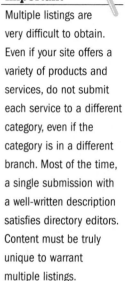

Important

Multiple listings are very difficult to obtain. Even if your site offers a variety of products and services, do not submit each service to a different category, even if the category is in a different branch. Most of the time, a single submission with a well-written description satisfies directory editors. Content must be truly unique to warrant multiple listings.

continues

❑ Yes ❑ No — If you have a business site, do you have a virtual domain name (such as *www.companyname.com*)?

❑ Yes ❑ No — Do all of your links, both internal links (to pages within your site) and external links (to other web sites), work?

❑ Yes ❑ No — Does your site have secure credit card processing (for sites that accept credit cards)?

❑ Yes ❑ No — If your site sells products, does your site have a return policy and a money-back guarantee?

❑ Yes ❑ No — If your site collects confidential information, does your site have an official privacy policy?

❑ Yes ❑ No — Does your site have a copyright notice? If so, is the most current year published?

❑ Yes ❑ No — Do visitors have to download a plug-in to view the site? Requiring a plug-in might cause a site to be rejected.

❑ Yes ❑ No — Does your site have at least six to eight pages of substantial content? Sites with too few pages generally get rejected.

❑ Yes ❑ No — Are both your web pages and your graphic images quick to download?

❑ Yes ❑ No — Is your site fully functional 24 hours a day, 7 days a week? Make sure your shopping carts, forms, search engines, and other dynamically generated functions work properly.

❑ Yes ❑ No — Have you tested all your forms to be sure they are working properly? Do forms have an appropriate Thank You page after your visitors click the Submit button?

❑ Yes ❑ No — Have you spell-checked all your content?

❑ Yes ❑ No — Do you have redirects on any of your pages? Most redirects are considered spam.

❏ Yes	❏ No	Does your site require a user name and password to view its contents? If so, have you provided directory editors with this information so that they can verify your site's content? Many sites are rejected if there is no substantial content outside a password-protected area or if you require your visitors to give you confidential information before viewing a site's content.
❏ Yes	❏ No	Did you perform extensive category research to choose the most appropriate categories for your site?
❏ Yes	❏ No	Did you select the most language-appropriate categories?
❏ Yes	❏ No	Is the title of your main site your official company or organization name?
❏ Yes	❏ No	Have you removed unnecessary punctuation, sales hype, and buzz words from your title?
❏ Yes	❏ No	Is your title written with all capital letters? You should remove all unnecessary capitalization.
❏ Yes	❏ No	Did you repeat the site's title or the category in the description? Editors do not like this.
❏ Yes	❏ No	Did you use abbreviations or acronyms in your description that are commonly understood? When in doubt, spell out the acronym.
❏ Yes	❏ No	Did you capitalize the first letter of the description?
❏ Yes	❏ No	Did you carefully review the current descriptions in your targeted categories for adherence to standard word count?
❏ Yes	❏ No	Does your description contain only a list of keywords? If so, review the current descriptions in your target categories again and rewrite following the editors' lead.

continues

❏ Yes   ❏ No   Did you highlight your most important products and services, using keywords, in your description?

❏ Yes   ❏ No   Did you highlight your unique selling propositions in your descriptions?

❏ Yes   ❏ No   Can directory editors easily find your most important products and services just by viewing your home page?

❏ Yes   ❏ No   Did you remove all sales hype from your description?

❏ Yes   ❏ No   If you submit additional pages within your site, is the information on those pages substantial and unique?

❏ Yes   ❏ No   Are additional pages submitted to categories in a different category branch than the main site?

❏ Yes   ❏ No   Do your additional page title and description contain keywords that clearly, concisely, and accurately describe the contents of the page?

❏ Yes   ❏ No   If it is within your budget, did you use the paid, expedited submission form?

❏ Yes   ❏ No   Did you verify whether your site is already listed in the directory? If so, you have to fill out a Change Request form.

❏ Yes   ❏ No   Did you create a log of all directory submissions information, including dates, names, titles, descriptions, and contact information?

❏ Yes   ❏ No   If your site has not appeared in the directory, did you wait at least three to four weeks before resubmitting?

❏ Yes   ❏ No   If you are suggesting an additional category, did you model that category after other categories that already exist in the directory?

❑ Yes	❑ No	If your submission was rejected, did you appeal within 30 days? Was your appeal written in a polite and professional manner?
❑ Yes	❑ No	Are all submissions tailored for each directory?

Most of the time, web site owners have only one chance to do it right with directories. Modifying a directory listing is very difficult, if not impossible. However, with proper planning and execution, web site owners can reap the rewards of directory listings years after submission.

Search Engine Submission

The guidelines for submitting to search engines are completely different from the guidelines for submitting to directories. With directories, a human editor evaluates your web site and ensures that it is placed in the most appropriate category. With search engines, no editors or categories are involved. In fact, over time, many search engines find a site without a direct submission guiding them.

Search engines begin finding web pages through lists of heavily used servers from major Internet Service Providers (ISPs). They also find web pages through the most frequently visited web directories, such as Yahoo!. Because the major web directories are a starting point for many search engine spiders, submitting your site to directories is actually the first step in effective search engine submission. The popularity boost can greatly affect search engine visibility.

Planning a Search Engine Submission Campaign

Many web site owners feel that they get maximum search engine visibility by having every single page on their site listed well in the search engines. This belief is a common misconception. Every page on a web site does not have to be optimized to obtain effective search engine visibility. In fact, many successful small business sites need only 20–25 optimized pages, and larger sites usually do not need more than 200 optimized pages.

The first pages you should submit to the search engines are the ones that are properly optimized. The first one on the list should be your home page. Some search engines ask only for your home page URL, opting to spider the rest of your site from the home page. Always be sure that your home page is properly optimized.

To get optimal visibility in search engine results, keywords and keyword phrases must be placed strategically throughout your web pages. To summarize, keywords need to be placed in the following locations:

- Title tags
- Visible body text
- Anchor text
- Within or near hypertext links
- Meta tags
- Alternative text

As discussed in Part 2, title tags, visible body text, and anchor text are considered *primary text* because all the major search engines place a great deal of emphasis on this text. Meta tags and alternative text are considered *secondary text* because not all search engines read and record this text.

To ensure that the search engines can find your optimized pages, your site designer should provide multiple means for the search engine spiders to find those pages. Effective cross-linking within your site is beneficial for both your site's visitors and the search engine spiders. If cross-linking is too difficult or time consuming to implement, creating and submitting a site map gives spiders access to many URLs within your site.

As stated, begin search engine submission with your home page and other optimized pages. In general, submit anywhere from one to fifty web pages at a time, depending on the search engine guidelines. Some search engines accept only five pages per day. Some search engines accept more. Always fall within the submission limits the search engines publish on their own sites.

Additionally, do not submit and then resubmit a web page to the search engines within one 24-hour period, even if you made legitimate changes to it. To a site owner, the change is a legitimate one, particularly if the page contained typographical errors. However, a search engine spider cannot determine that the submission of the same page within a 24-hour period is due to an honest mistake. To the search engines, the submission appears to be spam. So be patient, and wait a few days if you find that you made errors in your submission.

With free submissions, it can take anywhere from a few weeks to a few months for your pages to appear in the search results. If your search engine marketing campaign has specific deadlines, using pay-for-inclusion programs and pay-per-click search engines are your best options because of their quick turnaround time.

However, to succeed with both paid-inclusion programs and pay-per-click search engines, you need to remember their unique characteristics. Pages submitted to paid-inclusion programs must be properly optimized for them to rank well. Select only your best optimized, most targeted pages for paid-inclusion programs.

Effective pay-per-click advertising involves careful keyword research and selection as well as the writing of a series of ads. Designing appropriate landing pages for your pay-per-click advertising is also essential. Design landing pages and write a series of ads *before* you sign up for any pay-per-click program.

Search Engine Submission Checklist

To avoid possible spam penalties and wasted time and effort, review your site using the following checklist to be sure that the site is ready for submission:

❏ Yes	❏ No	Are you creating web pages with content your target audience is genuinely interested in reading?
❏ Yes	❏ No	Does your content contain highly focused keyword phrases rather than phrases that are too general and competitive?
❏ Yes	❏ No	Are you optimizing your web pages for at least three to five keywords at a time?
❏ Yes	❏ No	Are you using regionally specific keywords, when applicable?
❏ Yes	❏ No	Are you using the most commonly used variations of your keywords, based on your keyword research?
❏ Yes	❏ No	Does each optimized page contain a unique title?
❏ Yes	❏ No	Are you using multiple keywords in your title tags (using the power combo strategy) when appropriate?
❏ Yes	❏ No	Are your most important keywords (a) appearing above the fold and (b) throughout each optimized page?
❏ Yes	❏ No	Are you using keywords in hypertext links, whenever possible?
❏ Yes	❏ No	Does each optimized page have at least one call to action?
❏ Yes	❏ No	Does each optimized page contain a unique meta-tag description?
❏ Yes	❏ No	Do your meta-tag descriptions contain both targeted keyword phrases and a call to action?
❏ Yes	❏ No	Does each optimized page contain a unique meta-tag keyword list?
❏ Yes	❏ No	Does each set of meta-tag keywords contain words and phrases that you actually use within the visible body text?

❏ Yes   ❏ No   Do you place common misspellings of your keywords within your meta-tag keywords?

❏ Yes   ❏ No   Do your graphic images contain descriptive keywords within the alternative text attribute, when appropriate?

❏ Yes   ❏ No   Do you provide at least two means of navigating your site: one for your visitors and one for the search engines?

❏ Yes   ❏ No   Does your site have a site map, to assist both your visitors and the search engine spiders?

❏ Yes   ❏ No   If your site uses frames, is your site navigable with and without the frameset?

❏ Yes   ❏ No   If you are using JavaScript on your site, did you place the JavaScript in an external .js file and place the Robots Exclusion Protocol on that file?

❏ Yes   ❏ No   If you are using Cascading Style Sheets (CSS) on your site, did you place the style sheets in an external .css file?

❏ Yes   ❏ No   Do you have any redirects on your site? If so, have you placed the Robots Exclusion Protocol on pages that use redirects?

❏ Yes   ❏ No   Are your optimized pages placed in the root directory (along with your home page) on your web server?

❏ Yes   ❏ No   Is your robots.txt file placed in the root directory on your web server? Did you remember to transfer your robots.txt file before you transferred any other web pages to your server?

❏ Yes   ❏ No   Are you using subdomains instead of subdirectories if you find that your subdomains contain unique and substantial content?

❏ Yes   ❏ No   If you are submitting pages to non-U.S. search engines, are you writing your pages in the appropriate language?

continues

❏ Yes	❏ No	If it is within your budget, did you submit your optimized pages to pay-for-inclusion (PFI) programs?
❏ Yes	❏ No	If you use pay-for-placement (PFP) advertising, are your purchases based on detailed keyword research and selection?
❏ Yes	❏ No	If you use PFP advertising, do you carefully monitor your bids to get the best search engine visibility at the most reasonable cost?
❏ Yes	❏ No	Did you name your web pages something that your target audience can remember and spell easily, using keywords whenever possible?
❏ Yes	❏ No	Did you design or select a series of landing pages for your PFP advertising? If the landing pages do not contain substantially unique content, did you place the Robots Exclusion Protocol on those pages?
❏ Yes	❏ No	Do the search engines and your site visitors view the same page? (The only exception to this rule is sites that participate in XML-feed programs.)
❏ Yes	❏ No	Do you submit the maximum allowable number of pages per day for each of the major search engines?
❏ Yes	❏ No	Do you avoid submitting the same pages twice within a 24-hour period?
❏ Yes	❏ No	Do you resubmit to a search engine only if a page has dropped from the index or if a page's content has changed significantly?

The time between page submission and the addition of the page to the search engine index is called the search engine lead time. You will not see results in your site statistics software until the lead time has passed.

Position Checking Software

Many search engine marketers like to check positions using automated query software to verify whether a page has been added to the search engine index and to see how the page ranks.

Unfortunately, all the major search engines frown on this practice. The goal of this practice is primarily to tweak a site for positioning purposes, not to create content that truly benefits end users. Furthermore, the use of automated position checking software places a considerable load on the search engines' servers. For these reasons, many search engines have banned the software from their indices.

Too many search engine marketers focus on positioning only—without viewing the web site online marketing process. Top positions are useless if your target audience is not clicking the links to your site and becoming customers. Therefore, when checking the effectiveness of your search engine marketing campaign, do not rely on position checking software. Rather, monitor your site statistics software to see how your target audience is finding and using your site.

Monitoring Your Site Statistics

Measuring the effectiveness of your web site is crucial for maintaining a successful online presence. Site statistics software, also known as traffic analysis software, can help you understand how visitors use your site.

With traffic analysis data, web site owners can learn which pages their target audience members respond to and which pages they don't. For example, if a particular web page ranks well in the search engines but the traffic analysis shows the vast majority of visitors leave the site after viewing only that single page, the web site owner knows that he or she must rewrite or redesign the page.

The traffic analysis data categories that can assist web site owners with visitor conversions are as follows:

- Top referring URLs

- Top search phrases

- Top paths through site

Top Referring URLs or Sites

With an effective search engine marketing campaign, your target audience usually finds a web site via a search engine, directory, or an industry-related site. Figure 4.6 shows the top referring URLs for a marine web site.

Figure 4.6
WebTrends report showing the top referring URLs. Other excellent traffic analysis software includes DeepMatrix LiveStats and Accrue Software's Pilot HIt List.

Top Referring Sites		
	Site	Visits
1	No Referrer	5,817
2	http://www.google.com	3,550
3	http://search.yahoo.com	875
4	http://www.sailingshow.com	659
5	http://search.lycos.com	598
6	http://search.msn.com	480
7	http://dir.yahoo.com	340
8	http://www.nyboating.ny.us	316
9	http://search.aol.com	302
10	http://www.looksmart.com	301
11	http://sg.google.yahoo.com	299
12	http://www.clickz.com	295
13	http://www.overture.com	289
14	http://www.oregonmarine.com	284
15	http://www.altavista.com	206
16	http://aolsearch.aol.com	193
17	http://hotbot.lycos.com	193
18	http://search.excite.com	191
19	http://www.yachtingmag.com	190

Your traffic analysis software can show you the sites your target audience uses the most to find your products and services. Generally, most sites receive quality traffic from 10–20 search engines and directories.

Does your reporting show that your site gets the most quality traffic from Inktomi? Then you know that you should write effective title tags and meta-description tags because Inktomi displays the content of those tags in its search results. If you know that your target audience uses Inktomi, to guarantee your optimized pages are always in the Inktomi index, participating in Inktomi's pay-for-inclusion program might be a wise investment.

Does your reporting show that your site gets the most quality traffic from Google? Then the meta-tag content doesn't matter because Google rarely uses meta-tag content. However, purchasing pay-for-placement services on Google, called Premium Sponsorships or AdWords, might be a good investment to increase your site's visibility.

Does your site get the most quality traffic from Yahoo!? Yahoo! offers Sponsor Matches (PFP ads through Overture), Sponsor Listings (through Yahoo!), and banner advertising to help increase your site's visibility.

Traffic analysis reporting is also helpful for monitoring your site's link popularity. When someone adds a link to your site, you can see when that link was added in your traffic analysis software and determine if a reciprocal link is worthwhile. By carefully analyzing the link popularity of the other sites that link to your site, you can find other non-competitive sites that might be useful.

Search Phrases

Traffic analysis software can give you the keywords and keyword phrases your target audience types into search engine and directory queries to find your site. Figure 4.7 shows an excerpt from a report showing Google users' top search phrases for a sample web site.

Figure 4.7

Sample excerpt from a WebTrends report showing the top keyword phrases used to find a web site through Google.

Top Search Engines with Search Phrases Detail			
Engines	Phrases	Phrases Found	% of Total
Google	oregon marine authorized dealer signup	127	1.44%
	oregon marine authorized dealer	109	1.23%
	oregon marine dealer login	106	1.20%
	oregon marine corporate	95	1.07%
	oregon marine news archives	94	1.06%
	oregon marine board	87	0.98%
	oregon marine stock	83	0.94%
	oregon marine press releases	78	0.88%
	oregon marine email newsletter	78	0.88%
	oregon marine news	77	0.87%
	find boat dealer	72	0.81%
	oregon marine authorized dealers	71	0.80%
	oregon marine investor relations	70	0.79%
	supplier login	64	0.72%
	boat dealers	58	0.65%
	owners circle	57	0.64%
	custom boats	57	0.64%
	oregon marine promotional offers	57	0.64%
	oregon marine dealers	57	0.64%
	bid on contracts	56	0.63%

Based on these words, you can adjust your web copywriting to make current and future web pages more search engine friendly.

For example, is your target audience interested in a particular set of products? Maybe you can write some tips or guidelines for selecting the most appropriate product. Does this set of products have unique features and benefits? Maybe you can write unique product descriptions using the keywords your visitors are typing into search queries.

The top search phrase data can also help your web copywriters write better for Frequently Asked Questions (FAQs) pages.

Top Entry Pages

An effective search engine marketing campaign, through optimization and pay-per-click programs, connects the search results to specific pages on your web site. When people click on a link to a web page, be it from search engine results, directory results, or another web site, they want to go directly to the page that gives them the information they need. Visitors do not necessarily want to go to your home page, nor do they want to perform another search on your site. The pages that your visitors land on are called entry pages or landing pages.

In an optimization campaign, the most popular landing pages are probably the most search engine–friendly pages on your site. In a pay-per-click campaign, the most popular landing pages are the ones that correspond to your most effective ads.

Figure 4.8 shows an excerpt from a report showing top entry (landing) pages for a sample web site.

Figure 4.8

Sample WebTrends report on the top entry pages.

Top Entry Pages			
	Page	% of Total	Visits
1	Welcome to Oregon Marine Inc. Quality Boat Builders http://www.oregonmarine.com/	24.99%	4,624
2	Promotional Offers http://www.oregonmarine.com/promos/	9.68%	1,791
3	Dealer Locations http://www.oregonmarine.com/locations/	8.52%	1,577
4	Oregon Marine – Products http://www.oregonmarine.com/products/	8.03%	1,487
5	Oregon Marine – Corporate News http://www.oregonmarine.com/news/	6.53%	1,208
6	Corporate Information http://www.oregonmarine.com/corporate/	5.89%	1,090
7	Owner's Club http://www.oregonmarine.com/club/	5.81%	1,075
8	Oregon Marine – Employment Opportunities http://www.oregonmarine.com/corporate/jobs.asp	4.92%	911
9	Dealer Home http://www.oregonmarine.com/dealers/	4.76%	882
10	Supplier Home http://www.oregonmarine.com/suppliers/	4.51%	836
11	Oregon Marine Sailboats http://www.oregonmarine.com/products/sailboats/	4.49%	831
12	Merchandise http://www.oregonmarine.com/store/	4.31%	798
13	Owner's Club Home Page http://www.oregonmarine.com/club/club_home.asp	1.40%	260

	Page	% of Total	Visits
14	**Oregon Marine – Investor Relations** http://www.oregonmarine.com/ corporate/investors.asp	0.84%	156
15	**Accessories for Your Boat** http://www.oregonmarine.com/store/ accessories/	0.70%	130
16	**Logo Clothing** http://www.oregonmarine.com/store/ clothes/	0.56%	105
17	**Oregon Marine Powerboats** http://www.oregonmarine.com/ products/powerboats/	0.49%	91
18	**Stock Ticker** http://www.oregonmarine.com corporate/ticker.asp	0.35%	65
19	**Owner's Club – Message Board** http://www.oregonmarine.com/club/ messageboard.asp	0.32%	60
20	**Oregon Marine Club Newsletter** http://www.oregonmarine.com/club/ newsletter.htm	0.31%	58
Total for the Pages Above		97.49%	18,035

Traffic analysis software can also show your site's top exit pages and single access pages. If the vast majority of your top entry pages are also listed as your top exit pages in your traffic analysis reports, your target audience might not be responding favorably to your site's entry pages, even if they are search engine friendly.

Single access pages are web pages that your visitors view once; they then leave your site. If the vast majority of your landing pages are single access pages, you know that the site's content and design are not engaging your target audience. Therefore, you know that you need to rewrite and redesign your landing pages to encourage your visitors to stay on your web site.

Not only should you know your top entry pages, but also you should know how visitors are clicking through all the links on your site. Are your site's visitors doing what you want them to do? Are they subscribing to your newsletter, filling out a form, downloading your demo software, calling your sales office, or making a purchase? Converting visitors to customers is equally as important as obtaining search engine visibility.

Top Paths Through the Site

When your design team has created an effective set of landing pages, you need to determine how visitors are navigating your site. The "top paths through site" reporting illustrates how visitors are navigating your site, beginning with your entry pages.

Figure 4.9 shows an excerpt from a report showing top paths for a sample web site.

Figure 4.9

Sample excerpt from a WebTrends report showing the top paths through a site.

Top Paths Through Site by Starting Page			
Starting Page	Paths from Start	% of Total	Visits
All Entry Pages	1. Oregon Marine - Corporate News http://www.oregonmarine.com/news/ 2. Oregon Marine - Latest Press Releases http://www.oregonmarine.com/news/press.asp	1.61%	299
	1. Supplier Home http://www.oregonmarine.com/suppliers/ 2. Supplier Login Authentication http://www.oregonmarine.com/suppliers/scripts/authenticate.asp 3. Suppliers - Your Current Contracts http://www.oregonmarine.com/suppliers/supplier_home.asp	0.97%	181

Starting Page	Paths from Start	% of Total	Visits
	1. Oregon Marine - Latest Press Releases http://www.oregonmarine.com/corporate/jobs.asp 2. Jobs http://www.oregonmarine.com/corporate/scripts/job_display.asp	0.78%	146
	1. Welcome to Oregon Marine Inc. Quality Boat Builders http://www.oregonmarine.com/ 2. Oregon Marine - Latest Press Releases http://www.oregonmarine.com/news/press.asp	0.54%	100
	1. Welcome to Oregon Marine Inc. Quality Boat Builders http://www.oregonmarine.com/ 2. Supplier Home http://www.oregonmarine.com/suppliers/ 3. Supplier Login Authentication http://www.oregonmarine.com/suppliers/scripts/authenticate.asp 4. Suppliers - Your Current Contracts http://www.oregonmarine.com/suppliers/supplier_home.asp	0.54%	100

This type of reporting illustrates the effectiveness of your site's navigation scheme and calls to action. If visitors arrive at your site and are not converting, you know that you have to modify the site to get a higher conversion rate.

The best way to judge the effectiveness of a web page is to modify one item at a time. For example, let's say you create a page that has excellent search engine visibility but no conversions. One item that might increase the page's conversion rate is to add some text at the top of the page that encourages visitors to pick up the phone and call a customer service representative. If that web page is in a pay-for-inclusion program, it can be respidered very quickly. Measure the results for a period of at least two to four weeks.

Another call to action might be to use a small banner (120×60 pixels) instead of HTML text.

Measuring the success or failure of landing pages over time helps you develop better web pages for both your target audience and the search engines.

Important

Whenever testing the effectiveness of a landing page, remember that the search engines consider pages with identical or nearly identical content to be spam. Therefore, test your landing pages consecutively on the crawler-based search engines. If you are testing pages on the pay-per-click search engines, remember to place the Robots Exclusion Protocol on the mirror pages so that the crawler-based search engines do not index them.

How to Resubmit a Site

If your site is listed in one or more of the major directories, most of the time, search engines find your new and updated pages without resubmission. Therefore, resubmission is not a necessity. However, resubmission alerts the search engine spiders and directory editors that you have made changes to pages on your site.

The search engine spiders usually find your site's new information each time they visit your site, generally every two to eight weeks. Directories are different. Remember that editors are sorting through hundreds of submissions per day. They might not notice the subtle changes on your site. So, if your business has significantly changed, if your URL or company name has changed, or if your site clearly belongs in a different category, resubmission to the directories is essential to preserve the factual representation of your web site in the directories.

Modifying a Directory Listing

When your site has been added to a directory, you should not have to request a modification unless your business name, company location, domain name, or URL has changed. Another good reason to request a listing modification is if your company no longer offers a product or service that is shown in your site description.

For example, suppose your business no longer offers a service that is shown in your site description. Directory editors are more than happy to modify that description because the description no longer illustrates, accurately, the contents of your web site. If your business no longer offers a specific product and that product is reflected in the directory category, directory editors allow you to change your category. Editors want the information in their directories to be accurate.

One of the simplest changes to request is a regional listing. If your site has a regional listing and your main office is no longer in that region, directory editors want you to change the listing to the more appropriate region. Quite often, if you modify the physical address on your web site, a directory editor notices and moves your site to the more appropriate regional category. It is always best to point out this modification to the editors right away rather than wait for an editor to discover it.

Careful record keeping can make the change process move more smoothly. If you have a tracking or order number, the initial date(s) of submission, and the other relevant information, directory editors can locate your site more easily and make any suggested modifications.

If a directory has a Change Form, fill out the form exactly as requested. If a directory allows paid, expedited submissions with their Change Form, use this option. The change request will be processed more quickly, and the change will appear more quickly in the search results.

Most directories do not allow for expedited submission, however, and the change requests might take some time to process. Again, careful record keeping is essential to get the best results.

With a directory, your site must be reviewed first, accepted into the directory, and then added to the database. The time between submission and addition to the directory database is called the lead time. The lead time for directory submission is generally between three to four weeks.

If your change request has not been added to a directory within a specified lead time, resubmit the Change Form to the directory. Wait another three to four weeks to give directory editors time to evaluate and process your suggested modifications.

In the event that your change request is not processed after three submissions, it is safe to contact a directory representative through email. Immediately following your third change request, send an email to the appropriate editor. Figure 4.10 shows a sample email to Yahoo! requesting a category and a description change for the fictional TranquiliTeas web site.

Figure 4.10

Sample email requesting a change to a Yahoo! listing.

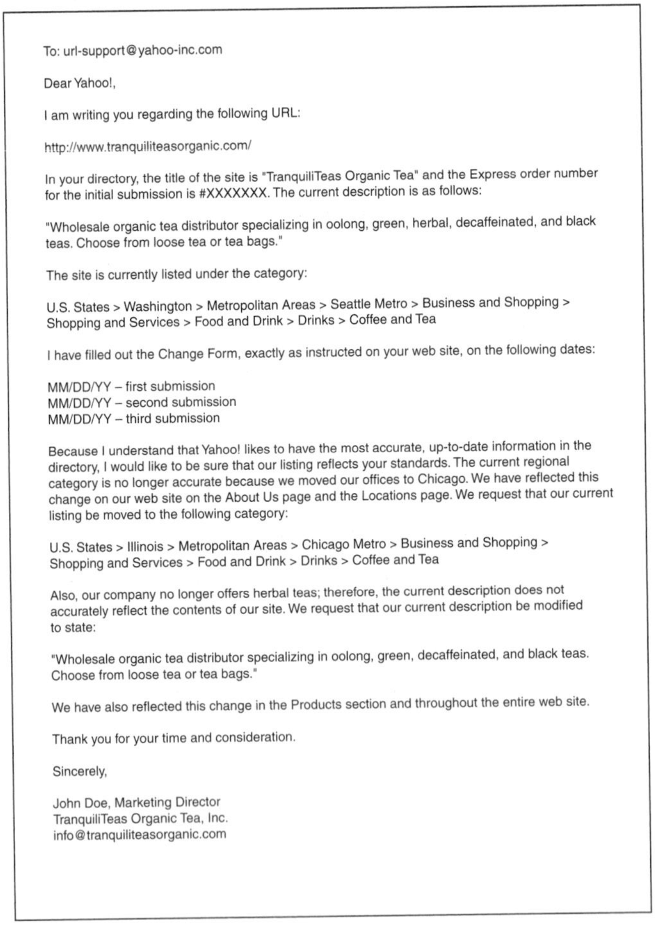

To: url-support@yahoo-inc.com

Dear Yahoo!,

I am writing you regarding the following URL:

http://www.tranquiliteasorganic.com/

In your directory, the title of the site is "TranquiliTeas Organic Tea" and the Express order number for the initial submission is #XXXXXXX. The current description is as follows:

"Wholesale organic tea distributor specializing in oolong, green, herbal, decaffeinated, and black teas. Choose from loose tea or tea bags."

The site is currently listed under the category:

U.S. States > Washington > Metropolitan Areas > Seattle Metro > Business and Shopping > Shopping and Services > Food and Drink > Drinks > Coffee and Tea

I have filled out the Change Form, exactly as instructed on your web site, on the following dates:

MM/DD/YY – first submission
MM/DD/YY – second submission
MM/DD/YY – third submission

Because I understand that Yahoo! likes to have the most accurate, up-to-date information in the directory, I would like to be sure that our listing reflects your standards. The current regional category is no longer accurate because we moved our offices to Chicago. We have reflected this change on our web site on the About Us page and the Locations page. We request that our current listing be moved to the following category:

U.S. States > Illinois > Metropolitan Areas > Chicago Metro > Business and Shopping > Shopping and Services > Food and Drink > Drinks > Coffee and Tea

Also, our company no longer offers herbal teas; therefore, the current description does not accurately reflect the contents of our site. We request that our current description be modified to state:

"Wholesale organic tea distributor specializing in oolong, green, decaffeinated, and black teas. Choose from loose tea or tea bags."

We have also reflected this change in the Products section and throughout the entire web site.

Thank you for your time and consideration.

Sincerely,

John Doe, Marketing Director
TranquiliTeas Organic Tea, Inc.
info@tranquiliteasorganic.com

The person who made the initial submission to a directory should be the person sending the change request email. If a different person is sending this email, be sure to mention the initial submitter's name and email address in a short paragraph at the beginning of the letter. Let the editors know that you are the new person responsible for your web site.

Free Submission

Check your site statistics software regularly to see when your site has been modified in a directory. If your site has not been modified in a directory within three to four weeks, resubmit. Keep track of your dates of submission, categories, descriptions, and titles.

In the event that your site is not accepted into a directory after three submissions, contact a directory representative via email.

Paid Submission

If a paid submission is within your budget, use this method for directory resubmission. The turnaround time is much faster.

If Your Submission Is Rejected

Submissions are rejected for a variety of reasons. The site might be submitted to the wrong category. The site might not offer truly unique content. The web server might not have been functioning properly when a directory editor was evaluating a submission. The designer might have left some Under Construction pages on the site. The description might not accurately reflect the contents of the site being submitted.

If your submission is rejected, try to find out the reason the site was rejected. If you can find out the specific reason, it is easier to appeal the decision. For example, if your site was rejected because it contained Under Construction pages, those pages can be easily removed.

Other rejections are not so easily appealed. In one situation, I encountered a web site owner created a unique glossary of over 1,000 terms on her site. The content was truly unique because it encompassed a specific industry, and most of the definitions were not available in other glossaries currently listed in the directory. After the main site was accepted, the web site owner submitted this glossary to an additional category. Figure 4.11 shows an email excerpt from Yahoo! explaining the initial reason the additional listing was rejected.

Figure 4.11

Excerpt from a Yahoo! rejection email.

We're sorry to report that we've decided not to include your site in the Yahoo! directory. The URL appears to be part of a larger site that is already listed in Yahoo!. After reviewing both your URL and the existing URL that encompasses it, we've determined that the existing listing is adequate for users to find your site.

The Yahoo! Express Terms of Service state that in order to be listed in the Yahoo! directory, a site must meet the following minimum criteria:

"The site must contain substantively unique content that is not already accessible in the Yahoo! directory."

In general, rather than separately listing every subpage of a large site, we try to find the core or hub page of the site and point users to that. Our users appreciate this because it means they do not have to sift through multiple listings from the same site, and it gives your site more prominence because it won't get lost among many separate listings of other sites.

If you have questions, or would like to request a reconsideration of this decision, please email us within thirty days by replying to this message.

If a submission is rejected, you have about 30 days to appeal the decision. When appealing through email, be polite. Directory editors are human beings. They are looking out for the best interests of their end users. If they rejected your submission, they have reasons to do so, even though you might not agree with them.

Figure 4.12 shows a sample email we helped our client write to Yahoo! to appeal a rejection. After reviewing the contents of this email, the additional listing was accepted. (Note that some words are changed to preserve confidentiality. Modified words and URLs are placed in italics.)

Remember that editors are looking out for the best interest of their directories and their end users. They are not looking out for the best interest of your individual web site. If they feel that your resubmissions meet their guidelines, your site will be accepted and/ or modified.

Dear Yahoo!,

I respectfully disagree with your evaluation of the following URL and would like you to reconsider:

<url:http://www.companyname.com/page.html>

The Express order number for this submission is *#XXXXXXX*.

The reason given for the rejection was:

"The site must contain substantively unique content that is not already accessible in the Yahoo! directory."

Before I submitted this URL for inclusion, I carefully reviewed the contents of the category. There is no glossary specifically written for (*target audience*) in this category. I clicked on all the URLs in the category to be sure that the information represented by the submitted URL contained unique content.

Also, based on the reasoning presented to me, I see some inconsistency. For example, the URLs:

http:// food.company1.com/resources/glossary/
http://www.company2.com/glossary/

Both the home pages and glossaries of the aforementioned sites are accessible in the Yahoo! directory, and an editor/surfer appears to find the additional content acceptable. Furthermore, when I performed a search on *keyword1* glossary, *keyword2* glossary, or *keyword3* glossary, no relevant glossaries appeared in Yahoo!.

Because of the other listings in this category, and because I performed multiple searches for this particular topic, I felt that this would be good, unique content to appear in Yahoo!.

I understand that Yahoo! gets spammed all the time, and I understand the reasoning behind the rejection. I hope you understand that I did not submit this site without researching the various categories and clicking the links to sites already listed in Yahoo!. I performed searches on other glossary sites to be sure that the content in this glossary was unique. In fact, it contains over 1,000 definitions. All the other glossaries in this category contain fewer than 500 definitions.

Please reconsider your decision. I really did exhaustive research before I submitted to be sure that the content was unique and that it would serve a useful purpose to your visitors.

Thank you for your time and consideration.

Sincerely,

Jane Doe, Marketing Director (or official title)
Company Name
info@companyname.com

Figure 4.12
Sample appeal letter sent to Yahoo!.

Search Engine Resubmission

As stated, crawler-based search engines find your new and updated pages without resubmission. Therefore, resubmission is not always necessary.

Sometimes, due to technical reasons, a page might be dropped from a search engine index. For example, your web host might have upgraded or rebooted your server when a search engine spider visited your site, making it impossible or difficult for the spider to access your pages. Pages that have been dropped can be safely resubmitted, as long as they are not spam pages.

If a page is already in a search engine index, do not resubmit the page unless you have updated it with new and significant information. If the information is significant, visitors should be able to view that information change in a standard web browser. Changes in your visible body text, and the addition or modification of a product photo, constitute a significant change. An insignificant change would be rewriting a meta-tag description or a title tag purely to increase search engine positioning.

To verify whether your web pages have been added or deleted from a search engine, go to each search engine in the following list and type the respective string. Replace *companyname.com* with your domain.

- **AltaVista:** *url:companyname.com*

- **Google:** *site:companyname.com companyname.com*

- **Any Inktomi-based search engine:**
  domain:companyname.com

- **Fast Search** (*www.Alltheweb.com*):
  url.all:www.companyname.com

Site Maintenance

Web sites are always works in progress. Companies continually add and remove products and services. Open job positions are often placed in an employment section of a corporate site. Public relations divisions are constantly writing and distributing press releases. Software companies offer new-and-improved versions of their software and technical support documents. News sites change content every day.

Web technology is also continually changing. How browsers display web pages changes over time. A site that was perfectly designed for cross-browser compatibility two years ago might not look as presentable on newer browser versions.

It is not uncommon for corporate web sites to be redesigned every two to three years. If you know your site is going to change and it already has excellent search engine visibility, how can you preserve some of that visibility? The following sections will tell you how.

Error 404 Pages

Not surprisingly, many sites that undergo redesigns lose some search engine visibility. If a web page has been removed or deleted from a site, the search engine results link to a page that has a 404 Not Found error message. By default, the server returns a 404 Not Found error page when a URL has been renamed or deleted from a server.

How do think your site's visitors might react to the Error 404 page shown in Figure 4.13? Will they try to retype a similar filename to try to access your site's information? Will they go back to the search engine results and click a link to another site? In all likelihood, your site will lose quality traffic if the links from the search engines go to default Error 404 pages.

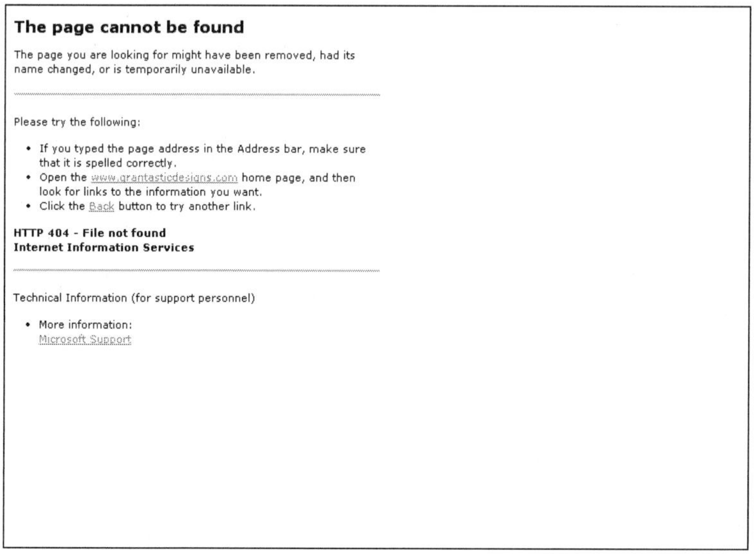

The page cannot be found

The page you are looking for might have been removed, had its name changed, or is temporarily unavailable.

Please try the following:

- If you typed the page address in the Address bar, make sure that it is spelled correctly.
- Open the www.grantasticdesigns.com home page, and then look for links to the information you want.
- Click the Back button to try another link.

HTTP 404 - File not found
Internet Information Services

Technical Information (for support personnel)

- More information:
  Microsoft Support

Figure 4.13

A default Error 404 page on my own web site, GrantasticDesigns.com.

One way to keep visitors on your site is to create a custom 404 page based on the data you gather from your traffic analysis software. Which pages of your web site are the top landing pages? What keywords are your visitors typing into search queries? What do you want your visitors to do when they land on your 404 page?

By continually analyzing and using your traffic analysis data, you can build a custom 404 page that keeps potential customers on your site. For example, in the fictional TranquiliTeas site, the site owners might have determined that the most popular sections of the site are the Products, Recipes, and Tea Facts sections. Within the Products section, visitors are most interested in oolong, green, herbal, and black teas. Within the Tea Facts section, visitors are most interested in the history of tea and the Japanese tea ceremony. The custom 404 page can reflect these three sections and highlight the targeted keywords within the HTML text on the page, as shown in Figure 4.14.

The search engines do not want dead links in their indices. The search engine spiders find these dead links over time. As a courtesy, let the search engines know that pages no longer exist after a site redesign. Submit the non-existent URLs to the search engines to their Add URL form. The search engines record the URL as an Error 404, and the links in the search engine results are removed.

Figure 4.14

Apple has a beautifully designed custom 404 page that clearly benefits its target audience. Apple highlights the three areas that are of the highest interest to its target audience, and also provides a series of text links for other popular sections of the site.

File Naming

A custom 404 page can help with links from the search engines, but it is not as effective with sites that link directly to individual web pages. Web site owners that have sites with a large number of links to them from industry-related sites, professional organizations, educational institutions, and so forth have to contact each site individually to let them know of any URL changes.

With a little foresight and planning, web developers can save a considerable amount of time in preserving their site's link popularity. Whenever possible, try to keep the same filenames and directory structures for the site redesign. As long as you make the pages accessible to the search engine spiders in the redesign, the search engines merely respider the pages and reflect the page modifications in their search results. Then, a site's link development can be preserved.

For example, using the fictional TranquiliTeas web site, the About Us page's URL is this:

www.tranquiliteasorganic.com/about.html

Suppose the CEO no longer wants to call this page About Us but rather Company Information. The site design can reflect the name change in the masthead, navigation buttons, and text links. However, the filename does not have to change to companyinformation.html; the filename can still remain about.html.

Redirects

Another way site owners can let both search engines and end users know that a web page no longer exists is to provide redirects to the new web page. However, there can be potential problems with this solution because many unethical search engine marketers like to use redirects to spam the search engines.

One ethical way to redirect site visitors and search engine spiders to new URLs is to use the HTTP 301 (permanent) redirect. This type of redirect indicates that a resource (web page) has moved permanently, and the client (which is the web browser) should always use the new URL. Because the configuration of this redirect depends on the type of server on which your site is hosted, your web host or your programmer can help you set up this type of redirect.

Another way to redirect is to use JavaScript or meta-refresh tags to point to the new URL. As long as visitors can view (for at least 30 seconds) a page instructing users to bookmark the new URL, the search engines generally do not consider the redirect to be spam. However, with these types of redirects, dead links still exist in the search engines' indexes temporarily. Thus, you should be sure to create custom 404 pages to make your site more user friendly.

Conclusion

Planning effective search engine and directory submission campaigns is crucial to your site's search engine visibility. Directories generally give web site owners one chance to submit correctly. With the crawler-based search engines, spiders should be able to find your pages without direct submission as long as the URLs exist on your web server.

A web site is always a work in progress. Technology and visitor preferences constantly evolve. With successful search engine marketing and careful traffic analysis, web site owners can continually modify their sites for their visitors and maximum search engine visibility.

part 5

Best Practices: The Dos and Don'ts of Search Engine Marketing

Introduction

Parts 1–4 of this book presented strategies for creating a search engine–friendly web site. These strategies help increase your site's search engine visibility, and they also benefit your site's end users.

To keep their search results relevant and accurate, search engines actively work to thwart excessive and unethical optimization tactics. *Spamdexing*, commonly referred to as spam, is the taking of extreme or excessive measures to achieve top search engine positions. Spam is also the use of any words, HTML code, scripting, or programming on a web page that is not meant to benefit the end user experience.

Many search engine marketing firms spend a great deal of time utilizing spam techniques to gain top search engine positions for their clients, particularly if clients do not want to modify their existing sites to be more search engine friendly. Unfortunately, some web pages that gain top positioning through spam techniques do slip through the search engines' spam filters. However, positions gained from spamming are generally sporadic and short-lived.

Another reason to avoid spam is that the search engines can penalize or permanently ban your web pages from their indices if they detect the usage of spam techniques. Your competitors or human "spam cops" can also spot the use of spam techniques on web pages. Do not discount your competitors. They compete for the same online visibility you desire, and if they can eliminate a site from top positions because of spam, they will not hesitate to report your site to the search engine Spam Police.

If a site is banned or penalized, it is placed on a search engine blacklist. The only way to have your site removed from the blacklist is to contact the search engine staff member who actually banned or penalized your site. Then you must convince that person that you no longer practice the spam techniques that got your site banned. The odds of contacting the exact person who penalized your site are not very high. In addition, if your site is readmitted into the search engine indices, any future web pages from your site are subjected to higher scrutiny.

Spamming the search engines is not an effective use of time or money. The amount of time it takes to "trick" the search engines can be better spent on developing a more effective web site, one that pleases both your target audience and the search engines.

What Exactly Is Spam?

As much as we all would like the search engines to give us clear guidelines on what does and does not constitute spam, we have to accept that it is an unrealistic expectation. Whenever a search engine presents a clear-cut spam guideline, unethical search engine marketers try to implement exceptions to the guideline. Then the search engines must update the guideline to include the new exceptions to the guideline, and so on, and so on. It's a never-ending process. Thus, the search engines present general rather than specific guidelines as to what constitutes spam.

Search engine spam is more about *how and to what extent* a marketing technique is used rather than *if* a technique is used. Thus, the search engine Spam Police do not automatically penalize a site for using a design technique if that design technique is used in an appropriate manner. For example, a site that uses invisible DHTML layers for drop-down menus, such as the Position Technologies site (see Figures 5.1 and 5.2), are not penalized because the invisible layers serve a navigation purpose. However, if a design or writing technique is used to deliberately trick a search engine into offering inappropriate, irrelevant, redundant, or poor-quality search results, a site can be penalized for spamming.

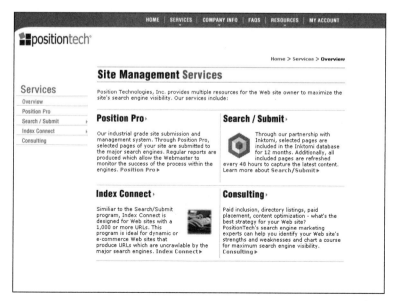

Figure 5.1

Position Technologies uses DHTML layers as part of its navigation scheme. The menus are not visible to site visitors at first.

Figure 5.2

When a visitor places his or her cursor over the top navigation or the side navigation, the menus appear. Because the menus are meant to be seen by the site's visitors, the invisible DHTML layer is not considered spam.

To determine whether a search engine marketing strategy is spam, ask yourself the following questions:

- Does your web site's actual content benefit your target audience and end users?

- Would you perform a search engine marketing strategy if the search engines did not exist?

- Are you building pages primarily for search engine positioning?

If you answered "yes" to the first and second questions and "no" to the third question, then in all likelihood, the search engine Spam Police will not consider the use of your design or writing strategies to be spam.

Types of Spam

If a search engine representative discovers that a web site owner is deliberately trying to trick the search engines into giving a page higher relevance than it deserves, the individual page, or even the entire site, can be penalized. Most of the time, a search engine engineer modifies the algorithm so that the spam pages no longer appear at the top of search results. In more extreme cases, the page itself, or the whole site, is removed from the search engine index. Therefore, avoid the types of spam discussed in the following sections.

Promoting Keywords That Are Not Related to Your Web Site

To gain top search engine visibility, many spammers place words on their web pages that are not related to the pages' actual content. For example, many people take the most popularly searched-for words (such as "sex" or a celebrity name) and place those words inside a meta tag. This is done only because the word is popular, not necessarily because the word relates to the content of a web page.

As a general rule, if you are not using a keyword or a keyword phrase on the visible content of your pages, do not place unrelated words in your meta tags, titles, alternative text, or any CSS layers.

Keyword Stacking

Keyword stacking is the repeated use of a keyword or keyword phrase to artificially boost a web page's relevancy in the search engines. Keyword stacking, at its simplest level, looks like the following:

```
organic tea organic tea organic tea organic tea organic tea organic tea
organic tea
tea tea tea tea tea tea tea tea tea tea tea tea tea tea tea tea tea
tea tea tea tea tea tea
```

This type of text can be placed in any HTML tag, including the title tag, meta tags, alternative text, and so forth. It can also be placed inside invisible layers and the <noframes>, <noscript>, and <input type="hidden"> tags. It can even be placed at the very bottom of a web page where people are not likely to view the text.

No matter where this type of text is placed, it is still considered spam because the words are gibberish and are clearly written to boost relevancy, not to benefit a site's end users.

Keyword Stuffing

Keyword stacking and keyword stuffing often have the same meaning. Some search engine marketers differentiate the two forms of spam. Keyword stacking often refers to the writing of the gibberish "sentences." Keyword stuffing usually refers to placing the gibberish "sentences" inside graphic images or layers.

For example, many unethical search engine marketers create a small, transparent image called blank.gif, clear.gif, spacer.gif, or shim.gif. Its size is from 1×1 pixels to 25×25 pixels. Then they place a series of keywords in the alternative text of the graphic image. The HTML code for keyword stuffing generally looks like the following:

```
<img src="images/blank.gif" alt="organic tea organic teas Organic Tea
Organic Teas ORGANIC TEA ORGANIC TEAS">
```

If such text does not describe the graphic image or the page on which it is placed, the search engines consider the text to be spam.

Hidden Text

As stated, for web pages to appear at the top of search results, the words that your target audience types into a search query must be used on your web pages. One way to place keywords on your web pages without changing the look and feel of your site design is to hide the text or make it invisible. Hidden keywords and keyword phrases are supposed to be visible to search engine spiders, but not to site visitors.

Unethical search engine marketers can make text invisible in multiple ways:

- Using colored text on a same-colored background, with <font> tags, tricky graphic images, and Cascading Style Sheets.

- Using hidden text in HTML forms tag <input type="hidden"> even though a web page does not contain a form.

- Placing keywords inside a <noframes> tag even though the page does not contain a frameset.

- Placing keywords between the <noscript></noscript> tags if there are no scripts on a web page. The <noscript> tag is text that is meant to display in the event that a script is not executed. It is not meant as a "secret hiding place" for keyword stacking.

- Using hidden layers in style sheets, either by placing layers on top of each other or by placing the layers outside the browser screen.

As a general rule, anything on a web page that is not meant to be seen or detected at any time by your target audience is considered spam. Because most browsers support frames and JavaScript, there is little or no need to use <noframes> and <noscript> tags. Furthermore, the search engines have been aware of keyword stuffing in these tags for years now, and they place little or no relevance on this text.

Tiny Text

Many spammers understand that hidden text can get their pages penalized, so they often place keywords at the bottom of a web page. They format this text with an extremely small typeface and usually in a color that is not the exact same color as a background, but light enough so that it is difficult to read.

Even though tiny text is visible, it is often illegible. If the text on your web pages is too tiny for your site's visitors to read, the tiny text is also considered spam.

Hidden Links

The true purpose of creating hypertext links and navigation buttons (graphic images) is to have people click them. Unethical web marketers who create links that end users cannot easily detect are, in essence, deceiving end users. Therefore, hidden links are generally considered spam.

Ways of hiding links include the following:

- Using the same font attributes for a hypertext link as your regular text

- Hiding hypertext links in punctuation marks

- Hiding hyperlinks in transparent images

- Hiding hyperlinks in invisible layers

- Hiding hundreds or thousands of links inside a small graphic image

Artificial Link Farms and Web Rings

In an attempt to boost the link component of a search engine algorithm, many spammers try to create multiple web sites whose sole purpose is to link to each other. Free-for-all (FFA) web sites are an example of artificial link farms.

All the search engines make it very clear that linking to "bad neighborhoods" can get a site into trouble. Though no one can control which web sites link to your site, you have total control over which sites you link to. Therefore, if your site links to another site that is considered a "bad neighborhood," your site can be penalized.

Creating web rings for the sole purpose of increasing popularity can also be considered spam, especially if the sites linking to each other are not related. For example, a dating service web site has nothing to do with an auto parts web site.

As a general rule, if a hyperlink is not created to be read or followed by humans, it is probably spam.

Page Swapping, Page Jacking, and Bait-and-Switch

Page swapping, also called bait-and-switch spam, occurs when an optimized web page is submitted to the search engines, and then the page is "swapped" for a different one after a top search engine position has been attained. Search engines end up viewing an optimized page; end users wind up viewing a different page altogether.

The reasoning behind this type of spam is to prevent others from stealing a page's search engine "secrets." Unfortunately, page swapping often happens with stolen content. Unethical search engine marketers find a high-ranking web page and copy its content. Sometimes, they change the company name but nothing else. The page with the stolen content is submitted to the search engines. After the stolen page gets a top search engine position, a different web page is placed on the server. The practice of stealing content from other web sites is called *page jacking*.

Bait-and-switch spam occurs in directories as well. To artificially boost link popularity, unethical web marketers submit a "fake" web site to the directories. After the site is accepted, another web site is put up in its place.

Page swapping is a difficult practice to maintain. No one knows when or how often a search engine spider visits a site. Thus, a swapped page's position is always temporary. Furthermore, if content is stolen from a web page and the original author discovers the online thievery, the spammer could be faced with a copyright and/or trademark lawsuit.

Redirects

Another way that spammers switch web pages is by using a redirect. A *redirect* is HTML coding, programming, or scripting that is placed on a web page so that page visitors are sent to a different URL after a specified period of time, often zero seconds. One of the most common ways to redirect is a meta-refresh tag, which looks like the following:

```
<META HTTP-EQUIV="refresh" content="0;
URL=http://www.domainname.com/differentpage.html">
```

With redirection, spammers create an optimized page for a particular keyword phrase. The optimized page, with the redirect, is submitted to the search engines. If the optimized page gets a top search engine position, anyone clicking the link to this page is automatically sent to a different page called a *destination page*. The destination page does not contain the same content as the optimized page. In fact, the destination page often does not contain the same keywords as the optimized pages.

To combat this type of spam, many search engines do not accept pages with any type of redirection other than the HTTP 301 (permanent) redirect. Most of the time, the search engines list the destination page, not the page that contains the redirect.

If you find yourself in a situation where your design calls for a redirect, the redirect timing must last long enough for your site's visitors to read the content. Most of the time, 15 seconds does not cause a spam penalty. Another solution is to place the Robots Exclusion Protocol on any page that contains a redirect.

Mirror or Duplicate Pages

Both search engines and their end users do not want the same web sites dominating search results. For this reason, most search engines now cluster their search results. *Clustering* generally enables only one or two pages per web site to be displayed in the top search results.

All too often, spammers duplicate or slightly modify a web page. Then, the spammers submit to a search engine hundreds or thousands of pages with only tiny modifications. For example, two pages might have identical content and different title tags, and two other pages might have identical content and different meta tags. If any of the submitted pages rank well for a specific keyword phrase, all the pages with slight modifications can dominate a search engine's top search results.

Think about any search you performed that showed the same company over and over again. If you did not like the information the first time you visited the company's site, you would not like it the second, third, fourth, or fifth time either.

Duplicate content is a common occurrence with affiliate and reseller sites. Affiliates and resellers are essentially providing the same information on their web sites as the original corporate site. Again, if you, the end user, did not like the information presented on the corporate site, in all likelihood, you would not like the same information on an affiliate site.

Thus, search engines tend to reject affiliate and reseller sites due to duplicate content. If they find duplicate web pages or web sites, they try to eliminate at least one of them.

Doorway Pages, Gateway Pages, and Hallway Pages

Doorway pages, *gateway pages*, and *hallway pages* are not created for the benefit of a site's visitors. They are created specifically for obtaining high search engine positions. That is the main reason the search engines consider doorway pages to be spam.

Doorway page companies generally create thousands of pages for a single keyword or keyword phrase. All these pages are fed to the search engines, often through the free submit pages. Because doorway pages are built specifically to rank, the search engines indices are essentially polluted with web pages containing unnecessary information. Doorway pages are not very pleasant to look at, and they often contain so much gibberish that they have to be cloaked.

Cloaking

Cloaking is the technique of feeding search engine spiders one web page and feeding all other end users a different web page. All the major search engines consider cloaking to be spam. The only time that search engines accept cloaking is through a trusted feed program.

Domain Spam and Mirror Sites

Domain spam is the practice of purchasing multiple domain names and building sites with identical or nearly identical content in them. The purpose of utilizing domain spam is to get multiple listings in directories to achieve link popularity and more traffic. The resulting link popularity in the directories helps boost search engine visibility.

A warning sign that you might be dealing with domain spam is if you hear the terms "micro-site" or "mini-site." This type of spam can also be done with subdomains.

Search engines and directories respond to domain spam by removing all the mirror sites. If the domain spam is particularly egregious, they permanently remove all the sites from their indices.

Typo Spam and Cybersquatting

Web site owners who purchase domain names for the sole purpose of tricking end users into visiting their sites can be considered spammers. For example, a cybersquatter might purchase the domain name Yahhoo.com (note the extra "h") to try to steal traffic from Yahoo!.

Google is particularly picky about this form of spam. They penalize sites that cybersquat. In fact, cybersquatting is illegal in many countries.

Deconstructing Common Misconceptions

Unfortunately, the search engine marketing industry is riddled with myths and misinformation. All too often, search engine marketers mix sales hype with facts just to make a sale. In addition, many amateur search engine marketers rely on their personal experiences rather than tested results. To help you select a reputable, reliable search engine marketing firm, you should become aware of the following search engine myths.

Guaranteed Placement or Your Money Back

A credible, experienced, and knowledgeable search engine marketer can demonstrate results from past performance but cannot guarantee future results. Why? Except for pay-for-placement (PFP) search engines, no one can guarantee top positions because there are third parties—the directory editors and the search engines—who have all the control. In fact, all the major search engines have some sort of disclaimer stating that they ultimately decide which web sites to include in their indices.

Search engine marketers can guarantee that they perform proper keyword and category research and that they use optimal HTML coding and suitable submission techniques. However, they cannot state, with absolute certainty, that their efforts result in top search engine positions.

Search engine marketers like to guarantee results so that they can tell a target audience what they want to hear. I often compare search engine marketing to being a stockbroker. No stockbroker can guarantee future earnings. In the same vein, no search engine marketer can guarantee future search engine positions.

Search Engine Marketing Guarantees Permanent Positions

Search engines do not want the same sites appearing over and over again in the same positions. They constantly modify their algorithms, sometimes daily, so that the same sites *do not* always appear in the same positions.

What does this mean to you? It means that having a goal of "permanent" top positions is an unrealistic expectation. A more realistic expectation is to have consistent, quality traffic from the search engines over time.

The Goal of Search Engine Optimization Is to Achieve Top Positions

This myth is very widespread and inaccurate. The goal of search engine optimization is to make a web site more "findable" in the search engines. If a web site receives consistent, qualified traffic from the search engines over time, the search engine marketing campaign is successful.

Generally speaking, most web sites receive between 6–7 percent of their overall traffic from the search engines. A successful search engine marketing campaign should deliver qualified traffic at least in the double digits.

Submit Your Site to Thousands of Search Engines

If you ever receive an email that makes this statement, consider it to be spam. Most of a site's qualified traffic comes from the top 10–20 search engines, directories, and industry-specific web sites. In all likelihood, participation in these programs gets your site listed in many FFA search engines and directories. FFA listings are worthless, especially because the major search engines consider FFA sites to be spam.

Search Engine Visibility Reports

If you receive an unsolicited "visibility" report in your email, you are probably not dealing with a reputable search engine marketing firm. Here is why:

- The report you received was unsolicited. If you really wanted a search engine visibility report, you would have requested one.

- The company that sent you the report probably selected a very general keyword phrase or a set of keywords that is not important to your business. No one knows what keywords are your most profitable selections just by viewing your web site.

- If you actually perform keyword searches on the search engines, you will find that your site is appearing more frequently than indicated in the visibility reports. Many of these visibility reports are inaccurate. The search engine marketing company is just trying to scare you into using their services.

- If you have a new web site, in all likelihood, your site will not appear in the search engines for at least one to three months. All search engines have lead times, which is the time between web page submission and when the page appears in the search engine index. Again, this is a tactic used to scare you into using their services. Your site will probably appear in the search engines after the lead time has passed.

Don't fall for the sales hype from a company sending you visibility reports. Your site-statistics software tells you whether your site is receiving search engine traffic.

Search Engine Optimization Does Not Deliver a Good Return-On-Investment (ROI)

Currently, there is a widespread belief that if a company can pay for a position, why should the company bother embarking on a search engine optimization campaign? Search engine optimization and search engine advertising are two different online marketing strategies.

Search engine advertising relies far more on payment than relevancy. Granted, a pay-per-click search engine such as Overture does not let search engine advertisers buy any keyword they want. The landing or destination pages for the advertising must contain some relevant content. However, nothing on the landing page determines positions. Ultimately, what determines positioning is how much the advertiser is willing to pay.

Simply optimize your entire web site so that there is a good chance that your web pages will appear at the top of search engine queries for your selected keywords and keyword phrases. When a site is properly optimized, search engine spiders do not have a difficult time finding and spidering a site. Quite often, with a search engine–friendly site, paid submission and paid advertising are not even necessary.

Many businesses never use pay-per-click advertising and yet, they still get excellent ROI. Personally, I have witnessed many sites receiving millions of dollars in increased sales within months of launching a search engine–friendly web site. Some of the web pages used as examples in this book have generated this type of ROI.

Search Engine Traffic Is Not as Good as Leads from Traditional Marketing Methods

Search engine traffic is often better than leads from traditional marketing and advertising (direct mail, public relations, radio, television, and so on) because people who come to your site through the search engines are actively seeking information about your products and services.

When analyzing cost per lead (CPL) data, you'll find that costs can be much lower for search engine marketing than for more traditional marketing methods.

Effective Search Engine Marketing Should Be Done In-House by the Webmaster

Most companies delegate search engine marketing responsibilities to a single webmaster or web site developer. In my experience, the IT department is a poor selection for relegating search engine marketing. The IT department might be responsible for creating a search engine–friendly web site that downloads quickly, but the IT department usually is not responsible for a web site's content. Usually an Editorial or Marketing department is responsible for a site's content, and they know that the actual content of the page is equally as important as the design. Furthermore, an effective search engine marketing campaign also involves link development, a responsibility which usually falls under the Marketing department.

The fact is that search engine marketing involves talent in web copywriting, site design and layout, technology, site submission and monitoring, site analysis, and so forth. In all likelihood, one person with multiple responsibilities cannot effectively handle all these responsibilities and keep up with the ever-changing search engines. Many search engine marketing firms specialize in all aspects of optimization and submission.

You Don't Have to Change Your Site to Achieve Top Positions

This statement is rarely true. If you hear this type of statement from a search engine marketer, in all likelihood, you are dealing with a cloaking company. All the major search engines consider cloaking to be spam. Thus, if you work with cloaking companies, you should know that your site might be penalized for spamming.

If you are purchasing positions on a pay-per-click search engine such as Overture, you might not have to change your site. However, if you are purchasing a search engine optimization (SEO) campaign, you have to modify your site.

A search engine optimization campaign involves rewriting some of your content so that keywords are more prominent and frequently used. Quite often, a site's navigation scheme might not deliver keyword-rich content to the search engines. In addition, you might need to modify the navigation scheme or participate in a pay-for-inclusion (PFI) program.

A Client List and Testimonials on a Web Site Indicate a Reputable SEO Firm

Just because a search engine marketing firm displays an impressive client list does not necessarily mean that the firm practices ethical search engine marketing. You should ask a search engine marketing firm if any of its strategies have resulted in any spam penalties. If a search engine marketing firm is constantly building micro-sites or purchasing domain names specifically for search engine positioning, you might not be dealing with an ethical search engine marketer.

Note that many reputable search engine marketing firms sign non-disclosure agreements (NDAs) with their clients. Thus, they are not permitted to display all or part of their client lists on their web sites. However, because most firms that want to hire a search engine expert ask for references, firms that have NDAs should still have at least three references that they can give you.

Conclusion

Utilizing spam techniques does not guarantee that your web pages get top search engine positions. Even if spam techniques work, the search engine positions are short-lived. After the search engines or competitors discover the spam, the site(s) utilizing spam are either penalized or permanently banned from the search engines. Then the spammers have to build another web site, another set of web pages, and begin the whole search engine marketing process all over again. This cat-and-mouse game can become very time consuming and expensive.

Web pages with quality content and an acceptable search engine–friendly design consistently perform better on the search engines than spam pages. Because the pages contain quality content and the search engines have access to that quality content, there is no cat-and-mouse game. Sites that are optimized from the very beginning of the design and redesign process need little tweaking after the foundation is in place. Building a site for your target audience and following search engine best practices is one of the most cost-effective components of a search engine marketing campaign.

Resources

Introduction

The list of web sites and books that follows contains resources that I consistently use as references whenever I build a new web site or redesign an existing one. These resources contain books, marketing companies, and reputable search engine marketing newsletters that will help web site owners build search engine–friendly web sites that enhance the end-user experience.

Web Sites

Adventive
www.adventive.com/

This is one of the best marketing resources on the web. Adventive contains moderated discussion groups on sales, public relations, search engine marketing, online promotion, wireless communications, and effective web site design. The popular I-Search Discussion Group is located here.

High Rankings Advisor
www.highrankings.com/archives.htm

The High Rankings Advisor is an informative and witty, free weekly email newsletter written by search engine expert Jill Whalen. Jill keeps no secrets when it comes to optimizing sites for search engine visibility. It also contains excellent interviews with timely, accurate information.

Microsoft bCentral Daily Digest
http://digest.bcentral.com/

This is a free, moderated discussion list focused on web site design and marketing. Topics frequently covered include search engine marketing, graphic design, Hypertext Markup Language (HTML) coding, and more. Over 135,000 members make this list a great place to learn. It is published five days a week.

Microsoft bCentral Submit It!
http://submitit.bcentral.com/

This is a time-saving site submission and optimization service for small businesses. It offers an optimization check to ensure that your pages are ready for submission, a keyword selection tool, and rank checking and Inktomi inclusion features.

PositionPro
www.positionpro.com/

PositionPro is a web-based service that crawls a web site much like a search engine. PositionPro analyzes the web site's content and provides valuable insight into how the search engines will view it. Included in the service are tools to help you optimize your content, ranking reports, and easy access into Inktomi and FAST paid inclusion programs.

Position Technologies, Inc.
www.positiontech.com/

Position Technologies is the leading provider of search traffic solutions. Through its partnerships with the leading search engines and value-added services, Position Technologies provides a unique platform for businesses to manage their search engine visibility and traffic.

Search Engine Forums
www.searchengineforums.com/

This is an online forum for discussions about current topics relating to search engine marketing. Top search engine experts moderate and contribute to forum discussions. Representatives from the major search engines and directories sometimes contribute to discussions.

Search Engine Optimization Tips
www.submit-it.com/subopt.htm

This gives tips on search engine–friendly design, keyword phrase selection, copywriting, and meta-tag optimization. It also includes search engine lead times for submitting a web site.

Search Engine Watch
www.searchenginewatch.com/

If you bookmark only one web site about search engine marketing, this is the one. It is the most reputable source of information on the search engines. Danny Sullivan's Search Engine Reports are a "must -have" for all web site designers and online marketers.

SearchDay

www.searchenginewatch.com/searchday/

SearchDay is a free newsletter from Search Engine Watch, featuring web search news, reviews, tools, tips, and search engine headlines from across the web. Beyond breaking news, SearchDay also features tips and techniques for sharpening your web searching skills, reviews of specialized search sites and tools, interviews with important people in the world of search, and a variety of additional search-related content.

SEO Consultants Directory

www.seoconsultants.com/

Directory of professional, ethical search engine marketers who follow all the guidelines set forth by the search engines and directories. It is a great resource for finding search engine marketers who do not spam the search engines.

Ten Steps to Building Links to Your Site

www.bcentral.com/articles/marketing/134.asp

Inbound links and "link popularity" are a very important part of any online marketing campaign. This article describes the tools required to build links and includes step-by-step instructions for organizing your campaign and locating the best links for your site.

Traffick.com

www.traffick.com/

This is a search engine marketing site that provides feature articles from top search engine experts and search engine news. The Traffick Directory provides links related to portals, search engines, vertical portals, web browsers, and web tools.

Webmaster World

www.webmasterworld.com/

This is an online forum for discussions about current topics relating to site design and search engine marketing. Representatives from the major search engines and directories sometimes contribute to discussions.

Books

Designing Web Usability: The Practice of Simplicity
Jakob Nielsen
New Riders Publishing
www.useit.com/jakob/Webusability/

Search engines, directory editors, and end users prefer sites that are simple and easy to use. Though not all advice presented in this book is search engine friendly, the information will help web site owners create sites that enhance the end-user experience and increase sales conversions.

Don't Make Me Think: A Common Sense Approach to Web Usability
Steve Krug
New Riders Publishing
www.sensible.com/

If I had to select only one book that would be required reading in a web site design class, this one would be it. Even though *Don't Make Me Think* is classified as a usability book, it is a must-read for all web site designers who plan on creating a user-friendly web site. It also provides usability reviews and site design problem-solving tips.

Homepage Usability: 50 Websites Deconstructed
Jakob Nielsen and Marie Tahir
New Riders Publishing
www.useit.com/homepageusability

Usability gurus Jakob Nielson and Marie Tahir present 113 guidelines for a user-friendly home page and analyze the home pages of popular web sites such as About.com and Microsoft. This is a great book for determining the effectiveness of your home page.

The Invisible Web: Uncovering Information Sources the Search Engines Can't See
Chris Sherman and Gary Price
CyberAge Books
www.invisible-Web.net/

Enormous expanses of the Internet are unreachable with standard web search engines. This book provides the key to finding these hidden resources by identifying how to uncover and use invisible web resources. Mapping the invisible web, when and how to use it, assessing the validity of the information, and the future of web searching are topics covered in detail.

Net Words—Creating High-Impact Online Copy
Nick Usborne
McGraw-Hill
www.nickusborne.com/

Nick Usborne speaks, writes, and consults on strategic copy issues for business online. For web sites, emails, and newsletters, he crafts messages that drive results. This book is a guide to creating copy that connects with customers and increases sales conversions. This is one of the best web copywriting books available.

Web Redesign | Workflow That Works
Kelly Goto and Emily Cotler
New Riders Publishing
www.web-redesign.com/

Planning is one of the most cost-effective things a web site owner can do, especially when it comes to creating search engine–friendly designs. Kelly Goto and Emily Cotler provide a framework for a cohesive web workflow plan that saves web site owners time, money, and headaches. Read this book before designing your web site.

Glossary

404 error

File not found. This error occurs when the host server cannot find the specific file that a search engine spider or browser requests.

A

Above the fold

Refers to the first screen viewed on a computer monitor when a document is opened.

Absolute link

Hyperlinks that include the complete URL, which is the domain name, pathname (if used), and filename.

Adjacency

Search specification that requires words typed into a search query to be next to or near one another.

Agent name delivery

The process of delivering specific web pages to a search engine spider by means of the spider's agent name. For example, the agent name of Google's search engine spider is Googlebot. With this process, search engine spiders and end users do not view the same page. See *cloaking*.

Algorithm

The mathematical formula used to determine how web pages are ranked in a search engine's or directory's search results.

Alternative text

In HTML, text placed inside the image source tag. If a graphic image does not appear on a browser screen, the alternative text appears in place of the graphic image. The same text appears when end users view a web page with a text-only browser. Also known as *alt text*.

Anchor text

In HTML, text that is placed between the <a> and </a> tags. Commonly referred to as a text link.

Applet

A small program written in the Java programming language that usually runs in a web browser, as part of a web page. Search engine spiders currently do not record the text inside a Java applet.

B

B2B

Abbreviation for Business to Business. A B2B web site sells products and services to other businesses.

B2C

Abbreviation for Business to Consumer. A B2C web site sells products and services to consumers and the general public.

Bait-and-switch

The process of submitting one web page to a search engine or directory and substituting a different page with unrelated or spam content on the server after the search engine or directory has recorded the information about the initial web page.

Below the fold

On a web page, content that is "below the fold" requires that a user scroll vertically to view that content.

Best of the Web

The elite Inktomi database currently comprised of over 115 million documents that come from Inktomi's natural crawling of the web. Web sites listed in this index are the most popular documents on the web through Inktomi's link (popularity) analysis. Abbreviated as BOW.

Boolean search

A search on a computer database, such as a search engine, for keywords that best describe your topic using Boolean operators such as AND, OR, and NOT.

Breadcrumbs

A form of text navigation showing a hierarchical linking structure of a web site. The current location within the site is indicated by a list of pages above the current page in a hierarchy, leading up to the home page. A typical set of breadcrumb links might look like this: Home > Products > Teas > Green Tea.

Bridge page

Another term for a doorway page. See *doorway pages*.

Browser

The software used to view, manage, and access web pages by interpreting hypertext and hyperlinks. The two most common browsers are Netscape Navigator and Microsoft Internet Explorer.

C

Call to action

The intended response a web site owner wishes site visitors to take when they view a web page. Various calls to action include order, purchase, subscribe, download, and click here.

Cascading Style Sheets (CSS)

A feature of HTML developed by the W3C. They enable web designers and end users to create style templates (sheets) that specify how different text elements (paragraphs, headings, hyperlinks, and so on) appear on a web page. Style sheets can also be used for positioning elements on a web page. Currently, not all browsers express CSS formatting in the same manner.

CGI

Abbreviation for common gateway interface. CGI refers to programs used to produce content for browser delivery. Common CGI programming languages include Perl, C, Java, and Visual Basic.

Classification

The process of organizing information into topical categories, usually in a hierarchical structure.

Click-through or click-thru

The process of clicking a link from one web page to go to another web page. In search engine marketing, it is the process of clicking a link from a search results page to a specific web page.

Click-through popularity or click-thru popularity

In search engine marketing, the number of times end users click the link from search engines to a web site and how long end users stay on the site after they click the link from the search engine. Some search engines use click-through popularity to determine relevancy. Also known as *click tracking*.

Cloaking

The process of delivering custom content to a search engine spider that is hidden from site visitors. With cloaking, search engine spiders see one page, and visitors view another page with different content.

Clustering

Listing only one or two pages from each web site in a search engine's or directory's list of search results.

Comment tag

An HTML tag used to hide content from browsers. Comment-tag content is placed between the <!-- and --> symbols. Most search engines ignore the content placed between these symbols.

Concept search

A search for documents related to a keyword or keyword phrase. Different from a search specifically containing the keyword itself.

Content page

Another term for an information page. See *information page.*

Conversion rate

The measure of the number of specific calls to action divided by the total number of unique page visitors. For example, if 10 visitors purchase a product or service and 100 visitors view the web page, the page has a conversion rate of 10 percent.

Cookie

A message given to a web browser by a web server. One of the main purposes of cookies is to identify web site users/visitors and possibly prepare customized web pages for them.

Counter

A program or script that measures the number of hits on a web page. Can also measure the number of page views on a web site.

CPA

Abbreviation for cost per action. Type of advertising in which a web site gets paid each time an end user performs a desired action.

CPC

Abbreviation for cost per click. Type of advertising in which a web site gets paid each time an end user clicks a link to the advertiser's web site.

CPM

Abbreviation for cost per thousand. Type of advertising in which a web site gets paid based on the number of impressions. Calculated in blocks of 1000.

Crawler

Another word for a search engine spider. See *spider*.

Cross linking

Linking among web pages within the same web site.

D

Dead link

A link to a web page that does not exist on a web server.

Deep linking

Linking to content that is two or more directories deep within a web site. Can also be linking directly to individual web pages within a site, rather than to the home page.

Destination page

The web page a visitor is taken to after clicking a search engine listing or advertisement. Also known as a *landing page*.

Directory

Web site that focuses on listing web pages or sites by specific categories, using human editors to manually place web sites or web pages into the categories. Commonly called a "human-based" search engine.

Directory enhancement

The process of selecting the most appropriate category (or categories) in a directory and writing a keyword-rich description that accurately describes the content of a web site or web page.

DNS

Abbreviation for Domain Name System. The DNS translates URL text addresses (such as companyname.com) into a numeric Internet address (such as 201.214.12.6).

DNS lookup

The process of converting a unique IP address (of a site visitor) to its domain name. Often used in site statistics software to analyze server log files.

Domain name

Generally, a text address that corresponds to one or more numeric IP addresses. An exclusive name that identifies a web site, such as companyname.com.

Doorway domain

A web site that consists mostly or solely of doorway pages. A doorway domain's only purpose is to rank well on the search engines and to ultimately redirect traffic to a different site.

Doorway pages

Web pages created specifically for obtaining top search engine positions and not to benefit end users. Computer-generated doorway pages are usually created to rank high on specific search engines and are often cloaked.

Download

The process of retrieving information from a main source to a peripheral device. Browsers download web pages from a server.

Dynamic HTML

An HTML extension that enables web pages to react to the end users' input, such as displaying a web page based on the type of browser or computer end users are using to view the page. HTML and CSS rely on JavaScript to make web pages interactive.

Dynamic IP

An IP address that changes every time a user connects to the Internet.

Dynamic URLs

The URL of a dynamic web page. Dynamic URLs typically contain characters such as ?, =, %, +, cgi, or cgi-bin.

E

Entry page

The first page an end user views after clicking a link to a web site. Also known as a *landing page*.

F

Fake copy listing

A web page that has achieved a top search engine position by stealing the contents of another web page.

False drop

A web page retrieved from a search engine or directory that is not relevant to the query used.

FFA

Abbreviation for free-for-all links. FFA web pages contain a collection of indiscriminate, often unrelated, links to other web pages. FFA links are commonly used to artificially boost link popularity and are considered spam by the major search engines.

Filter words

Common words that search engines remove when adding web page information to their full-text indices because they tend to slow down search queries without improving the results. Common filter words are as follows: the, a, an, or, for, of, but, is, and it.

Focus page

A web page that contains quality content about a specific topic. Also known as an *information page*. See *information page*.

Frames

An HTML technique that enables web site designers to divide the browser screen into two or more sections. Each section, or frame, is a single web page.

Full-text index

A database, or index, containing every word of every web document, including filter words and stop words. Can also refer to an index without filter and stop words included.

Fuzzy search

A search that retrieves matches for partially spelled or misspelled words. Fuzzy matching techniques reduce words to their root and then try to match all forms of the word. Fuzzy search is based on "fuzzy logic engineering," which is a very advanced mathematical discipline. Simply put, it enables you to say "maybe," "almost," or "close to" in computer code.

G

Gateway domain

See *doorway domain*.

Gateway page

See *doorway pages*.

Gibberish

Web site content that has no logical, sensible meaning when viewed by site visitors.

GIF

Abbreviation for Graphics Interchange Format. A type of bitmap graphic image commonly used on web sites. GIFs contain 256 colors and are displayed in the most commonly used browsers.

H

Hallway page

A web page created specifically to link doorway pages on a web site.

Hidden text

Text on a web page that is not visible to end users in a browser, at any time, but is visible to search engine spiders. Considered spam by all the major search engines if used to artificially increase keyword density.

Hit

A single request made to a web server for an object on your web site. The object can be an HTML file, a graphic image, or any other embedded object, such as a sound file, in your web pages.

HTML

Abbreviation for Hypertext Markup Language. A cross-platform, text-formatting system for creating web pages, including text, images, sounds, frames, and animation.

HTTP

Abbreviation for Hypertext Transfer Protocol. The system used to transfer data between a web server and a browser.

Hypertext link

A word or set of words placed inside an anchor tag.

I

Image map

A single graphic image, generally in a GIF or JPEG format, containing multiple hyperlinks.

Inbound link

A link from an external domain to a web site, bringing traffic to that site. Inbound links are used to measure link popularity.

Index

A searchable database of words pointing to documents created by search engine software.

Indexer

The part of the search engine that processes and places spidered, or crawled, web documents into a database. The indexer typically processes a document by removing all tags, storing links in a queue, removing filter words, looking for stop words, and storing the document in a searchable database.

Information page

A static web page that contains quality content about a specific topic. The page is written for a site's target audience but formatted for easy search engine spidering.

Invisible web

Web sites or pages that search engine spiders cannot or will not crawl because the content is locked up in a database.

IP address

A unique number that identifies every computer on the Internet. Currently, an IP address consists of four, 32-bit numbers (from 0 to 255) separated by periods, such as 255.195.12.13.

IP delivery

A type of cloaking technique where customized content is delivered to a site visitor based on the visitor's IP address. Because search engines have unique IP addresses, content delivered to the search engines is not the same content delivered to site visitors.

IP spoofing

The act of sending messages to a computer using an IP address from a trusted source to gain unauthorized access to that computer. IP spoofing is illegal in many countries.

ISP

Abbreviation for Internet service provider. An ISP is a company that provides access to the Internet.

J

Java

A programming language created by Sun Microsystems that enables small applications to run on different types of computers and operating systems. Currently, search engines do not record the content inside a Java applet.

JavaScript

An open-source scripting language developed by Netscape that enables web designers to create more animated and dynamic web pages.

JPEG

Abbreviation for Joint Photographic Experts Group. A type of graphic image commonly used on web sites. JPEGs can contain millions of colors and are displayed in the most commonly used browsers. Best format for photographs, images containing gradients, or the presentation of millions of colors.

K

Keyword

A single word typed into a search engine query. Also a single word that accurately describes the contents of a single web page or web site.

Keyword buy

A term used in search engine advertising in which advertisements appear when a keyword or set of keywords is typed into a search query.

Keyword density

A measure of the number of times keywords occur within a web page's text divided by the total number of words on a web page. Search engines have unique algorithms for calculating keyword density.

Keyword domain name

A domain name that contains one or more keywords.

Keyword phrase

A set of words typed into a search engine query. Also a set of words that accurately describes the contents of a single web page or web site.

Keyword prominence

Refers to how "high up" on a web page a keyword appears. Generally, if keywords are visible on the first screen on a web page without site visitors having to scroll, the words are said to have high keyword prominence.

Keyword proximity

Refers to how close keywords are to each other on web pages.

Keyword stacking

Placing gibberish sentences and phrases on a web page in order to artificially boost keyword density, keyword prominence, and keyword proximity. Keyword stacking often occurs in title tags, meta tags, and invisible text.

Keyword stuffing

Placing gibberish sentences and phrases inside graphic images or CSS layers. Often has the same meaning as *keyword stacking*.

L

Layers

Attribute in CSS. A rectangular section, or layer, of HTML code that can be placed on a web page by assigning X, Y, and Z coordinates, measured in pixels.

Link farm

A collection of indiscriminate, often unrelated, web sites that link to each other to artificially boost link popularity.

Link popularity

Refers to the number and quality of inbound links to a web site from other web sites. One of the highest quality inbound links is a link from a major directory such as Yahoo!.

Link rot or linkrot

A link from a search engine, directory, or other web site that results in a 404 error page after a web developer modifies a web site with new URLs or removes pages from a web server.

M

Meta refresh

Attribute in a meta tag in which one URL is replaced with another URL after a specified period of time. A method of redirecting end users from one URL to another.

Meta revisit

Attribute in a meta tag in which web designers instruct the search engine spiders to return to a web page within a specified period of time. Search engines do not honor this attribute.

Meta tag

An HTML tag, placed between the <head> and </head> tags, that gives information about the content of a web page, such as what HTML specifications a web page follows or description of a web page's content. A meta tag, however, does not affect how a web page is displayed on a browser. For online marketing, the most common uses for meta tags are the keyword, description, and robots exclusion attributes.

Mirror domains or mirror sites

Multiple copies of web sites, often on different servers, with the exact same, or similar, content. Used to artificially boost link popularity and search engine visibility.

Mirror pages

Multiple copies of web pages, often on different servers, with the exact same, or similar, content. Most mirror pages are doorway pages tailored for a specific search engine.

N

Navigation button

A graphic image, generally in a GIF or JPEG format, that links to a single URL.

noframes

An element commonly used on framed pages. Content placed between the <noframes> and </noframes> tags display when a browser does not support frames or is configured not to display frames. Because almost all browsers support frames, search engines either ignore or place low weight on the content inside the <noframes> tags.

noscript

If a browser does not support a scripting language or if an end user has disabled client-side scripting in a browser, content between the <noscript> and </noscript> tags is displayed. This element enables web developers to display alternative content in the event a script is not executed.

O

Obfuscation

The act of misrepresenting web page content to site visitors. Similar to cloaking, search engine spiders see one page, and visitors view a page with different HTML code and content.

Optimization

The process of designing, writing, coding (in HTML), and submitting web pages to the search engines to increase the probability that your web pages will appear at the top of search engine queries for selected keywords and key phrases. The process of making a web page as perfect or effective as possible for end users and the search engines.

Outbound link

A link from a web site to a different web site with a different domain name.

P

Page views

In site statistics software, the total number of times users view a single web page.

PageRank

A numeric value that represents how popular a web page is based on Google's link analysis calculations. Part of this numeric value is the quality and quantity of links pointing to a web page.

PDF

Abbreviation for portable document format. Created by Adobe Systems in its software program Adobe Acrobat as a universal browser. A PDF document uses formatting information from many different desktop publishing applications, such as InDesign and QuarkXPress. Files can be downloaded over the web and viewed page by page, provided the user has installed the necessary plug-in, Adobe Acrobat Reader.

PFI

Abbreviation for pay for inclusion. In a PFI program, in exchange for payment, a search engine guarantees that a web page will (a) be included in a search engine index, (b) be added to the search engine index within days, and (c) be respidered regularly within a specified period of time.

Positioning

In a search engine or directory, the process of ordering URLs so that the most relevant sites appear at the top of search results for a particular query.

Power combination

The first three words in a title tag that, when typed in any combination in a search query, will contain a keyword phrase.

PPC

Abbreviation for pay per click. A type of search engine advertising model where the advertiser pays a specified amount of money to the host every time an end user clicks a link to the specified site.

Precision

The quality and degree of accuracy with which a search engine lists documents that match a query.

Proximity search

A search in which users specify that documents returned in search results should have the words (entered into the search query) near each other.

Q

Query

A request for specific information from a database.

Query processor

The part of the search engine software that matches the words typed in a search query with the web page that is most likely to have the information for which end users are searching.

R

Ranking

See *positioning*.

Reciprocal links

The mutual exchange of links from one site to another.

Relative link

A link that does not include an entire domain name, subdirectory (if used), and filename together in the URL. A link that is defined by its relative position to the current URL.

Relevancy

A search engine's numeric measure of how well a particular URL matches terms entered in a search query.

Robot

A software program that search engines use that visits every URL on the web, follows all the links, and catalogs all the text of every web page that (a) contains text, and (b) that can be visited or crawled. Also known as a *spider* or *crawler*, but the term "robot" is more and more commonly associated with automated agents.

Robots Exclusion Protocol

A text file that you place on your server that instructs search engine spiders to not spider and record the information in specified areas on your web site. The same function can also be utilized using the meta-robots tag.

S

Search engine

Software that searches an index or database and returns relevant matches based on the information typed into a query.

SERP

Abbreviation for search engine results page.

Server

In search engine marketing, a computer that delivers web pages to browsers and search engine spiders.

Spam

The act of taking extreme or excessive measures to achieve top search engine positions. Spam also can be the act of using any words, HTML code, scripting, or programming on a web page that is not meant to benefit the end user experience.

Spider

Software used by a search engine to find and retrieve web pages to include in its index.

Splash page

A web page, commonly the home page, that consists either of (a) a large graphic image and a link instructing visitors to "Enter" a web site, or (b) a Flash animation, a link to skip the Flash animation (Skip Intro), and a redirect to a new page after the animation is completed.

Static IP address

An IP address that remains constant, or the same, every time a person logs on to the Internet.

Stemming

Stemming is the ability for a search engine to search for variations of a word based on its root. For example, if the word "running" is typed into a search query, search engines that utilize stemming might also display documents that contain the word "run."

Stop words

Extremely common words that the search engines will not record. This is done to save space on their servers and to speed up searches. Examples of common stop words include the, a, an, for, and, but, to, and so forth. Also known as *filter words*.

T

Text link

See *anchor text*.

Title

The text placed between the <title> and </title> tags on a web page.

Traffic

The number of unique visitors to a single web site.

U

Unique visit

Represents a single, unique viewer who has visited a web site within a specified time period.

Upload

Act of copying a file from your computer to another computer.

URL

Abbreviation for uniform resource locator. Address referring to the location of a file on the Internet. In terms of search engine marketing, it is the address of an individual web page element or web document on the Internet. Every web document and web graphic image on a web site has a URL.

V

Virtual domain

A term used by web hosting services when multiple domains are hosted on a single web server. Each web site hosted on that server can have a unique domain name, called the virtual domain.

Visit

Represents one unique viewer who has visited a web site. One site visitor can view many web pages.

W

Web copywriting

The process of writing content specifically for display on web pages, including potential search result pages.

Web site

A collection of web pages, usually found under one domain, generally formatted in HTML, that contain text, graphic images, and multimedia effects such as sound files, video and/or animation files, and other programming or scripting elements such as Java and JavaScript.

X

XHTML

Abbreviation for Extensible Hypertext Markup Language. XHTML is a hybrid of XML and HTML. Web pages designed in XHTML should look the same across all platforms.

XML

Abbreviation for Extensible Markup Language. XML enables web site designers to create customized tags to describe data.

Z

Z-index

In CSS, the z-index property sets the stacking order of an element, usually a layer. Layers with greater z-index numbers will appear in front of layers with lower z-index numbers.

Chapter 1, excerpted from

Speed Up Your Site: Web Site Optimization

Andrew B. King

0-7357-1324-3

Speed Up Your Site: Web Site Optimization shows you how to shrink the size of your web pages and reduce their complexity for maximum speed. Not everyone has cable modems or the luxury of a T1 line. With 56.6K modems still in many households, it's increasingly important for web sites to be optimized for faster download times. Face it, consumers are impatient. By maximizing page display speed, bailout rates are reduced and bandwidth costs are minimized. The result is happier users and happier bosses. This book emphasizes valid code and languages like HTML, CSS, JavaScript, and PHP. Everything that goes into creating a web site is covered, from optimizing HTML and XHTML, to CSS, graphics, JavaScript, multimedia, and server-based techniques. Throughout the book, real-world examples illustrate the techniques discussed, with before and after code and percentage savings. Finally, 20 popular web sites are analyzed over time, reviewing how their size and complexity have changed since 1996.

1

Response Time: Eight Seconds, Plus or Minus Two

People hate to wait.

You're the fourth person in a six-person line at the supermarket. You spot a clerk moving toward the closed register in the next lane. Is she going to open it? If you bail out too early and she's just looking for bags, it's the back of the line for you. Wait too long and the clerk could call over the next person in line. What do you do?

On the Internet, this kind of choice is simple. If the page you're waiting for takes more than a few seconds to open, you just bail out to another site. No bodies to jostle, no icy stares from the slower crowd. Just exercise your freedom of choice with a twitch of a finger. To hell with the owners of the slower site you just left. Survival of the fittest, right? It's all rosy—unless, of course, you happen to be the owner of that slower site and it's a part of your business. In that case, it's a good thing you have this book.

In survey after survey, the most common complaint of Internet users is lack of speed. After waiting past a certain "attention threshold," users bail out to look for a faster site. Of course, exactly where that threshold is depends on many factors. How compelling is the experience? Is there effective feedback? This chapter explores the psychology of delay in order to discover why we are so impatient, and how fast is fast enough.

Lack of Speed Is the Most Common Complaint

Slow web sites are a universal phenomenon. Researchers have confirmed our need for speed in study after study:

- "GVU's Tenth World Wide Web User Survey," by Colleen Kehoe et al. (1999) `http://www.gvu.gatech.edu/user_surveys/survey-1998-10/tenthreport.html`—Over half of those surveyed cited slow downloads as a problem.

- In "The Top Ten *New* Mistakes of Web Design" (1999) `http://www.useit.com/alertbox/990530.html`—Jakob Nielsen found that 84 percent of 20 prominent sites had slow download times.

- *Designing Web Usability: The Practice of Simplicity* by Jakob Nielsen (New Riders Publishing, 2000)—"…fast response times are the most important design criterion for web pages."

- In "System Response Time and User Satisfaction: An Experimental Study of Browser-based Applications," in *Proceedings of the Association of Information Systems Americas Conference* (2000), John Hoxmeier and Chris DiCesare found that user satisfaction is inversely related to response time. They said that response time "could be the single most important variable when it comes to user satisfaction."

The study of this psychology is called *Human-Computer Interaction* (HCI). This chapter focuses on the speed aspects of HCI. How does delay affect user satisfaction? Why do we become so frustrated when we have to wait? This chapter distills this research into understandable language and web page design guidelines.

Flow: The Compelling Experience

It's one thing to optimize a web site for speed and get satisfactory results. It's quite another to help your users achieve flow. *Flow* is an optimal state that is characterized by intense yet effortless concentration, a sense of being at one with a larger good, clarity of goals with challenges met, and actualization. Is it possible that optimal web design can lead to users experiencing this optimal state? You'll find out in Chapter 2, "Flow in Web Design."

With the rapid expansion of the web and increasing bandwidth, you would think that the problem of slow system response would have gone away. As you learned in the Introduction, the opposite is true: Consumer sites are actually becoming slower.[1] In fact, Zona estimates that over $25 billion in potential sales is lost online due to web performance issues. HCI research is just as relevant today as it was a decade ago.

Speed: A Key Component of Usability

Speed is a key component of usability, which helps determine system acceptability.[2] How acceptable a system is determines its adoption rate. With over half of the IT projects deployed in the U.S. abandoned or underutilized,[3] it is important to make systems and sites (many of which are big IT projects themselves) that people actually use.

---

1. Zona Research, "The Need for Speed II" [online], (Redwood City, CA: Zona Research, 2001 [cited 9 November 2002]), available from the Internet at `http://www.keynote.com/downloads/Zona_Need_For_Speed.pdf`. Found that although B2B sites have doubled their speed, consumer sites have become 20 percent slower.
2. Brian Shackel, "Usability—context, framework, definition, design and evaluation," in *Human Factors for Informatics Usability*, ed. Brian Shackel and Simon Richardson (Cambridge, UK: Cambridge University Press, 1991), 21–37.
3. Thomas K. Landauer, *The Trouble with Computers: Usefulness, Usability, and Productivity* (Cambridge, MA: MIT Press, 1995). "…sadly, most reengineering efforts fail." A sobering book on computers and productivity.

Shackel's Acceptability Paradigm

Part of our psyche, it seems, is devoted to understanding whether a particular system will have a big enough payoff to warrant the necessary expenditure of our time and energy. Brian Shackel characterized this paradigm as "system acceptability," which is a tradeoff between three dimensions:

- **Utility**—Or perceived usefulness. Is it functionally efficient?
- **Usability**—Or perceived ease of use. Can users work the system successfully?
- **Likability**—The user's subjective attitude about using the system. Do users feel it is suitable?

All of these factors are weighed against each other and the cost of using the system (see Figure 1.1). Seen through Shackel's lens, when users make decisions about using a web site, they weigh how useful it will be, its perceived ease of use, its suitability to the task, and how much it will cost them both financially and socially. That's why sometimes we are willing to put up with difficult sites if the reward for doing so is large enough.

Figure 1.1
Shackel's Acceptability
Paradigm.

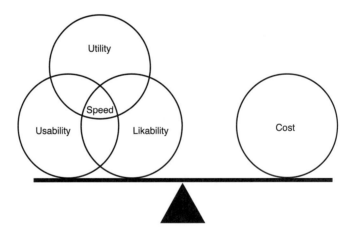

Traditionally, HCI research has focused on the quantification of Shackel's second dimension, usability. There is compelling evidence, however, that the utility of a technology should first be measured before any usability analysis occurs.[4,5] If you can't accomplish a task, it doesn't matter how easy the system is to use. Likability, Shackel's third dimension of acceptability, is most closely associated with "flow,"[6] or emotional appeal.

User Experience and Usability

The relative importance of usability changes over time. At first, usability has a strong effect on system use. As users gain more experience, they become more confident and believe they can accomplish more tasks with a desired level of performance (also known as *self-efficacy*[7]). As a result, ease of use fades in importance and utility, and likability increase in relative importance. Usability then indirectly influences usage through utility (usability -> utility -> usage).

Designers tend to favor ease of use over utility. Davis found that utility has far more influence on usage than usability, however. "No amount of ease of can compensate for a system that does not perform a useful function."[8]

Speed plays a key role in all of these dimensions, especially usability and likability, so it is an important determinant of system acceptability and usage. In other words, how responsive your site is will in large part determine its adoption rate, which in turn affects your bottom line.

---

4. Fred D. Davis, "Perceived Usefulness, Perceived Ease of Use, and User Acceptance of Information Technology," *MIS Quarterly* 13 (1989): 319–340. Found that perceived usefulness "had a significantly greater correlation with usage behavior" than perceived ease of use.

5. Brian R. Gaines, Lee Li-Jen Chen, and Mildred L. G. Shaw, "Modeling the Human Factors of Scholarly Communities Supported Through the Internet and World Wide Web," *Journal of the American Society for Information Science* 48, no. 11 (1997): 987–1003.

6. Mihaly Csikszentmihalyi, *Beyond Boredom and Anxiety: Experiencing Flow in Work and Play* (San Francisco: Jossey-Bass, 1975). This landmark book introduced the concept of flow to the public.

7. Albert Bandura, *Self-Efficacy: The Exercise of Control* (New York: W. H. Freeman, 1997).

8. Davis, "Perceived Usefulness," 333.

A Brief History of Web Performance

Soon after the birth of the web, HCI researchers started studying online environments. Networked environments like the Internet add another dimension to the mix—namely, network latency. Unlike the closed computing environments that HCI researchers studied in the past, on the Internet the delay between requesting a resource and receiving it is unpredictable. The more resources a page has (graphics, multimedia), the less predictable the response rate.

Initially researchers studied the effects of fixed response times on user satisfaction. Later studies simulated variable response rates for more real-world results. Their metrics changed from user satisfaction and performance to measures such as attunability, quality of service, quality of experience, and credibility.

In the late 1990s and early 2000s, researchers started looking at Shackel's likability dimension by studying the effects of download delays on user perceptions of web sites, flow states,[9] and emotional appeal.

Users form negative impressions from web site delays. Users perceive fast-loading pages to be of high quality, while they perceive slow-loading pages to be of low quality and untrustworthy. A user's tolerance for delay also decreases with experience. These topics are covered in more depth later in this chapter.

In fact, slow-loading web pages can cause users to believe that an error has occurred, because the computer has not responded in an appropriate amount of time.[10]

Affective Computing

Some researchers theorize that if a computer could respond "supportively" to delay-induced frustration, any negative emotional effects could be mitigated. According to

---

9. Donna L. Hoffman and Thomas P. Novak, "Marketing in Hypermedia Computer-Mediated Environments: Conceptual Foundations," *Journal of Marketing* 60 (July 1996): 50–68.
10. Jonathan Lazar and Yan Huang, "Designing Improved Error Messages for Web Browsers," in *Human Factors and Web Development*, 2d edition, ed. Julie Ratner (Mahwah, NJ: Lawrence Erlbaum Associates, 2002).

Pre-Attentive Recognition

In their classic book on the psychology of human performance, Wickens and Hollands describe parallel processing in visual searching, or *pre-attentive recognition*.[11] We can recognize features much more quickly on the screen using color or grouping than we can locate a word in a body of text. That's why links default to blue; this helps us locate them immediately.

---

11. Christopher D. Wickens and Justin G. Hollands, *Engineering Psychology and Human Performance*, 3d ed. (Upper Saddle River, NJ: Prentice Hall, 1999), 84–89.

researchers who have studied "affective computing," computers can respond to human emotions in order to lower frustration levels.[12]

Using galvanic skin response and blood volume pressure, Scheirer found that random delays can be a cause of frustration with computers.[13] Rather than ignoring their frustration (the most common condition) or letting them vent, a supportive approach gave users the most relief from frustration.[14] Perhaps we'll soon hear something like: "I'm sorry I'm so slow, Dave. Would you like me to speed up this web site?"

User-Rated Quality Models

More recently, researchers have been attempting to create a grand unified theory of web site quality from a user's perspective. How do users rate web sites? Why do they return to particular web sites and buy products? WebQual™, an overall measure of web site quality, is composed of twelve distinct measures derived from existing research.

---

12. Rosalind W. Picard, *Affective Computing* (Cambridge, MA: MIT Press, 1997).
13. Jocelyn Scheirer, Raul Fernandez, Jonathan Klein, and Rosalind W. Picard, "Frustrating the User on Purpose: A Step Toward Building an Affective Computer," *Interacting with Computers* 14, no. 2 (2002): 93–118.
14. Jonathan Klein, Youngme Moon, and Rosalind W. Picard, "This Computer Responds to User Frustration: Theory, Design, and Results," *Interacting with Computers* 14, no. 2 (2002): 119–140.

WebQual™ can accurately assess the overall perceived quality of web sites. Response time and emotional appeal both play a major role in perceived web site quality.[15]

Automated Quality Testing

WebTango researchers have developed an automated web site quality rating tool.[16] Their system, which is empirically based, automatically measures web site structure and composition in order to predict how experts will rate sites. Based on web designs judged by experts (Webby Awards), their 157-factor model, which includes page performance, had an average accuracy of 94 percent when quantifying good, average, and poor pages. However, some of the measures of good design are counterintuitive (for more Bobby accessibility errors, see `http://bobby.watchfire.com/`).

Essentially a mining tool, WebTango analyzes existing web pages to create profiles of good and bad designs, and then applies this data to the design of new sites. This interactive "quality checker" is analogous to a grammar checker for web sites (see Figure 1.2).

Figure 1.2
Web site structure: From information to experience design.

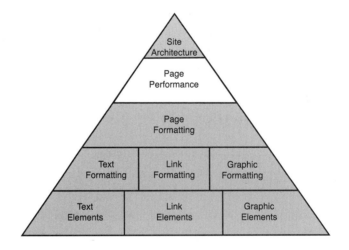

15. Eleanor T. Loiacono, Richard T. Watson, and Dale L. Goodhue, "WebQual™: A Web Site Quality Instrument," *American Marketing Association: Winter Marketing Educators' Conference* 13 (Austin, Texas: American Marketing Association, 2002): 432–438. A 12-factor web quality super-model from a user's perspective. See also `http://www.webqual.net/`.

16. Melody Y. Ivory and Marti A. Hearst, "Improving Web Site Design," *IEEE Internet Computing, Special Issue on Usability and the World Wide Web* 6, no. 2 (2002): 56–63. Available from the Internet at `http://webtango.ischool.washington.edu/`.

Set Performance Goals

Usability professionals routinely set usability metrics and goals for particular systems. Web performance is no different. Choose a performance goal for your site, and strive to achieve that goal for all of your pages. Because usability guidelines can be subjective, Shackel suggests quantifying usability in measurable terms.[17] Here is an example of a performance goal checklist:

- **Effectiveness**—Display high-traffic pages faster than eight seconds on 56Kbps modems; display useful content within the first two seconds. Other pages should display useful content in no more than 12 seconds on 56Kbps modems.

- **Learnability**—Achieve a 95 percent success rate on finding particular products within 30 seconds.

- **Flexibility**—Give users the ability to find products by browsing or searching.

- **Attitude**—With an attitude questionnaire on a 5-point scale from "very good" to "very bad," score 80 percent in good or above and only 2 percent below neutral.

- **Overall usability**—Meet 75 percent or more of Nielsen's 207-point usability checklist.[18]

17. Shackel, "Usability—context, framework, definition, design, and evaluation," 27.
18. Jakob Nielsen, Rolf Molich, Carolyn Snyder, and Susan Farrell, *E-Commerce User Experience* (Fremont, CA: Nielsen Norman Group, 2001). This invaluable book revealed the mythical 207 usability design guidelines.

Response Time and User Satisfaction

Shneiderman posed the question best: "How long will users wait for the computer to respond before they become annoyed?"[19] Researchers say "it depends." The delay users will tolerate depends on the perceived complexity of the task, user expertise, and feedback. Variability also plays an important role in delay tolerance. Users can tolerate moderate levels of delay variability, up to plus or minus 50 percent of the mean.

19. Ben Shneiderman, "Response Time and Display Rate in Human Performance with Computers," *Computing Surveys* 16, no. 3 (1984): 265–285. Keep it under 1 to 2 seconds, please.

A number of studies have attempted to quantify computer response times versus user satisfaction. Robert Miller found three threshold levels of human attention:[20]

- **0.1s**—One tenth of a second was viewed as instantaneous.

- **1.0s**—A one-second response time was needed for users to feel they were moving freely through an information space.

- **10s**—A response time below 10 seconds was required for users to keep their attention focused on the task.

Miller proposed that the ideal response time is around two seconds.

Shneiderman agreed with Miller that a two-second limit is appropriate for simple tasks, as long as the cost is not excessive. Shneiderman found that users "pick up the pace" of computer systems, that they were more productive at shorter response rates, and that they "consistently prefer the faster pace," below 1 to 2 seconds.

Although users prefer shorter response rates, the optimum system response time (SRT) depends on task complexity. Fast SRTs cause input errors while longer response times tax short-term memory and frustrate users. Users want consistency in response times.

Because surfing the web is mainly a low-complexity activity, users prefer faster response rates. Usage studies empirically confirm this need for speed; most pages are viewed for less than a second and few for more than 10 seconds.[21]

---

20. Robert B. Miller, "Response Time in Man-Computer Conversational Transactions," in *Proceedings of the AFIPS Fall Joint Computer Conference* 33 (Montvale, NJ: AFIPS Press, 1968), 267–277.

21. Bruce McKenzie and Andy Cockburn, "An Empirical Analysis of Web Page Revisitation," in *Proceedings of the 34th Hawaii International Conference on System Sciences* (Los Alamitos, CA: IEEE Computer Society Press, 2001). Found that web page revisitation is over 80 percent, visits are short, and bookmark lists are long.

An Interview with Ben Shneiderman, Ph.D.

I talked to Dr. Ben Shneiderman, one of the leading experts on HCI, to find out more about the relationship between speed and user satisfaction on the web.

Andy King: How does speed relate to usability and success on the web?

Ben Shneiderman: Usability plays a key role in web success stories…design, graphics, navigation, organization, consistency, etc. all play important roles. Speed is also vital—it's hard to get users to like a slow interface, and satisfaction grows with speed. Google is a good example of an excellent service that is even more valuable and appreciated because it is fast. Speed is the strongest correlate of user satisfaction.

King: Why do we prefer shorter response times?

Shneiderman: Lively interaction keeps the engagement high. For most people, wasted time, especially while just waiting for something to happen, is annoying.

King: What happens when we exceed our attention threshold (8 to 12 seconds)?

Shneiderman: Users not only grow frustrated, but they forget their next step, and have to reconstruct their intentions…often making mistakes that only exacerbate their frustration.

King: What do you think of the flow construct for user satisfaction on the web?

Shneiderman: Rapid movement through complex sequences of actions that move users toward a desired goal contributes to the flow experience. Users should be working just at the right level of challenge, accomplishing something they desire. There is a great thrill of finding what you want, and getting it rapidly so you can move on to the next step.[22]

---

22. Ben Shneiderman, email to author, 24 August 2002.

System Response Time Guidelines

Shneiderman suggests the following guidelines for system response times:[23]

- Users prefer shorter response times.

- Longer response times (> 15 seconds) are disruptive.

- Users change usage profiles with response time.

- Faster is not always better. Users tend to increase the rate of interaction, which may cause corresponding increased error rates.

- Users should be advised of long delays.

- Modest variability in response times is acceptable (plus or minus 50 percent of the mean).

- Unexpected delays may be disruptive.

- Response time should be appropriate to the task:

  - Typing, cursor motion, mouse selection: 50 to 150 milliseconds

  - Simple frequent tasks: 1 second

  - Common tasks: 2 to 4 seconds

  - Complex tasks: 8 to 12 seconds

23. Ben Shneiderman, *Designing the User Interface: Strategies for Effective Human-Computer Interaction*, 3d ed. (Reading, MA: Addison-Wesley, 1998). An excellent HCI book for designers.

Negative Impressions and Perceived Quality

The speed at which your pages display can affect user perceptions of the quality, reliability, and credibility of your web site. Ramsay, Barabesi, and Preece studied the effects of slow-loading pages on user perceptions of web sites.[24] Using delays of two seconds to two minutes (with an interval of 19.5 seconds), they asked users to rate pages on eight

24. Judith Ramsay, Alessandro Barabesi, and Jenny Preece, "A psychological investigation of long retrieval times on the World Wide Web," *Interacting with Computers* 10 (1998): 77–86.

criteria including "interesting content" and scannability. They found that pages with delays of 41 seconds or longer were perceived to be significantly less interesting and harder to scan. Note that the pages in this study loaded incrementally.

Perceived Usability

Jacko, Sears, and Borella studied the effects of network delay and type of document on perceived usability. They found that perceived usability of web sites was dependent on the length of delay and on the media used in web documents. When delays are short, users prefer documents that include graphics. When delays lengthen, however, users prefer text-only documents because graphics are viewed as contributing to the delay. As users become more experienced, their sensitivity to delay increases, increasing the need for "delay reduction mechanisms."[25]

Perceived Quality of Experience

Morris and Turner found that perceived quality of experience (Shackel's utility dimension) affects the adoption rate of IT.[26] How users perceive the quality of a system can affect how much they will actually use it.

They found that interface "enhancements" (graphics, animation, sound, etc.) had little effect on quality of experience "although these features may be aesthetically pleasing…they do little to remove actual barriers to the users' goal attainment."

Perceived Quality of Service

The speed at which your pages display affects their perceived quality and reliability. Bouch, Kuchinsky, and Bhatti investigated the effects of delay on perceived QoS in order to find an acceptable QoS level for e-commerce transactions. They tested delays

---

25. Julie A. Jacko, Andrew Sears, and Michael S. Borella, "The effect of network delay and media on user perceptions of web resources," *Behavior & Information Technology* 19, no. 6 (2000): 427–439.

26. Michael G. Morris and Jason M. Turner, "Assessing Users' Subjective Quality of Experience with the World Wide Web: An Exploratory Examination of Temporal Changes in Technology Acceptance," *International Journal of Human-Computer Studies* 54 (2001): 877–901.

from 2 to 73 seconds for both non-incremental and incrementally loaded pages.[27] Users rated latency quality versus delay on a scale of high, average, to low (see Table 1.1).

Table 1.1   Web Page Quality Rating versus Delay

Quality Rating	Range of Latency: Non-Incremental Display	Range of Latency: Incremental Display
High	0–5 seconds	0–39 seconds
Average	> 5 seconds	> 39 seconds
Low	> 11 seconds	> 56 seconds

The results show a mapping between objective QoS and the users' subjective perception of QoS. Pages that displayed quickly (<= 5 seconds) were perceived to be of high quality with high-quality products. Pages that displayed slowly (> 11 seconds) were perceived to be of low quality and untrustworthy. In fact, slower pages caused some users to feel that the security of their purchases may have been compromised, and they abandoned their transactions.

Figure 1.3 shows the actual data behind Table 1.2 for the non-incremental display. This figure plots the number of low, average, and high ratings versus latency. The range where high ratings turn to low is between 8 to 10 seconds for non-incremental downloads, closely matching what Nielsen and others have found.

Figure 1.3
Latency quality ratings show a drop-off at around 8 to 10 seconds.

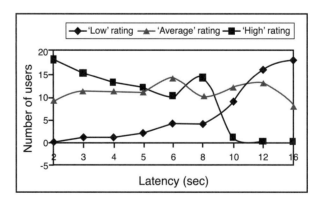

---

27. Anna Bouch, Allan Kuchinsky, and Nina Bhatti, "Quality is in the Eye of the Beholder: Meeting Users' Requirements for Internet Quality of Service," in *Proceedings of CHI2000 Conference on Human Factors in Computing Systems* (New York: ACM Press, 2000), 297–304.

Users tolerated nearly six times the delay for pages that displayed incrementally, although this tolerance decreased with usage. Test subjects rated pages as "average" with delays up to 39 seconds, and "low" with delays over 56 seconds.

The researchers also tested user requirements for speed by allowing them to click "increase quality" if they found the web page delay to be unacceptable. The average tolerance was 8.6 seconds with a standard deviation of 5.9 seconds. They attribute this large deviation in acceptable download times to contextual factors like web experience and user expectations. *The longer users interact with a site, the less they tolerate delays.*

Users will tolerate longer delays with tasks they perceive to be computationally complex. Users expect database access or complex calculations to take longer than displays of cached or static pages. Users form a conceptual model of system performance, which influences their tolerance for delay.

Credibility

Fogg et al. found that slow-loading pages reduce ease of use, which reduces credibility (or trustworthiness and expertise). Only difficult navigation was found to hurt credibility more.[28]

Bailout Rates and Attention Thresholds

The *bailout rate* is the percentage of users who leave a page before it loads and start looking for a faster, more engaging site. In their first "Need for Speed" study of 1999, Zona Research found that pages larger than 40K had bailout rates of 30 percent.[29] Once the designer reduced the same page to 34KB, the bailout rate fell to between 6 and 8 percent, a dramatic decrease for just a few kilobytes. When fat pages were reduced to the recommended maximum of 34K, readership went up 25 percent.[30] These are averages,

---

28. B. J. Fogg et al., "What Makes Web Sites Credible? A Report on a Large Quantitative Study," in *Proceedings of the SIGCHI Conference on Human Factors in Computing Systems* (New York: ACM Press, 2001), 61–68.
29. Zona Research, "The Economic Impacts of Unacceptable Web-Site Download Speeds," *Zona Market Bulletin* [online], (Redwood City, CA: Zona Research, 1999 [cited 9 November 2002]), available from the Internet at `http://www.keynote.com/solutions/assets/applets/wp_downloadspeed.pdf`. The oft-quoted "Need for Speed I."
30. Jacob Nielsen, *Designing Web Usability*, 49.

and users with faster connections and processors will experience faster downloads, but they can also become frustrated.

Zona's second study, "Need for Speed II," took into account dynamic transactions in order to modify the so-called "8-second rule."[31] They recommend that web site designers of dynamic sites cut an additional 0.5 to 1.5 seconds off connection latency in order to stay at the same level of abandonment compared with static web pages. As the web moves from a "plumbing" (pipes delivering pages) to a "transaction" (a series of dynamically generated pages) model, they argue that "cumulative frustration" plays an important role in user satisfaction.

Cumulative Frustration and Time Budgets

Users can change the way they browse a site as they request and view additional pages. As they become more proficient, their learning "spills over," and users reduce their expected number of page views on returning visits. Clickstream-based analysis suggests that visitors trade off the number of pages requested and the time spent at each page.[32] Users may set "time budgets" for particular tasks, even though the tasks may take multiple pages to complete.

Provide Feedback for Longer Tasks

Without effective feedback, users will wait only so long for your pages to load. For longer delays, you can extend the time that users are willing to wait with realistic feedback. Displaying your pages incrementally, a crude form of feedback, can extend user tolerance for delays.

Myers found that users prefer percent-done progress indicators for longer delays.[33] These linear progress bars lower stress by allowing experienced users to estimate completion

---

31. Zona Research, "The Need for Speed II" [online], 2001.

32. Randolph E. Bucklin and Catarina Sismeiro, "A Model of Web Site Browsing Behavior Estimated on Clickstream Data" [online], (Los Angeles, CA: UCLA, 2001 [cited 9 November 2002]), available from the Internet at http://ecommerce.mit.edu/papers/ERF/ERF129.pdf.

33. Brad A. Myers, "The Importance of Percent-Done Progress Indicators for Computer-Human Interfaces," in *Proceedings of the ACM Conference on Human Factors in Computing Systems* (New York: ACM Press, 1985), 11–17.

times and plan more effectively. Such progress bars are commonly used in download managers.

Bickford found that with no feedback, half of his test subjects bailed out of applications after 8.5 seconds. Switching to a watch cursor delayed their departure to an average of 20 seconds. "An animated watch cursor was good for over a minute, and a progress bar would keep them waiting until the Second Coming."[34]

Dellaert and Kahn found that wait time negatively affects consumer evaluation of web sites, but that this effect could be mitigated by providing information about the delay.[35] Delay information reduces uncertainty between expected and actual delays. For longer delays, they found that countdown feedback, a form of percent-done indicator, was better than duration feedback.

They also found that delays before viewing pages are less frustrating than delays while viewing pages. In other words, any delay *after* a page has loaded—for example, a sluggish response while users are interacting with the page—is worse than delays *before* a page has loaded.

Response times below two seconds are ideal, but current bandwidths make this speed impractical, so we settle for 8 to 10 seconds. What does this mean for web page design?

Page Design Guidelines

Page size and complexity have a direct effect on page display speed. As you learned in the Introduction, the majority of current users are at 56Kbps or less. That trend will continue until at least 2004, with international users lagging behind until 2007. Table 1.2 shows the maximum allowable page size needed to meet three attention thresholds at different connection speeds (derived from Nielsen, *Designing Web Usability*, 2000).

---

34. Peter Bickford, "Worth the Wait," *Netscape's Developer Edge* [online], (Mountain View, CA: Netscape Communications, 1997 [cited 10 November 2002]), available from the Internet at `http://developer.netscape.com/view-source/bickford_wait.htm`.

35. Benedict G. C. Dellaert and Barbara E. Kahn, "How Tolerable Is Delay? Consumers' Evaluations of Internet Web Sites after Waiting," *Journal of Interactive Marketing* 13, no. 1 (1999): 41–54. Found that countdown feedback nearly negates the negative effects of waiting for the web for retrospective evaluations.

Table 1.2   Maximum Page Size for Various Connection Speeds and Attention Thresholds

Bandwidth	Attention Threshold		
	1 Second	2 Seconds	10 Seconds
56.6Kbps	2KB	4KB	34KB
ISDN	8KB	16KB	150KB
T1	100KB	200KB	2MB

These figures assume 0.5-second latency.

You can see that 34KB is about the limit of total page size to achieve the 10-second attention threshold at 56Kbps. Under 30KB would be an appropriate limit for 8.6 seconds at 56Kbps. This is total page size, which includes ads and graphics. Assuming a 10KB banner ad and some small graphics, your HTML should be at most around 20K.

Designers who violate the 30KB limit will pay for their largess with lost sales, increased bailout rates, and increased bandwidth costs.

The Limits of Short-Term and Working Memory

Chunking is important to the working of short-term memory. For example, we do not easily retain the number 7545551212 but have much less difficulty with 754–555–1212. There are three *chunks* and we know where to expect boundaries. Our short-term memory is limited in the number of "chunks" of information it can hold. As we gain expertise with an activity, we tend to think more abstractly and acquire shortcuts, increasing our overall chunk size and thus increasing how much we can perceive and accomplish.

Shneiderman and others suggest that delays increase user frustration due to the limits of short-term and working memory. Depending on complexity, "people can rapidly recognize approximately" three to "seven 'chunks' of information at a time, and hold them in short-term memory for 15 to 30 seconds."[36]

36. Shneiderman, "Response Time and Display Rate in Human Performance with Computers," 267–68.

George Miller's original (and entertaining) "The Magical Number Seven, Plus or Minus Two"[37] study was subsequently shown to be a maximum limit to short-term memory span for simple units of information along one dimension. Broadbent argued that the basic unit of memory is closer to three, where each chunk can perhaps hold three further chunks.[38] LeCompte showed that as word length or unfamiliarity increases, memory span decreases, and Miller's maximum memory span should really be three to cover 90 percent of the population.[39] Mandler said that the magic number is closer to five.[40] Some 44 years after Miller's original paper, Kareev found that the effect of capacity limitations of working memory forces people to rely on samples consisting of seven plus or minus two items, for simple binary variables.[41]

People make plans on what to do next, and form solutions to problems while waiting between tasks. Longer delays (11 to 15 seconds) tax the limits of short-term memory and frustrate users who cannot implement their plans, and errors increase. Extremely short response times also increase errors, but lower their cost, improving productivity and encouraging exploration. More complex tasks require the use of working memory, which slows the optimum response rate. Given their druthers, users prefer short response times to long ones.

---

36. Shneiderman, "Response Time and Display Rate in Human Performance with Computers," 267–68.

37. George A. Miller, "The Magical Number Seven, Plus or Minus Two: Some Limits on Our Capacity for Processing Information," *Psychological Review* 63 (1956): 81–97. "My problem is that I have been persecuted by an integer…"

38. Donald E. Broadbent, "The Magic Number Seven After Fifteen Years," in *Studies in Long-Term Memory*, ed. A. Kennedy and A. Wilkes (New York: Wiley, 1971), 3–18.

39. Denny C. LeCompte, "Seven, Plus or Minus Two, Is Too Much to Bear: Three (or Fewer) Is the Real Magic Number," in *Proceedings of the Human Factors and Ergonomics Society* 43rd Annual Meeting (Santa Monica, CA: HFES, 1999), 289–292.

40. George Mandler, "Organization in Memory," in *The Psychology of Learning and Motivation*, ed. K. W. Spence and J. T. Spence 1 (San Diego: Academic Press, 1967), 327–372.

41. Yaakov Kareev, "Seven (Indeed, Plus or Minus Two) and the Detection of Correlations," *Psychological Review* 107, no. 2 (2000): 397–402.

So what have we learned from all this? Speed of response is certainly one factor in user satisfaction on the web. Consistency of response times is another. But some researchers say that modeling human behavior in real-time environments with fixed performance metrics (like response times below 10 seconds) is too simplified. What we need is a more holistic approach.

Attunability

Some HCI researchers say that it is not so simple: users "attune" to a particular system's response rate regardless of its duration.[42] Ritchie and Roast say that user satisfaction with web performance is more complex than simple numeric response times. Users form a mental model of systems they are dealing with based on system response characteristics. To form this model, users perform a "selection and adjustment [of] *subjective time bases*, and adapting the rate at which the environment is monitored to meet its particular pace."[43] *Attuning* is the process of forming this mental model and adapting our expectations to a particular system's response rate.

Consistent response times and adequate feedback help users attune to a system's pace. Inconsistent response times and poor feedback reduce the "attunability" of a particular system, and "temporal interaction errors" ensue. Thus "the less variable the duration of a particular task, the more likely that users can attune to the environment"[44] and the more accurately users can distinguish tasks of differing duration.

Humans can attune to a remarkably varied range of response rates, anything from years to seconds. Everyone knows that postal mail takes a matter of days, that Domino's delivers pizza within minutes, and that traffic lights change in a matter of seconds. The web is different, however.

---

42. Innes Ritchie and Chris Roast, "Performance, Usability, and the Web," in *Proceedings of the 34th Hawaii International Conference on System Sciences* 5 (Los Alamitos, CA: IEEE Computer Society Press, 2001).

43. Chris Roast, "Designing for Delay in Interactive Information Retrieval," *Interacting with Computers* 10 (1998): 87–104. Introduced the notion of attunability.

44. Ibid., 91.

The Chaotic Web

On large decentralized networks like the web, the effects of latency can exceed the effects of improvements in performance. Conventional performance engineering and evaluation are not possible in this environment.

Chaotic large-scale systems like the web can introduce non-deterministic delays. An external object in a web page can take anywhere from tens of milliseconds to what seems like an eternity (30 to 40 seconds or longer) to download. Rigid performance metrics such as response times under 10 seconds can be less important than consistent response rates.

To meet the needs of users, you need to provide an environment with characteristics to which they can attune. Consistency of response times and feedback allows users to better "attune" to system delays.

Consistent Response Rates

The key to attunability is to minimize the variability of delays. Variability is the difference between the slowest and fastest possible response rates. "The larger this variation, the less well system delays can be associated with a task," and the lower the system's attunability.[45] By minimizing this range, you allow users to model your system more easily and adjust their performance expectations.

Design for Attuning

Designing for attuning implies the adoption of transparency as an architectural principle.[46] By offering feedback mechanisms as pages and objects download, you can ensure that users will minimize "temporal interaction errors" associated with inconsistent response times.

---

45. Ibid., 94.

46. Chris Roast and Innes Ritchie, "Transparency in Time," in *Proceedings of the Workshop on Software Architectures for Cooperative Systems* (Philadelphia: IFIP Working Group 2.7/13.4, 2000).

The idea is to offer feedback that matches user expectations. Linear progress bars, which match user expectations, can be used to give users real-time feedback. Server load, cache state, and file sizes can be displayed with server-side includes. All of these performance cues are designed to let the user know how the system is performing and form a mental model. Here is an example SSI for file size cue:

```
<a href="thisfile.zip">download this file</a>
(<!--#config sizefmt="abbrev" -->
<!--#fsize file="thisfile.zip" -->)
```

This code automatically displays the file size of the referenced file so the user can gauge how long it will take.

The antithesis of this concept is the Windows file copy animation. The system portrays the activity as an animation of pages flying across at a constant rate, independent of the actual progress being made. This is like a spinning watch cursor, which has no relation to the progress bar. The non-linear progress bar stalls near the end of the scale, while pages keep flying (see Figure 1.4). A better solution would be to create a linear progress bar, and change the animation to filling up a page or removing it entirely.

Figure 1.4
The non-linear Windows file copy animation.

Users "attune" to the speed of the web's response. If your pages are slower than average or are inconsistent in size, users tend to tune out and go elsewhere. Optimizing the size of your pages and making them respond consistently can help users establish a rhythm as they surf through your site. Throw in a compelling experience, and some sites can attain the most elusive of web site goals, flow. You'll learn more about flow in Chapter 2, "Flow in Web Design."

Summary

The research suggests that without feedback, the length of time that users will wait for web pages to load is from 8 to 12 seconds. Nielsen recommends the average of 10 seconds. Bickford, Bouch, and Shneiderman found that most users will bail out of your page at around 8 to 8.6 seconds. Without feedback, that is the limit of people's ability to keep their attention focused while waiting.

If you provide continuous feedback through percent-done indicators, users will tolerate longer delays, up to 20 to 39 seconds, although their tolerance decreases with experience. Users will be more forgiving if you manage their delay experience with performance information. They will also tolerate increased delays if they perceive the task to be computationally complex, like a database access. Try to minimize response time variability by keeping page response times uniform to maximize attunability.

This research suggests the following web page design guidelines:

- Load in under 8.6 seconds (non-incremental display).
- Decrease these load times by 0.5 to 1.5 seconds for dynamic transactions.
- Minimize the number of steps needed to accomplish tasks—to avoid cumulative frustration from exceeding user time budgets.
- Load in under 20 to 30 seconds (incremental display) with useful content within 2 seconds.
- Provide performance information and linear feedback.
- Equalize page download times to minimize delay variability.

Web designers exceed these limits at their peril. Users associate slow-loading pages with inferior quality products and services, compromised security, and low credibility. Lower user satisfaction can lead to abandoned web sites and shopping carts.

Online Resources

- `http://www.hcibib.org/`—HCI Bibliography offers human-computer interaction resources, by Gary Perlman.

- `http://www.keynote.com`—Keynote Systems offers web site performance measurement and research.

- `http://www.mercuryinteractive.com`—Mercury Interactive offers web site performance measurement products and services.

- `http://www.useit.com`—Jakob Nielsen's usability portal includes his biweekly newsletter, Alertbox.

- `http://www.webcriteria.com`—Web Criteria offers automated usability tools (Site Analyst) that can find e-commerce bottlenecks to increase conversion rates.

Index

inform IT

YOUR GUIDE TO IT REFERENCE

New Riders has partnered with **InformIT.com** to bring technical information to your desktop. Drawing from New Riders authors and reviewers to provide additional information on topics of interest to you, **InformIT.com** provides free, in-depth information you won't find anywhere else.

Articles

Keep your edge with thousands of free articles, in-depth features, interviews, and IT reference recommendations—all written by experts you know and trust.

Online Books

Answers in an instant from **InformIT Online Books'** 600+ fully searchable online books.

POWERED

Safar

Catalog

Review online sample chapters, author biographies, and customer rankings, and choose exactly the right book from a selection of more than 5,000 titles.

New Riders
www.newriders.com

HOW TO CONTACT US

VISIT OUR WEB SITE

WWW.NEWRIDERS.COM

On our web site you'll find information about our other books, authors, tables of contents, indexes, and book errata. You will also find information about book registration and how to purchase our books.

EMAIL US

Contact us at this address: **nrfeedback@newriders.com**

- If you have comments or questions about this book
- To report errors that you have found in this book
- If you have a book proposal to submit or are interested in writing for New Riders
- If you would like to have an author kit sent to you
- If you are an expert in a computer topic or technology and are interested in being a technical editor who reviews manuscripts for technical accuracy
- To find a distributor in your area, please contact our international department at this address: **nrmedia@newriders.com**

- For instructors from educational institutions who want to preview New Riders books for classroom use: Email should include your name, title, school, department, address, phone number, office days/hours, text in use, and enrollment, along with your request for desk/examination copies and/or additional information.
- For members of the media who are interested in reviewing copies of New Riders books: Send your name, mailing address, and email address, along with the name of the publication or web site you work for.

BULK PURCHASES/CORPORATE SALES

The publisher offers discounts on this book when ordered in quantity for bulk purchases and special sales. For sales within the U.S., please contact: Corporate and Government Sales (800) 382-3419 or **corpsales@pearsontechgroup.com**. Outside of the U.S., please contact: International Sales (317) 581-3793 or **international@pearsontechgroup.com**.

WRITE TO US

New Riders Publishing
201 W. 103rd St.
Indianapolis, IN 46290-1097

CALL US

Toll-free (800) 571-5840 + 9 + 7477
If outside U.S. (317) 581-3500. Ask for New Riders.

FAX US

(317) 581-4663

New Riders

Publishing
the Voices
that Matter

OUR AUTHORS

PRESS ROOM

| web development | design | photoshop | new media | 3-D | server technology |

EDUCATORS

ABOUT US

CONTACT US

You already know that New Riders brings you the **Voices That Matter**.

But what does that mean? It means that New Riders brings you the

Voices that challenge your assumptions, take your talents to the next

level, or simply help you better understand the complex technical world

we're all navigating.

Visit **www.newriders.com** to find:

▸ **10% discount** and **free shipping** on all book purchases

▸ Never-before-published chapters

▸ Sample chapters and excerpts

▸ Author bios and interviews

▸ Contests and enter-to-wins

▸ Up-to-date industry event information

▸ Book reviews

▸ Special offers from our friends and partners

▸ Info on how to join our User Group program

▸ Ways to have your Voice heard

New
Riders

WWW.NEWRIDERS.COM

0789723107
Steve Krug
US$35.00

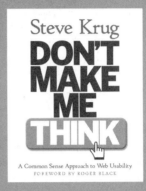

0735712026
Jesse James Garrett
US$29.99

0735712506
Christina Wodtke
US$29.99

0735712336
Molly E. Holzschlag
US$39.99

0735711968
Bob Baxley
US$45.00

073571150X
Joe Clark
US$39.99

VOICES
THAT MATTER™

New Riders

WWW.NEWRIDERS.COM